BOOKS BY ROBERT B. PARKER

THE GODWULF MANUSCRIPT
GOD SAVE THE CHILD
MORTAL STAKES

BOOKS BY ELMER A. LESLIE

OLD TESTAMENT RELIGION
ACQUAINTING YOUTH WITH CHRIST
THE COMRADESHIP HOUR

OLD TESTAMENT RELIGION

In the Light of
Its Canaanite
Background

ELMER A. LESLIE

**Professor of Hebrew and Old Testament Literature
in Boston University School of Theology**

ABINGDON-COKESBURY PRESS
NEW YORK ● NASHVILLE

Printed in the United States of America

DEDICATED
TO MY WIFE

CONTENTS

PREFACE

$\mathcal{T}$HE inception of this book came in 1925. Upon reading *The Religion of the People of Israel,* by the late Dr. Rudolf Kittel, of the University of Leipzig, the influence of the Canaanite civilization upon the development of Old Testament Religion presented itself to the author as a subject needing and inviting investigation. Since then it has been his major interest in research, pursued steadily in connection with his courses and assiduously during each summer. The privilege to him and his family of a Sabbatical year (1929-30) gave him a month of research in the library and Near East antiquities of the British Museum, three months of study and travel in Palestine, with trips to sites of archaeological investigation, conducted by Dr. Chester C. McCown, then director of the American School of Oriental Research in Jerusalem, and eight months of study in the Universities of Halle and Berlin.

Particularly fruitful for his project were the contacts enjoyed with the four members of the Old Testament department of the theological faculty at Halle: the late Dr. Hermann Gunkel, with his skill in seeing the life and literature of Israel in its total Near East context; Dr. Hans Schmidt, with his sensitiveness to the Palestinian color in the Old Testament; Dr. Kurt Galling, with his archaeological interest; and especially Dr. Otto Eissfeldt, who was keenly aware of the importance of the subject, and who introduced the author to the literary contributions of the late Dr. W. W. Graf von Baudissin. In Jerusalem great help was obtained

9

through conference with the outstanding French archaeologist of Palestine, Père L. H. Vincent, of the
Dominican *École Biblique et Ecole Archéologique
Francaise,* who counseled him regarding primary
sources for the study of Canaanite religion; and from
suggestions given by the chief American authority of
Palestinian archaeology, Dr. William F. Albright, now,
for the second term, director of the American School of
Oriental Research. In friendly, scientific response to
specific queries from the author, letters were received
from Dr. Stanley A. Cook, lecturer in Hebrew and
Aramaic of the University of Cambridge, and Dr.
Adolphe Lods, professor of Hebraic Language and Literature at the Sorbonne, which contained suggestions of
great value. To all these scholars thankful acknowledgment is herewith made.

The treatment of the Old Testament Religion here
presented is genetic in nature and dramatic in method.
The growth of the religion is traced down to the end of
the Babylonian exile, by which time its major concepts
had been expressed. The evolution of the religion is
interpreted as the unfolding of a drama. Footnote references to authorities have of necessity been reduced
to a minimum, but a reasonably full bibliography has
been appended to the text, most extensive for THE
CANAANITE BACKGROUND. This includes only such
books and articles as have proved to be helpful to the
author in the preparation of the volume. The order
of arrangement of the bibliography corresponds to that
of the chapters and subheadings within the chapters
of the book. It is hoped that this feature will enhance
the value of the work for pastors, students, and scholars

who are interested in the Old Testament field and who may welcome specific suggestions for pursuing the subject further. In this connection grateful acknowledgment is made to Mr. Walter B. Briggs, Assistant Librarian of the Widener Library at Harvard, and to Dr. Owen H. Gates, Librarian of the Andover-Harvard Theological Library, for their generosity and courtesy in permitting him access to their richly furnished Old Testament and Semitic sections, without which these studies could not have been carried on.

The author feels under sacred obligation to Dean Albert C. Knudson, whose creative teaching first kindled his interest in the scientific study of the Old Testament. Giving most generously of his time, he examined and criticized the manuscript while it was in the making. His counsel and persistent encouragement have been of inestimable help. He is also indebted to the Rev. Vernon A. Loescher, A.M., S.T.B., Jacob Sleeper Fellow, who typed the first draft of the manuscript, and whose interest and suggestions were most heartening. He is especially grateful to his assistant, the Rev. Otis R. Fischer, A.M., S.T.B., Roswell R. Robinson Fellow, who has read the entire manuscript with great care, offering many valuable suggestions, and who has prepared the index. The work is dedicated to one whose loyal devotion, unfailing encouragement, and sacrificial interest are a perpetual inspiration.

ELMER A. LESLIE.

INTRODUCTION

*T*HE land of Canaan has had an importance in the
history of civilization quite out of proportion to
its size. It was the bridge between Africa and Asia.
Here converged the great trade routes of the ancient
world. Across it passed the caravans of Babylonia and
Egypt. Through it marched the armies of Tiglathpileser
and Alexander the Great. And in our own times, upon
its soil one of the decisive military actions of the Great
War was fought.

It was the sensitive recipient of diversified streams
of culture. Here met and mingled the characteristic
contributions of the great nations of antiquity. Babylonians, Egyptians, Canaanites, Amorites, Hurrians,
Hittites, Aramaeans, Israelites, Philistines, Phoenicians,
Assyrians, Chaldaeans, Persians, Greeks, and Romans, to
speak only of the pre-Christian era, all successively made
unique and distinctive contributions to its life. It was
thus the meeting place and the melting pot of ideas and
ideals of the ancient world.

For the student of Israelite religion it has an interest
as fascinating as it is romantic. The land of Canaan
was the stage upon which was enacted one of the most
important dramas in the history of religion. For in the
center of those early converging streams of civilization
was Israel in the formative period of its tribal and national life. The drama of the growth of Israelite religion took place upon a stage which had already wit-
nessed an extensive history. The Canaanite civilization

13

was the immediate environmental influence which was
destined to play upon Israelite religion with terrible yet
vitalizing potency.   Most of these early streams of culture, from the Babylonians, the Egyptians, the Hurrians, and the Hittites, reached Israel primarily through
the mediatorship of the Canaanites.   The latter were
destined to transmit great religious values to Israel as
well as to stimulate mighty spiritual protests.   Hence to
recover dominant aspects of the Canaanite religion as
it existed during Israel's settlement and evolution will
be an important phase of our problem.

To this drama upon the age-long prepared stage of
Canaan there was the Hebrew Prelude in Canaan itself,
the epoch of the Hebrew Fathers, and the Israelite
Prelude in the Wilderness, the epoch of Moses.   To discover some characteristic features of the religion of the
Fathers and that of Moses will be a difficult but necessary aspect of our problem.

Then in swift succession come the three acts in the
drama which were played on the stage of Canaan.   The
first is "Clash and Transition."   One of the most dramatic moments in the religious history of the Near East
was when Israelites met Canaanites, when as nomads of
the Near East they made the transition to agriculturalists.   The second act is entitled "Yahweh or Baal."   It
describes the streams of Canaanite influence which
poured in upon Israel and interprets the early prophetic
protest to the consequent Canaanizing of Israelite religion.   The third act of the drama, "The Prophetic
Clarification," took place in the classic eighth century
B. C., the most creative single century of Israelite religious history, when the pioneering, penetrating minds

of Amos, Hosea, Isaiah, and Micah clarified the nature
and the requirements of Yahweh. These prophetic
teachers of Israel faced and gave pioneering answers to
the two deepest and most persistent questions of Israelite religion: (1) What is the nature of Yahweh, Israel's
God? (2) What does Yahweh require of his worshipers?

Lastly came "The Final Synthesis," the issue of the
drama. Dependent in part upon the insights of these
pioneer minds, came the seventh-century teachers, the
prophets Zephaniah, Nahum, Habakkuk, and the great
transitional religious teacher, Jeremiah. It remained
for the sixth-century prophets, Ezekiel and Deutero-
Isaiah, to bring the religious development of Israel to
its highest peak.

Our aim is to understand the main features of the
prophetic religion of Israel up to about 540 B. C., as it
took shape upon the soil of Canaan. We are to study
the development, clash, and interplay of two mighty
forces in Israel's growth. With penetrating clarity and
simplicity, Dr. F. M. Theodore Böhl has stated what
these forces are: "Israel stood on the border between
two ages. The religion of Sinai and the culture of
Canaan were the two conflicting factors in its history."
The author is of the opinion that the freshest and most
illuminating approach to the religion of Israel, as interpreted by the prophets from Amos to Deutero-Isaiah, is
through a vivid sense of the clash, grapple, and interpenetration of the Mosaic religion of the wilderness
with the civilization and religion of Canaan, consequent upon the invasion and settlement of the Israelites
in the land.

It was primarily this interpenetration that aroused

the prophets to utterance. It was this intermingling of radically diverse cultures which set for them their problem. They were not speculative thinkers, brooding in lofty isolation upon the meaning of God. They were, in the finest sense of the term, spiritual opportunists, defining with vigor and sensitive insight, under the smarting stimulus of an Israel rapidly becoming Canaanized before their eyes, the true nature and requirements of Yahweh. They were primarily the great protesters. But at the heart of their protests were profound interpretations of religion. Moreover, the influence of the Canaanite environment upon Israel was by no means limited to the rôle of a negative irritant. Into Israelite religion went from the soul of Canaan profound spiritual values. And no small part of our task will be to discover their nature and to estimate their worth.

CHAPTER I

THE CANAANITE BACKGROUND

THE earliest historical references to the land of Canaan appear in the Tell el-Amarna letters (Kinahhi, Kinahi, Kinahna, c. 1400 B. C.) and the Egyptian monuments from the reign of Seti I (Pe-Kanan, c. 1300 B. C.). According to these sources Canaan embraced the entire region of Semitic Syria, including Palestine. Both Gaza, in the extreme south of Palestine, and Laodicea, in the Lebanon region of the north, are designated in ancient sources as Canaanite cities. And the cuneiform tablets in the north Canaanite language, recently unearthed at Ras Shamra in northern Syria, clearly reveal that in the middle centuries of the second millennium B. C. Canaan extended yet farther north, embracing all Phoenicia. Even in Saint Augustine's day peasant Phoenician colonists in Africa called themselves Canaanites.

1. CANAANITES AND AMORITES

As early as 3500 B. C. the Canaanites are found in Syria, Palestine, and the adjoining Sinaitic peninsula. They came originally from Arabia, and for a time, as is evidenced archaeologically from Gezer and Mizpah (Tell en-Nasbeh), occupied certain areas simultaneously with the indigenous non-Semites. Upon first entering Phoenicia they dwelt in the inland region as agriculturalists and cattle raisers, which fact accounts for the unique relation to physical nature which re-

17

mained characteristic of the Canaanite fertility cults.
They gave their name to the land and for many centuries were the ascendant cultural force in Palestine
and Syria.

Closely related to the Canaanites were the Amorites,
who, early in the third millennium B. C., migrated from
Arabia.   We first meet them in the time of Sargon
(Sharrukin) the Great (2637-2582 B. C.), who made an
expedition to the land of "MAR. TUki," which designation is the Sumerian for "West Land," Amurru being
its Akkadian equivalent.   Amurru then embraced Palestine, Phoenicia, and Coele-Syria, a region which in
the lowlands had been partially settled by the Canaanites. They invaded Babylon from the west and founded
the first Babylonian or Amorite dynasty, the most important monarch of which was Hammurabi (1955-1913
B. C.).   They introduced into Babylonia their own
west Semitic gods, Dagon and Hadad.   Egyptian documents dating from this period (c. 2100 B. C.) reveal
them in Amurru as Bedouins, tribal in organization
and dominating the highlands, the coastal cities and
plains being held by the Canaanites.[1]   In the early
centuries of the second millennium B. C. the pressure of
the Hittites and the Kashites telescoped them west-
ward into the region which lay behind the coastal district of the Phoenician ports.   By Tell el-Amarna times
(c. 1400 B. C.) Amurru had practically become an administrative district under successive Amorite sheiks,
who were subject to the overlordship of Egypt.   It then
embraced the region north of Beirut as far as Arvad,
some forty miles north of Gebal, and included the

---

[1] K. Sethe: *Die Achtung feindlicher Fürsten* (1926).

Lebanon and Anti-Lebanon mountains.[2] The Amorites
as a people became extinct long before the Canaanites.
But a vigorous Amorite kingdom under Sihon occupied
the region of Transjordania from the Arnon to the
Jabbok, and from the wilderness to the Jordan, as late
as the Israelite invasion of Canaan.   (Numbers 21. 24;
Judges 11. 22.)

Racially and culturally the Canaanites and Amorites
were not essentially different from one another and are
rightly viewed as originally one people.   In biblical
usage "Canaanites" and "Amorites" designate the
dominant element in the population of Canaan before
the invasion of Israel, the J document preferring the
name "Canaanites," the E document, "Amorites." The
most important bit of geographical evidence we have,
Numbers 13. 29 (J), mirrors the fact that the oldest or
Canaanite section of the population, including the
Phoenicians, was chiefly lowland in character, commercial in the coastal regions, and agricultural in the inland.
The later or Amorite section was primarily highland in
character and better preserved the primitive Bedouin
nature, as is vividly illustrated by the intrigues of the
Amorite sheiks of the Tell el-Amarna age.   But just as
is the case with Scottish lowlanders and highlanders,
who, while having many elements of difference, nevertheless represent a cultural unity, so Amorites and
Canaanites shared in common the essential features of
their culture.

Situated as it was at the very heart of the "Fertile
Crescent," the land of Canaan became the recipient
across the centuries of many cultural contributions both

[2] O. Weber, in Knudtzon, *Die El Amarna Tafeln,* II, pp. 1131-6.

from Semites and from non-Semites, notably the Hurrians and Hittites. Yet no mere cultural syncretism
developed in Canaan. The most tangible and illuminating illustration of this is in the sphere of language. The
Canaanite language, as shown by its vocabulary and
syntax, to a marked extent retained its purity throughout its history. It developed, to be sure, through several
stages—Old Canaanite, Amorite, Hebrew, and Phoenician—but remained in its essence Canaanite to the end.[3]
Moreover, these stages of linguistic development coincide respectively with the four major ages in the cultural history of Canaan. These are the Old Canaanite,
which begins with the earliest Semitic occupation of the
land, but extends more particularly from c. 2600 to 2000
B. C.; Middle Canaanite, from c. 2000 to 1600 B. C; Late
Canaanite, from 1600 to 1200 B. C., and Recent Canaanite (Phoenician), from 1200 B. C. to 600 B. C. These
stages of Canaanite culture coincide respectively with the
Early, Middle, and Late Bronze Ages, and the Iron Age.

2. DEITIES

This Canaanite culture is defined by Dussaud as that
which unites Phoenician and Palestinian civilization
into one.[4] Our concern is solely with the religious phase
of Canaanite culture, viewed as the spiritual background upon which the religion of Israel developed. Of
outstanding importance are the deities of the Canaanite
religion. Some of these are importations from without,
especially from the Hurrians, Egyptians, and Babylonians. Whether introduced from without or indige-

---

[3] Compare H. Bauer and P. Leander: *Historische Grammatik der
hebräischen Sprache des Alten Testaments*, I, pp. 16, 19.
[4] R. Dussaud, in *Syria*, IX (1928), p. 139.

nous to Canaanite culture, the central feature of the Canaanite deities is their fertility character.

This is evident in the worship in Canaan during the Amarna age (c. 1400 B. C.) of the Mitannian-Hurrian Teshub, the storm god, and his female counterpart, Hepa, whose designation appears in a constituent part of the name borne by the Canaanite chieftain at Jerusalem, Ebed-Hepa (Abdi-Khiba).

The Egyptian deity Osiris, whose cult reaches back to great antiquity in Egypt, and who, as the corn or fertility god, had close correspondence with the Canaanite-Phoenician Adonis, was revered in Canaan. Moreover, the popularity of Horus, the son of Osiris, and the embodiment of the living king, is revealed by the "Horus eye" found frequently in Palestinian excavation, and which was viewed as having power to impart vital force. Hathor, goddess of love, the most ancient of the mother deities in Egypt, had great vogue in Canaan, and her characteristics influenced the portrayal of the Canaanite Ashtart, with whom she was early identified. Her symbol was a headdress composed of a solar disc between cow's horns. The Baalath (Lady) of Gebal was assimilated to her as early as the third millennium B. C. Isis, wife of Osiris and mother of Horus, was closely related to Hathor and was likewise identified with the Baalath of Gebal, where her relation to the Adonis cult gave her great prominence. The Egyptian form of Ashtart, goddess of love and fertility, in her most sensual expression was Qadesh, "Lady of Heaven" and "Mistress of the Gods."

The popularity of the Babylonian Nergal, god of war, pestilence, and the underworld, in Canaan was due to the fact that he was likewise the promoter of vegetation and the protector of the life of nature.[5] Shamash, the great Babylonian solar deity, was popular in Canaan, as the names of the old Canaanite towns Beth Shemesh and En Shemesh attest. Ramman (Rimmon), the Babylonian storm god, "the thunderer," was identified with the Canaanite Hadad and worshiped as a fertility deity of the Tammuz-Adonis type. The Babylonian Tammuz was worshiped primarily under his Canaanite form as Adonis. The feminine counterpart of Tammuz, conceived as his mother, sister, or wife, was Ishtar. She represented the Babylonian form of the old mother goddess brought into Babylonia by the earliest Semitic settlers. She personified the life-giving, death-dealing force of nature and in Canaan was worshiped primarily under the western form of her designation, Ashtart, by the Greeks called Astarte. Here again the vegetation nature of the Babylonian deities worshiped in Canaan is evident.

We come now to the Canaanite pantheon itself, where the same fertility feature is everywhere noticeable. At the head of the old Canaanite pantheon was El, a solar deity, "the father of years," "the king."[6] He was god in himself, god *par excellence*. Productivity of the earth was dependent upon him and was brought about annually by his ritualistic marriage with the *qedheshoth,* the wives of El. There were many localized manifestations or particular phases of El. He is called El-Elyon in the Old Testament (Genesis 14. 19). He

[5] E. Ebeling: *Tod und Leben nach den Vorstellungen der Babylonier,* p. 165.
[6] Ras Shamra, IAB., col. I, lines 4-10.

was identical with Elioun, of whom we learn from Philo of Byblos (contemporary of Hadrian), and with whom the recently discovered fertility deity Al Eyan of the north Canaanite texts from Ras Shamra was fused.[7] The aged aspect of El is emphasized in Philo's designation of him as El-Kronos. Another manifestation of El is the biblical El-Shadday (Exodus 6. 3), identical with "Sadidos," who, according to Philo, was a "son" of El-Kronos. Other local manifestations of El are the biblical deities El-Roi (Genesis 16. 13), El-Olam (Genesis 21. 33), and El-Berith (Judges 9. 46). Likewise a king deity and at Byblos identical with El-Kronos, was Malk (Milk), whose cult in Canaan is evidenced in the Tell el-Amarna age. In the Old-Testament sources he appears as Molech or Moloch. To him children were sacrificed. The worship of El carries us back to a pre-Baalism stage in Canaanite religion.

At the side of El was his feminine counterpart, Asherat-of-the-sea, "the mother of the gods," and the chief goddess of the Canaanites.[8] She was connected with the underground waters which created the fountains and springs.

Next in importance to El, as is clearly revealed in the new Ras Shamra texts,[9] was Baal. He was identical with Hadad, Baal *par excellence*,[10] the Canaanite god of lightning and thunder, storm and rain. He tended to coalesce with El, and Macrobius informs us that the

[7] W. F. Albright, in JPOS., XII (1932), pp. 190f.; H. Bauer in ZAW. (1933), p. 96.

[8] Ras Shamra, IAB., col. I, lines 10-16a.

[9] First mentioned in Ras Shamra IAB., col. I, line 14.

[10] Convincingly argued by M. J. Lagrange in ERS², pp. 88, 92-4, and accepted by R. Dussaud.

Syrians gave the name "Adad" ("Hadad") to the god
which they revered as first and greatest of all. The
symbol of Baal was the bull. Under the influence of the
Aton (Sun) religious reform of the Egyptian Ikhnaton,
"Baal in heaven" came to be viewed as the sun god,
and as early as c. 1360 B. C. he was called Bel Shame
(Lord of Heaven), which designation is also preserved
by Philo (Beel Samen), and appears in its Aramaean
form (Beel Shamin) at Hamath c. 800 B. C. The Babylonians identified him with Ramman, the Egyptians
with Sutekh, and the Mitannian-Hurrians with Teshub.
The local form of Hadad in the north was the god
Bethel (*hael Bethel;* Genesis 31. 13—so Dussaud), where
his symbol was the bull. He is identical with the Baity-
los of Philo of Byblos, for the name Bethel (house of
god) designated the deity and at the same time the
sacred stone (Baitylos=Bethel) in which he dwelt. An
ancient center of his cult was Luz (Genesis 28. 19),
which, because of the vogue his cult there enjoyed and
its fame as a pilgrimage center, came to be called by
the name of the deity, Beth-Bethel (House of Bethel),
which was then shortened to Bethel.

The term "baal" is a common noun denoting pos-
sessor, owner, or proprietor. As designating deity the
Baal embodies all that the tribe desires or values. Baal
differs from El, as S. A. Cook maintains, in representing
not the god in himself but some personal relationship,
a concept of the deity yet more basic than that of mere
ownership. The various Baalim (plural of Baal, *cf.*
Hosea 2. 13, 17) are rightly conceived as localized manifestations or particular expressions of the Baal *par
excellence.* Several of them we know by name. The

Baal of Harran, which city down to the Middle Ages
remained a famous center of Aramaean Semitic paganism impregnated by Mesopotamian and Canaanite elements, was called Sin.   Melqarth (king of the city)
was the Baal of Tyre.   Saphon (the Northerner) was
worshiped in the Lebanon.   Dagon (= Dagan), most
likely of Amorite origin, was worshiped in Canaan at
least as early as the Tell el-Amarna times, as the personal name Dagan-takala attests.   He had temples in
the south near Lachish and Eglon (Joshua 15. 41) and
in the region of Asher (Joshua 19. 27).   In the period
of the Israelite judges he was worshiped by the Philistines at Gaza (Judges 16), and at Ashdod (1 Samuel 5),
where temples of his cult existed.   The Philistines,
however, had taken over his worship when they entered
Canaan.   "Baal Dagan" appears on a Phoenician
cylinder seal from the seventh century B. C.[11]   He was
a grain god and later became a fish god, and, as is clear
from Philo of Byblos, his worship occupied a place of
great prominence in Canaanite religion.

Mekal was the Baal of Beth Shean (modern Beisan),
where his basic quality was omnipotence.   As the Baal
presiding over the destinies of Beth Shean he was identified with the Egyptian Sutekh, and likewise with the
Canaanite Resheph, god of storm and tempest.   He is
the celestial deity who agitates the heavens with lightning and thunder, and at the same time, the propitious
deity who gives life by dispensing the dew and rain.[12]

There were various Baalim which were distinguished

---

[11] So, A. H. Sayce: The "Higher Criticism" and the Verdict of the
Monuments, p. 327.

[12] H. Vincent: "Le Baal cananéen de Beisan et sa parèdre," in RB
Vol. XXXVII (1928), pp. 532-5.

by particular cultic features. Baal Marqodh, "Baal of the dance," was worshiped at Deir el-Kala near Beirut. Baal Marpe, Baal of healing, had his cult in Cyprus. Baal Hamman, "Baal of the pillar," was worshiped at Carthage, where thousands of votive steles were dedicated to him. The Baal Berith (Judges 9. 4) was the guardian of covenants at Shechem.

There were Baalim of mountains, such as Baal Peor (Numbers 23. 28; 25. 3), Baal Tabor, Baal Hermon (Judges 3. 3), Baal Carmel, Baal Lebanon, Baal Ras (Baal of the promontory), Baal Qarnaim, "the Baal of the two horned" mountain near Carthage, and Baal Zebul (Baal of the High House, so T. K. Cheyne), who was worshiped at Ras Shamra.

There were Baalim who were lords of specific cities, such as Baal Meon (Numbers 32. 38), Baal Shalishah (2 Kings 4. 42), Baal Hazor (2 Samuel 13. 23), Baal Sidon, Baal Tamar (Judges 20. 33), Baal Perazim (2 Samuel 5. 20), Baal of Tarsus, Baal of Gaziura, and Baal of Gebal.

At the side of the Baal (Lord) stood his feminine counterpart, the Baalath (Lady), a designation which is applied to the chief deity of Gebal (Byblos) as early as the third millennium B. C. The earliest known name of a Baalath was Asherat, a manifestation of Asherat-of-the-Sea. She was the feminine partner of Amurru, god of thunder and flood, and was given various titles, "Lady of the steppe, who belongs in the mountain," "Lady of sensuality and voluptuousness," and "The Bride of the King of Heaven."[13] Her symbol was the stump or stock of a tree (Hosea 4. 12) or a wooden post, both being

---

[13] H. Zimmern, in KAT³, pp. 432f.

familiar embodiments and emblems of the feminine principle in deity at the High Places, to which cultic objects she gave her name.

At Gebal, as we learn from later sources, the Baalath was Ashtart (= Astarte). Next to Asherat-of-the-Sea, she was the chief goddess of Canaanite-Phoenician religion. Her cult was very widespread, being practiced at Sidon, Ashkelon, in Cyprus, Sicily, Gaul, Carthage, and, as hundreds of Astarte figurines unearthed by archaeological research make unmistakable, throughout Palestine. These Astarte figurines were copies of specific idols of Astarte, of which there were three types, the first having its roots in Babylonia, the second in the Hittite civilization of Asia Minor, but influenced by Egyptian Hathor motifs, and the third in Aegean culture, particularly in its Cyprian phase. Ashtart, or Astarte, was the most usual Canaanite name of the great mother goddess, the goddess of love, fertility, and fecundity.

At Hieropolis, where her cult had merged with that of the Phrygian vegetation god Attis, the name of the Baalath was Atargatis, which means Atar (Aramaean for Ashtart), mother of Athe (Attis). She was originally a nature deity and as Atar Samain (Atar of Heaven) had a celestial character. She was a goddess of the life-giving power of water, as her marine character at Hieropolis, and as her fish-deity character at Ashkelon, attest. The dove and the fish were sacred to her.

At Beisan and at Ras Shamra the name of the Baalath was Anath. Her cult was widespread and popular. We encounter Anath as constituent parts of Amorite names of the first Babylonian dynasty (Zimrihanata, etc.), in a personal name, Anati, in the Tell el-Amarna letters, and as designations of a goddess in the Aramaic papyri from Elephantine, Anath Bethel, and Anath Yahu. The Palestinian place names, Beth Anath and Anathoth, attest her worship in pre-Israelite Canaan. In her primary significance Anath was a manifestation of the great mother and vegetation goddess. At Beth Shean (Beisan) she was "Lady of heaven and queen of all the gods." In the north Canaanite documents of Ras Shamra she was the sister-partner of Al Eyan and, as such, the chief vegetation goddess. A late inscription from Cyprus emphasizes her fertility nature in her characterization as "the strength of life." At Beth Shean she was distinguished by her noble character. The typical Egyptian portrayal of Anath which emphasized her warlike traits does not represent her primary aspect, which is rather that of a vegetation deity.

At Carthage the Baalath was Tanith, the female counterpart of Baal Hamman. She was called "face of Baal," by which is probably meant the female manifestation of the Baal principle. The name of the deity was probably Libyan, or North African, meaning "She of the Sky." Her nature, however, was strictly Canaanite, and as the supreme goddess of the Carthaginian area she was "mother of rain."[14] Tertullian, designating her "Virgin of Heaven," called her "the rain promiser."[15]

Whether worshiped in Babylonia as Ishtar, in Syria as Atargatis, in Egypt as Qadesh, in Ras Shamra and Beth Shean as Anath, in Carthage as Tanith, or in Canaan generally as Astarte, she was the great Semitic mother

[14] Allen H. Godbey: *The Lost Tribes a Myth,* p. 207.
[15] Tertullian: *Apology,* 9.

goddess and her worship had a tremendous hold upon
Canaan, as archaeological evidence in particular has
made clear. It endured in vigor throughout the entire
second millennium B. C. and the early half of the first.
We can, accordingly, realize most vividly the insidious
peril to Israelite Yahweh worship presented by this fertility aspect of Canaanite religion.

The basic concept of deity in the Canaanite religion
is the masculine-feminine, or what appears yet older
and more primitive as at Byblos, the feminine-mascu-
line principle. At Byblos, associated with the Baalath
of Gebal, was El-Kronos. Corresponding to Malk, the
king deity, we have Malkath, queen, as the characterization of a goddess. The partner of Amurru, "Lord of the
mountain," was Ashratu (Asherat), "Mistress of the
steppe." At Ras Shamra opposite El appeared Asherat-
of-the-Sea. Qadesh and Amurru were intimately connected as a divine pair at Ras Shamra. In Egyptian
representations Qadesh and Resheph appeared together.
Opposite Atargatis at Hieropolis was Hadad. At Beth
Shean Anath was the partner of Mekal. At Carthage,
beside Tanith stood Baal Hamman. The Old Testament is, therefore, quite accurate in designating
Canaanite religion as the worship of "the Baalim and
the Ashtaroth" (plural of Ashtart) (Judges 10. 6; 1
Samuel 7. 4; 12. 10).

The Canaanite religion shared in this basic masculine-feminine concept with the religions of the whole
Near East area. In Babylonia, beside Ishtar stood Marduk. In Egyptian religion, associated with Osiris was
his wife, Isis. And similarly in the Phrygian religion of
Asia Minor related to Ma or Cybele was Teshub. The

names of the deity varied, but throughout the whole
area this basic fertility aspect was always present.

Closely related to this basic masculine-feminine, or
fertility, aspect of Canaanite religion was the concept of
the dying-rising god. Clearly evident at certain centers
such as Byblos, Ras Shamra, Sidon, Tyre, and Carthage,
and no doubt extending throughout the centers of the
Canaanite-Phoenician religion, was the cult of the
young deity, sometimes the son, sometimes the brother
or lover of the feminine deity, who, coincident with the
languishing of vegetation, annually died. He was
mourned by his feminine partner and, coincident with
the renewal of vegetation, annually arose from the dead.

The earliest appearance in ancient sources of a deity
of this type in Canaan comes from the Thinite Age
3400-2980 B. C.). He is god of Nega, a district which
included the whole Lebanon region of which Byblos
was the major port. His name, Khay-Taou (so Dussaud), appears in Egyptian hieroglyphics upon a cylinder unearthed at Byblos by the French archaeologist
Montet. He represented particularly the spirit of tree
vegetation. On the same cylinder with him appears the
goddess of Byblos, who is represented in Isis-Hathor
fashion. This is the earliest known indication of the
dying-rising god cult in Canaanite territory. By the beginning of the second millennium B. C., the Babylonian
(Tammuz) form of this cult is evidenced at Byblos in
a personal name compounded with Damu (= Tammuz).

At Ras Shamra, in the now famous North Canaanite
epic of Al Eyan-Baal, we have an authentic glimpse of
a very ancient cult of this type. Here appear two fertility

deities, Al Eyan,[16] god of the spring rains which caused
vegetation to sprout forth anew, and Mot, the god of
the hot season, in which the grain ripens. These deities
were viewed as sharply antagonistic to one another.
Mot had to die if Al Eyan were to live. They represent
what Dussaud has suggestively maintained, "the division of Adonis." At a later time they were consolidated
into the one deity, Tammuz or Adonis. Al Eyan was
the brother of the goddess Anath, who lamented his
death, and Mot, his antagonist, was the enemy of Anath
and the object of her fierce attack.

The characteristic Canaanite designation of this dying-rising deity, however, came to be *Adhon*, "Lord,"
originally an appellative which the Greeks converted
into the proper name "Adonis." One of his beloved
titles was Naaman, "pleasant," "gracious," and it
appears in the place names Naman, north of Carmel,
and Numana, Namana in southern Palestine, c. 1500
B. C. In Tell el-Amarna times he was worshiped at
Arqa in northern Canaan. His holy city was Byblos
and his cult as described by Lucian (De Dea Syria, 6)
was already in existence by the eighth century B. C.,
and almost certainly had been practiced by the Canaanites centuries before that time. At Sidon and Carthage
this youthful deity was Eshmun, who was beloved by
Astarte, the latter there having the greater prestige of
the two.

But whether it were Khay-Taou in relation with the
goddess (Isis-Hathor type) of Byblos, or Al Eyan beloved by Anath, or Adonis-Eshmun beloved by Astarte,

---

[16] For the transliteration Al Eyan I follow W. F. Albright. Compare
Aleyin (Dussaud); Aleion (Chas. W. Harris).

this worship of the youthful dying-rising god in Canaanite religion represented a type of cult likewise practiced throughout the Near East. In Babylonia this deity was Tammuz, lamented and sought by Ishtar. In Asia Minor he was Attis, beloved by Cybele. In Egypt he was Horus, son of Osiris and Isis.

3. SACRED PLACES AND PERSONS

The earliest places of Canaanite worship were the dolmens, which were built by the Canaanites, most likely those of Amorite strain. Their formation consisted of two large supporting stones, across which a third large unhewn stone was laid horizontally, somewhat like a table. The dolmen is rightly viewed as a grave, a house for the dead, and there the cult of the spirits of the dead, the Rephaim, was carried on. These spirits were thought to be thirsty. The cup marks on the top of the dolmen, on the floor, or on nearby rock surfaces, were intended to hold water or wine poured out as gifts to mollify the spirits and secure their help.

The spirits of the dead inhabited mother earth, whose fountains made the fields productive. There being, to primitive thought, no clear demarcation between the conception of the spirits of the dead dwelling in mother earth and that of the earth or nature spirits, givers of fertility, the cult of the spirits of the dead passed over imperceptibly into the cult of the nature spirits.

We see here evidence of the origin of the agricultural and fertility aspect of the Canaanite religion. This principle of fertility, originally connected with the pow-

ers of the spirits of the dead, was detached from its
primitive association with graves and was connected
with such objects as gave evidence of productive power
—springs, trees, fruitful fields and valleys, wine and olive
presses. Moreover, this fertility principle was deified
and given an anthropomorphic explanation. The dying
of vegetation was consequent upon the death of the
powers, the deities, who gave fertility. The death of
Tammuz-Adonis, his descent to the underworld, caused
the death of vegetation. His resurrection from the
underworld brought the sprouting forth of the fresh
vegetation in the spring. And the peculiar vigor of
these conceptions in Canaan grows out of the nature of
the climate with its exceedingly long dry season, and the
brilliant change wrought in the spring as a result of
the former and latter rains. The cult associated with
the dolmens was motivated by sympathetic magic. To
pour out water unto these controllers of fertility was to
coerce the supply of water necessary for the productivity
of the soil.

Contemporaneous with the dolmen period and in
close relation to a dolmen necropolis in Transjordania,
is a monolith called Hagar el-Mansub. It is a rough
image of a phallus, a *maccebah* or pillar, and is a magical object of fertility and at the same time is the embodiment of the Baal of the place, in origin connected with
the spirits of the dead. The juxtaposition of this
maccebah with the dolmen suggests a possible original
connection between productivity in nature and productivity in human, perhaps also in animal life.[17]

The place of cult in early Canaanite religion was

---

[17] P. Karge: *Rephaim*, pp. 557ff., 621f., 608f.

open to the sky and in Old-Testament times was designated by the characteristic name *bamah*, or "High
Place." Much of our best knowledge of the High Places
comes from the Old-Testament polemic against them.
Every city had its High Place, where Baal and Astarte
were worshiped. It was usually situated on a high hill
in a region of great fertility. Luxuriant trees—oaks,
poplars, and terebinths—were present. There were altars for sacrifice and for the burning of incense. Every
High Place had at least one stone pillar, or *maccebah*.
It was the symbol of the Baal of the High Place and
represented the male principle of deity. Every High
Place also had its *asherah,* a tree, or sacred post of wood,
the symbol of the female principle of deity. The symbol
of Astarte at Byblos and at Paphos, however, was the
conical stone, and the wooden post represented Adonis
(Osiris). This is also, in one instance, in harmony with
the testimony of Jeremiah (2. 27).

Many Canaanite High Places have been discovered
in the course of the archaeological exploration of Palestine, notably at Beth Shemesh, Gezer, and Beth Shean.
At Beth Shemesh Elihu Grant found a stone table of
offerings with cup marks, a grooved channel, and a
basinlike depression for catching blood. Near by was a
hewn stone, one meter and a half long and the same in
circumference, evidently a *maccebah*, which fitted into
a stone socket not far away. At Gezer, which was
thoroughly excavated by R. A. S. Macalister, the most
significant result obtained was the uncovering of a great
central sanctuary, the High Place. The site was an open
space in the middle of the town and was probably
chosen because of the convenient presence of two

underground caves. It dates from 2500-2000 B. C., and represents the earliest Canaanite place of worship at Gezer. The first feature of the sanctuary was formed by the two underground caves which, when the High Place was constructed, were connected by a narrow, curved passageway. The larger cave of the two, forty feet in diameter, may have served as an assembly hall. The smaller cave, eight feet at its widest diameter, probably served as a holy of holies. It was the dark, inner chamber where the god was viewed as being immediately present. W. Robertson Smith maintains that the ancient holy of holies was originally a cave, a meara (so in Hebrew and Phoenician = mughara in Arabic). The holy of holies in the Jerusalem Temple was called the *debhir,* a term incorrectly rendered "oracle" but meaning, rather, the "part behind," the hindmost, innermost chamber, and probably dark as a cave would be.[18]

East of the cave was a rock-cut cistern sixteen feet deep which had evidently been used as a depository for refuse from the sacrifices, the bones found being those of human beings and of cows, sheep, deer, and goats. Surrounding the cistern there was an elaborate system of cup marks.

The most striking feature of the High Place at Gezer, however, was the alignment of eight, originally ten, monoliths, undressed pillars, standing in a gently curved line which was probably intended to be straight. Macalister thinks the second pillar, the smallest, is probably the surviving stone of an original pair which marked the High Place. The two would then represent the male divinity and his female companion. The top

---

[18] W. R. Smith: *The Religion of the Semites* (3d ed.), p. 200.

of this small pillar had several smooth spots which are best explained as the effect of the continued kissing by the succession of worshipers. Other pillars were added from time to time by the Canaanite chieftains of Gezer. One of them, the seventh in the series, seems to have been a sacred stone of another High Place which had been dragged to Gezer as a trophy of war.

At Beth Shean, Alan Rowe uncovered six Canaanite temples dating from c. 1500-1200 B. C. The most significant of the six was the one designated "the southern temple" of Thutmose III (c. 1500 B. C.), which combined an old Canaanite High Place containing a *maccebah* and a libation bowl, the original sanctuary in the level, with a temple that had altars and rooms. It thus represents the transition from a sanctuary open to the sky to the temple with the portions containing altars roofed over. Moreover, near the *maccebah* was found the now famous Mekal stele, which represented the Baal of Beth Shean in human form and dressed like Resheph, seated upon a throne, holding in his right hand the symbol of life and in his left the scepter of happiness. We see here a second significant transition— that from the representation of a god in the fashion of a stone pillar to his portraiture in human form. The northern temple at Beth Shean, dating from the time of Rameses II (c. 1272), was dedicated to Anath, "Queen of heaven and mistress of all the gods." The southern temple of Rameses II was dedicated to Resheph, Canaanite god of the underworld, and identical with Nergal. In the Philistine period the worship of Anath and Resheph continued at Beisan under the names of Astarte and Dagon, respectively (1 Chronicles 10. 10).

Fairly typical, in arrangement, of all six Canaanite
temples at Beth Shean was that of Seti I (c. 1300 B. C.).
An entrance court (1) with columns and architrave
above, led to an anteroom (2), which opened into a
court (3), partly surrounded by a low bench, in which
was situated a rectangular brick altar with a small stone
block in front of it. Two papyrus columns supported
the roof. From this court, steps led to the shrine containing the altar (4). A door in the anteroom opened
into a storeroom (5).

Similar Canaanite temples have been uncovered by
Macalister at Gezer, by Montet at Byblos, by Grant at
Beth Shemesh, by Badè at Mizpah, and by Welter at
Shechem.

At Tyre, where a temple had existed since c. 2750
B. C., in front there were two pillars, one of fine gold,
the other of emerald stone (Herodotus II, 44). The
same feature of the two pillars was present at the entrance to the temples at Byblos, Shechem, Taanach, the
temple of Atargatis at Hieropolis, and that of Aphrodite
(= Astarte) at Paphos in Cyprus.

The Canaanite temples served a twofold function.
Chief and foremost, the temple existed to house the
idol representing the deity. It was literally a Beth-El,
"a house of a god." The purpose of the sanctuary of
silver and gold, the holy of holies in the temple of Baal
at Ras Shamra, was to shelter the sacred objects, the
idols of silver and gold, where the Baal might keep
watch over them. The second function comes into
greatest clarity in the Ras Shamra myth. It was to bring
under regularity and control, by means of the rites of
the sacrificial cult, the fertility powers over which the

Baal presided—the thunder, the rain, and the dew. When the temple was constructed with a window open in the sanctuaries, a lattice in the midst of the temple, then Baal would give forth his holy voice, making a rift in the clouds, and the fertilizing waters of heaven would descend.

There were sacred persons in the Canaanite cult. There were priests and priestesses of Ashtart. There were also priests of a lower order, whose office it was to burn incense in the High Places (2 Kings 23. 5) and who, as Hosea attests, were officially connected with the cult of the bull deity of Bethel (Hosea 10. 5). Lucian saw 300 priests officiating at one time in the cult of Atargatis at Hieropolis, some sacrificing, some bringing libations, some bearing fire, and some tending the altar, all being clad in white vestments and wearing caps. The high priest, with whom Amaziah of Bethel may suggestively be compared (Amos 7. 10), was robed in purple and wore a golden tiara (Lucian, 42-3).

There were prophets of Baal, the earliest illustration of which is the noble youth of Byblos, of whom we learn in the romantic story of the Egyptian Wen Amon, dating from the early twelfth century B. C. While Zakar Baal, prince of Byblos, was offering a sacrifice, one of his noble youths was seized by the deity (that is, the Baal), and in a state of prophetic ecstasy which continued throughout the night the devotee uttered an oracle which was at once heeded by the prince.[19] But our clearest glimpse of these prophets is given in the vivid narrative of the ecstatic, orgiastic activities of the prophets of Baal over whom Elijah, the prophet of

---

[19] G. A. Barton: *Archaeology and the Bible* (5th ed.), pp. 410-14.

Yahweh, scored a signal triumph (1 Kings 18. 26-29). This is an authentic phase of the Canaanite-Phoenician cult of the Tyrian Baal Melqarth, described with fine objectivity and accuracy of detail by the Israelite historian.

Connected with the Canaanite sanctuaries were female sacred prostitutes called *qedheshoth* (singular, *qedheshah*) and holy men called *qedheshim* (singular, *qadhesh*). By both Phoenicians and Yahweh-worshiping Israelites these holy men were given the opprobrious name "dog" (Deuteronomy 23. 18). We understand them best when we view them as emasculated devotees of Astarte, corresponding exactly to the depraved and lewd devotees of the Syrian goddess Atargatis, whose disgusting coarseness and crass immorality is described by the Punic Lucius Apuleius. This is in harmony with Israelite evidence (Leviticus 18. 22) and accounts for the revulsion toward them felt by the finer moral sense of later Israel.

4. FESTIVALS

Two Canaanite festivals were an inheritance from nomadic times, the Festival of the New Moon (*hodhesh*), and the Festival of the Full Moon (*shabbath, shapatti*). They are not mentioned in the earliest codes of Israel (C. C., Exodus 20. 23–23. 33 and J Decalogue, Exodus 34), which fact implies their originally non-Yahwistic character. Hosea specifically associates these festivals with the Baal cult, designating them "days of the Baalim," and the sharp prophetic condemnation of them (Amos 8. 5; Hosea 2. 11, 13; Isaiah 1. 13f.) implies the same relationship.

The festivals most characteristic of Canaanite religion, however, were those associated closely with the turning points of the agricultural year, the Feast of Unleavened Bread (*hag hammaccoth*, Exodus 34. 18), the Feast of Weeks (*hag shabhuoth*, Exodus 34. 22), or of Harvest (*hag haqqacir*, Exodus 23. 16), and the Feast of Ingathering (*hag haasiph*, Exodus 34. 22). Although they appear in the biblical sources as features of the authoritative cult of Israel, we can penetrate to the essentials of their earlier observance in old Canaanite times.

The Feast of Unleavened Bread was a spring festival which lasted seven days (Exodus 34. 18). It came during the month of Abib, at the beginning of the grain harvest (Deuteronomy 16. 9). It was a sun festival, perhaps originally, as Oesterley thinks likely, a festival in honor of the sun god, and it was celebrated when the sun began to gather energy at the vernal equinox. It lasted seven days, during which no bread made with leaven was eaten. The distinctive rite of this feast was the waving of the first fruits to the Baal of the sanctuary (Leviticus 23. 11) as a species of fertility magic. "The exact prototype," as Dussaud calls it, of the festival as seen through Israelite sources, is found in the north Canaanite epic of Ras Shamra, which narrates the combat of Mot with Al Eyan. That portion of the cultic myth there given, which describes Anath's hunt for her brother, Al Eyan, whom Mot had put to death, and her destruction of Mot, took its origin from the ritual transactions of the feast. Seeing at her feet the last sheaf of grain (barley or corn), the sheaf in which Mot, god of the ripe harvest and destroyer of Al Eyan,

had taken refuge, Anath performs seven ritualistic acts.
1. She seizes the sheaf (= Mot), 2. cuts the ears, 3.
threshes them, 4. roasts the grains, 5. grinds them by
hand in a mill, and 6. scatters the grains thus ground
and crushed over the field. Then and only then, does
she 7. eat bread with leaven, for with the destruction of
the last sheaf (= Mot), the taboo on the harvest is
lifted.[20] The rite of the last sheaf symbolized the end
of the reign of Mot, just as the rite of the first sheaf
signified its beginning. The destruction of Mot makes
way for the resuscitation of Al Eyan, god of the nourish-
ing spring rains. The implication of the myth is that
during the seven days no leavened bread was eaten,
which corresponds with the biblical data as to its observance. The wave offering was accompanied by the burnt
offering of a male lamb one year old and a meal offering
of the first fruits (Leviticus 23. 12f.), "corn in the ear
parched with fire, bruised corn of the fresh ear"
(Leviticus 2. 14). In perfect harmony with the data
from this newly discovered source is the tradition regarding the Tammuz (= Adonis = Mot-Al Eyan) Festival as carried out at Harran. En-Nedim reports that
the women lament Tammuz because he was so cruelly
put to death, his bones ground in a mill and then
strewn in the wind. During this festival the women ate
nothing ground in a mill, but enjoyed only steeped
wheat, sweet vetches, dates, raisins, and other like
things.[21]

The Feast of Weeks, or Harvest (called Pentecost,

---

[20] R. Dussaud: "La mythologie phénicienne d'après les tablettes de
Ras Shamra," in RHR 1931, p. 390.

[21] D. Chwolsohn: *Die Ssabier,* Vol. II, p. 27.

compare Leviticus 23. 16, in the New Testament),
came seven weeks later and marked the end of the
joyous festivities of the corn and barley harvest. The
rite which alone distinguishes its observance from all
the other agricultural festivals was the offering of the
first fruits of the harvest in the form of a meal offering
of two loaves made of fine flour baked with leaven
(Leviticus 23. 17). It is possible that this practice in
Canaan echoed the Egyptian rite of the two cakes representing the eyes of Horus which were viewed as containing the essence of life. The aim of the offering
would then have been to strengthen the Baal and help
him in this magical fashion, in the renewal of vegetation.[22]

The most important Canaanite festival of all was the
great autumnal celebration held in Ethnaim, the first
month of the Canaanite year. It was a vintage festival,
and marked the end of the olive and vintage harvest
(Deuteronomy 16. 13). The most ancient name for it
is the Feast of Ingathering (Exodus 34. 22). It is the
earliest festival of which we learn from the records of
Israel, where it was celebrated at the temple of Baal-
Berith of Shechem. The worshipers "went out into the
field, and gathered their vineyards, and trod the grapes,
and held festival [lit., "made *hillulim*"], and went into
the house of their god, and did eat and drink" (Judges
9. 27). The celebration was accompanied by noise and
hilarity. A conspicuous feature of it, as we learn from
its annual celebration at Shiloh (Judges 21. 19-23), was
a dance (Exodus 32. 19) of the maidens in proximity
to the vineyards. The outstanding note of this festival

[22] W. O. E. Oesterley, in *Myth and Ritual*, p. 121.

was joy.[23] For seven days the Canaanites dwelt in booths made of "olive branches and branches of wild olive, and myrtle branches (a tree sacred to Astarte), and palm branches, and branches of thick trees" (Nehemiah 8. 15; compare Leviticus 23. 40), emblems of life and fresh vegetation, fertility and moisture. At the center of these rites was the vegetation idea. The plant pavilion (or, as it was called, the "booth" or "tabernacle") was a vegetation temple.[24] It is from these characteristic booths that the Deuteronomic name of the festival is derived, the Feast of Booths or Tabernacles (*hag hassukkoth,* Deuteronomy 16. 13).

5. SACRIFICE

One of the most characteristic elements of the Canaanite cult was the sacrificial system. Apart from what we can infer from Old Testament data, there are two primary sources for the sacrificial cult. The one is the Carthaginian system as revealed in two tables of sacrifices and dues, the Tariff of Marseilles, probably originally from Carthage, and the Tariff of Carthage, dating from c. 400 B. C. The other source is the north Canaanite texts of Ras Shamra recently discovered, which date c. 1400 B. C. and present vivid glimpses of a well-developed sacrificial system in Canaan as it was in effect shortly before the Israelite invasion. A comparison of the two primary sources reveals the essential continuity in religious concepts and sacrificial cult of late Canaanite with early Canaanite religion.

---

[23] Isaiah 30. 29; Deuteronomy 16. 15; Jeremiah 7. 34; Leviticus 23. 40.

[24] W. O. E. Oesterley, in *Myth and Ritual,* p. 142; H. Gressmann, in "The Mysteries of Adonis and the Feast of Tabernacles," in *Expositor* (1925), p. 430.

Animals sacrificed at Ras Shamra were bulls, castrated sheep, heavy and fat, rams, calves one year old, and sucking lambs. In addition to these the Phoenician tariffs included bulls, he-goats, kids, cocks, and pullets. There was already in existence before the Israelites entered Canaan a great variety of sacrifices. The most potent were the bloody sacrifices, but two birds could be substituted for a large animal. The following sacrifices were performed at Ras Shamra: the perfect offering, the peace offering, the sin offering, the sacrifice intended to secure justice, the sacrifice of thanksgiving for the rain, the whole burnt offering, the sacrifice of expiation, the offering made by fire, and the sacrifice of communion. Similar to the rite of the last sheaf in which Mot, god of the ripened harvest, had taken refuge, was the sacrifice of the stallion ass, covered with vine branches and leaves in which the spirit of the vintage harvest had taken refuge. Ordered by Asherat-of-the-Sea, the deities Qadesh-and-Amurru, having placed their hands upon the ass, just before the morning star appeared, sacrificed him upon the altar of the High Place, and then made their request of El, the great solar deity. The sacrificial rite which gave rise to this myth had as its motivation the renewal of the fruit-bearing power of the vine. Qadesh-and-Amurru there played a part similar to that of the rôle of Anath and Al Eyan in the rite of the last sheaf.[25]

The Phoenician tariffs likewise enumerate three types of animal sacrifices—the expiatory sacrifice, in which the body of the animal went to the priests; the sacrifice of communion, where the priests and the offerer

---

[25] II AB., cols. IV-V, 4-19; compare Dussaud in RHR 105, pp. 288ff.

shared in the sacrificial victim; and the whole burnt offering, the only animal sacrifice wherein some part did not go to the priests. There were also offerings of sacred first fruits, of food (grain or bread), and oil. There were likewise the meal offering of grain mixed with oil, and an offering of milk.

It is clear, especially from the Ras Shamra sources, that the dominating motive which underlay the sacrificial system was the desire to maintain by magical acts the regularity of the fertility processes in nature, particularly the rainfall, productivity of the soil, and fecundity in the flocks and herds. The offerings embodied a kind of coercive or co-operative magic. Bread was placed upon the tables of offering, while wine, "the blood of trees," was poured out in pots and goblets, food and drink for the fertility gods.

The most efficacious of all was human sacrifice, which was practiced in the early Canaanite cult and which was continued among the Phoenicians and Carthaginians until abolished under Hadrian in the second century A. D. Philo of Byblos, who in his late work based on Sanchuniathon gives much accurate information concerning early Phoenician religion, bears witness to it as an ancient practice at Byblos, where it had a propitiatory purpose. The rite gave rise to the myth that when a pestilence was raging, El-Kronos (=Malk=Molech), founder of Byblos, offered up his only son as a sacrifice to his father Ouranos (Heaven), the victim being viewed as "the price of redemption." Porphyry of Tyre records that in great calamities, such as war, drought, or pestilence, the Phoenicians sacrificed some of their dearest friends, who were selected by votes for the purpose. It was customary for rulers of city or nation to make such an offering. Similar to this and propitiatory in intention, was the sacrifice by Mesha, the Moabite king, of his eldest son as an offering to Chemosh, when an Israelite victory threatened. It was told by the Hebrew narrator whose home was in Canaan, and who was thoroughly familiar with the practice and motivation of such a sacrifice (2 Kings 3. 27). In Laodicea, in northern Canaan, the ancient custom of sacrificing a virgin to Athena (= Astarte) was later softened by the substitution of a stag.

Palestinian archaeology has revealed evidence of human sacrifice as foundation rites. At Megiddo, from Canaanite times, Schumacher found the body of a child buried in a jar at the foot of the city wall. Beside the skeleton lay a water jar with handle, and outside the bell-shaped cover of the jar there was a pottery eating-vessel. Several rows of stones surrounded this jar. In the east wall of the fortress, between the lowest layer of the foundation and the second layer, was found a jar enclosing the body of a child. The jar was covered by a small stone plate. It contained, along with the body, two small jars and an eating-vessel.[26] At Gezer[27] infants were buried in large, two-handled, pointed-base jars, the bodies being deposited head first and being accompanied inside or outside the jar with two or three small vessels. They were found over the whole area of the High Place. Many infants or very young children were found buried in jars and placed under the corners of houses from all the Semitic strata. In one case which

---

[26] H. Gressmann: *Altorientalische Bilder*, Nos. 228-9, and p. 71.
[27] R. A. S. Macalister: *The Excavation of Gezer* (3 Vols.).

seems unquestionably to suggest a foundation rite, the jar was under the wall, with its outer surface flush with the face of the wall. The vessels, lamps, and bowls, buried with the jar, were placed behind it, under the middle of the wall.

These seem to be in the nature of inaugural sacrifices. Any encroachment upon the domain of the Baal was fraught with peril. Special precaution to propitiate the divine powers had to be taken, hence, the erection of a building or wall was accompanied by human sacrifice. It is most likely that the intent of these rites was to guarantee fertility in the human, animal, and vegetable spheres.

Carthage was founded by Tyrians (c. 1200 B. C.) and as there Alexander's Hellenizing policy was least effective, the ancient Canaanite (Phoenician) rites of child sacrifice persisted into the early Christian centuries. At times, instead of sacrificing their own sons, the Carthaginians substituted slave boys secretly bred for the purpose. Or they would buy children for the purpose from poor people. Diodorus records a public sacrifice of two hundred sons of the nobility, at which no less than three hundred more who were liable to censure voluntarily offered themselves. He also describes the brazen statue of Saturn (= Melqarth = Molech, Moloch) with the palms of his hands extended and bent downward so that the child to be sacrificed, when laid upon them, would slip off and fall into a deep fiery furnace. And Plutarch tells how the mother would stand by without a tear or moan, while in the area before the statue the priests and devotees of the god would dance to the noise of flutes and drums in an orgy of ecstasy,

the loud tumult of which would drown the cries of
the victims, the sacrifice being the climax of the cult.[28]

In the sanctuary of Tanith, which probably dates
from the founding of Carthage and existed until its
destruction by Scipio, 146 B. C., Byron Khun de Prorok,
in 1921 and after, excavated thousands of urns containing the relics and bones of sacrificed children, ranging
from newborn babes to twelve years of age. They had
been passed through "the fires of Molech" (Malk =
Melqarth = Saturn) and then buried in the sanctuary.

6. THE ADONIS CULT

The most popular aspects of Canaanite-Phoenician
religion centered in the Adonis cult. A beloved feature
of this cult were the gardens of Adonis. They consisted
of baskets of earth in which the Canaanite-Phoenician
women planted various seeds and slips, such as barley,
corn, lettuce, anemonies, and other plants. They care-
fully watered them and forced them to grow rapidly,
only to wither as rapidly in the sun. After several days
they would throw them into the sea or the rivers. These
rites were of the nature of imitative magic, intended to
bring back the deity of the new spring life from the
world of the dead and to renew upon the earth the
fructifying waters.

The most famous centers of the Adonis cult were
Byblos, Aphaka, and Heliopolis. Lucian of Samosata
(born 125 A. D.), from personal observation and from
explanations given there by its adherents, knew the cult
as it was practiced at Byblos and gives the most accurate

---

[28] Diodorus: *The Historical Library*, II, pp. 422f.; Plutarch: *Moralia*,
II, 13; Tertullian: *Apology*, 9.

evidence of its nature. Annually lamentation rites were carried out by the women of Byblos. Such rites were being performed by the wailing women portrayed on the sarcophagus of Ahiram of Byblos (c. 1250 B. C.), discovered by Montet in 1923, where, with bodies bared to the waist and hair loosed, they are shown beating their breasts and laying their hands on the back of their heads. After this ritual wailing was concluded, they made offerings to the dead Adonis, shaving their heads in mourning as a form of magic, the hair thus offered being the symbol of life and being designed to restore the fertility deity to life. Women who refused thus to offer their hair were required to expose their persons for hire for the space of a day to foreigners, the hire money to be an offering to Astarte to secure her favor. On "another day" they alleged that Adonis was alive and they exhibited his effigy to the sky. At Byblos, where from the fourth millennium B. C. the relations with Egypt were intimate, the rites of the vegetation deity Osiris had so influenced the Adonis rites that some thought it was Osiris rather than Adonis whose death they mourned.[29]

Sacred prostitution as practiced at Byblos is also abundantly evidenced for Aphaka and Heliopolis. Aphaka was probably the scene of the Ras Shamra ritual of Mot-Al Eyan (= Adonis). Here at the chief source of the Nahr Ibrahim, the river of Adonis, where the vegetation is dense and luxuriant, the reputed burial place of Adonis (so Pseudo-Melito), there was

[29] Lucian: *De Dea Syria*, 6-7; H. Gressmann: *Altorientalische Bilder*, Nos. 665f. and pp. 190f.; W. Mannhardt: *Wald und Feld Kulte*, II, pp. 284ff.; Athanasius: *Oratio Contra Gentes*, 26.

one of the most highly reverenced of Astarte temples
which existed until destroyed, along with its cult, by
Constantine. Eusebius designates this great cultic center "as a school of wickedness for all votaries of impur-
ity," and records that along with other horrible and
infamous practices, unlawful commerce of women and
adulterous intercourse were perpetrated. At Heliopolis
(Baal Bek), where, still today, the most splendid temple
ruins in all Syria are to be seen, Eusebius informs us
that they dignified licentious pleasure with a distin-
guishing title of honor, and permitted their wives and
daughters to commit shameless fornication. Ancient
custom demanded that every virgin should be yielded
up to sacred prostitution with strangers in the temple [30]

The system of sacred harlotry so prevalent in the
Adonis cult, was deeply rooted in the whole north-
Semitic area, where there was a universal deification of
the reproductive forces of nature. It was most highly
developed in Babylonia, where there were three classes
of sacred women. There were (1) the "consecrated,"
who might be dedicated to any divinity by the father
of the devotee. There were (2) the hierodules of Ishtar,
generally called *qadishtu*, with which the Canaanite
qedheshoth were identical. They were a permanent
institution and bore no dishonor. There were (3)
those women, who in return for "hire" from a foreigner,
consecrated to the goddess before marriage the first

[30] Sozomen: *The Ecclesiastical History*, Bk. II, 10, Bk. III, 5; Socrates:
The Ecclesiastical History, I, 18; Eusebius: *Life of Constantine*, III,
55, 58. For similar practices in the Attis cults, see W. M. Ramsay:
Cities and Bishoprics of Phrygia, I, 94f. (Lydia); Strabo, XI, 14, 16
(Achilsena where Anaitu=Cybele): Strabo, XII, 2, 3, 6 (Comana of
Cappadocia, where Enyo=Cybele), and Strabo, XII, 3, 34, 36 (Pontic
Comana).

fruits of their virginity, the money thus secured being sacred to the goddess. In its ultimate purpose the rite was intended to insure fertility in women by the direct invocation of the goddess of fertility. The requirement that only a stranger could have relations with such a votary guards this cultic act from being a common love affair with a local lover (so E. S. Hartland). This type of sacred harlotry is found at Byblos and Heliopolis.[31]

The fullest ritual of the *qedheshoth* we possess is in the north Canaanite source in cuneiform, recently discovered at Ras Shamra, "The Birth of the Gracious and Beautiful Gods," in which they are called "the Wives of El." However it may have been enacted in the cult, the purpose of the ritual was to secure fertility in human and animal life.[32]

In their profoundest significance these rites of sacred prostitution were not the expression of common lust. Mannhardt has rightly maintained that "they are a symbolic and mystical expression of a religious idea," and "far-removed from animal intoxication and wild passion." We are fairest to the Canaanite concepts which they embodied when we stress their representative and substitutional features. Every woman devotee represented Astarte, and every foreigner who appeared and held union with her represented Adonis coming from the foreign region, the land of the dead.

By a method which may be called sympathetic magic, the *qedheshoth* and *qedheshim* sought to secure the

---

[31] Compare L. R. Farnell: *Greece and Babylon*, pp. 275f.; Herodotus, I, 199; *Epistle of Jeremiah*, 42f.; H. Zimmern in KAT², p. 423; S. A. Cook, in W. R. Smith's RS (3d ed.), p. 612.

[32] Ch. Virolleaud in Syria, XIV, pp. 129ff., lines 37-60; cf. G. A. Barton in JBL., Vol. LIII, p. 71.

blessings of fertility for their fields and vineyards, for their flocks and herds, and for their families. They were the official representatives of Astarte, the human vehicles, as Farnell rightly suggests, "for diffusing through the community the peculiar virtue or potency of the goddess, the much-coveted blessing of human fertility," and, indeed, fertility in all other areas of life as well.

The abiding and primary elements in the Adonis cult were the rites. But to interpret and explain these rites there arose, in a variety of versions, the Adonis myth. We find it in its earliest known Canaanite form in the Epic of Mot-Al Eyan (= Adonis) from Ras Shamra, which, while dating from the thirteenth century B. C., was probably composed between 1700 and 1500 B. C. Al Eyan met his death at the hands of Mot. Anath, sister of Al Eyan, being overcome by her affection for him, her heart being moved "like the heart of the wild cow for her calf, like the heart of the ewe for her lamb," lamented his brutal killing for days and months. At the end of lamentation she took hold of Mot by the shoe and raised her voice in mingled grief and rage, crying, "Mot, give me my brother." Attacking Mot fiercely, she destroyed him. At the death of Mot, Al Eyan was resuscitated and placed upon his throne.[33]

The later and most common version is as follows: Adonis, a shepherd and hunter, while hunting on Mount Lebanon, was wounded by a boar. Aphrodite (= Baalath = Astarte), who saw him weltering in his

---

[33] IAB., col. I, lines 10-13a; col. II, lines 4-12; cols. III-IV, lines 1-2; col. VI, lines 30-38.

blood, leaped down from the sky, rending her garments and her unbraided hair, smiting her bared breasts with her palms, and crying out in bitter and passionate lamentations. As a perpetual monument of her sorrow she ordained an annual representation of his death and an annual imitation of her wailing.[34]

Macrobius gives a solar interpretation of the myth which implies the presence in it of the resurrection motif. As Adonis was wounded by the wild boar, so the sun is wounded, as it were, by the rough winter and withdraws from the upper hemisphere of heaven to the lower hemisphere of the earth. At the spring equinox it returns to the heavenly sphere. This represents the resurrection of Adonis.[35] This same resurrection motif is implied in the annual designation of the festival of "the awakening of Melqarth," a deity of the Adonis type which was celebrated at Tyre in the spring (February-March). And it is further implied for the cult at Byblos where, succeeding the lamentation, the people alleged that Adonis was alive.

[34] Ovid: *Metamorphoses*, X.
[35] Macrobius: *Saturnalia*, I, 23.

CHAPTER II

THE RELIGION OF THE HEBREW FATHERS

*T*HE stage was ready for the opening act in the dramatic evolution of Old Testament religion. But ere the curtain rose a prelude of major importance was enacted in part in the wilderness and in part in Canaan. The first phase of this prelude was the epoch of the Hebrew fathers. The second phase was the epoch of Moses. In the present chapter we are concerned with the religion of the Hebrew fathers—Abraham, Isaac, and Jacob—and shall deal solely with the most distinctive and uniquely characteristic features of that religion.

The biblical term "Hebrew" and that appearing in nonbiblical sources as "Habiru," come from the same root, which means "to cross," "to pass," that is, from place to place, in nomadic fashion. The term was not originally racial. The "Habiri" was one committed to a particular mode of living and the whole Habiru movement, which emerges into the light of historical record in Babylonia (Akkad) in the middle of the third millennium B. C., probably received its original impulse from nomadic Semitic tribesmen. There gradually developed among these Habiru, however, a certain ethnic character and in the Tell el-Amarna period an influx of Aramaean stock gave them the Aramaean quality which they have in Old Testament times.

In the earliest sources they were nomadic plunderers who served as mercenary troops in the service of Babylonians, Kashites, Egyptians, and especially the

Hittites. Their penetration into Canaan in the Tell el-Amarna age is rightly understood as the southernmost stage of the invasion of Syria and Palestine by Shubbiluliumash, the founder of the New Hittite kingdom (c. 1380-1350 B. C.). These recognized mercenaries in the service of the Hittites were then sweeping everything before them. Egyptian dominion in Syria and Palestine was not strong enough to resist them. Canaanite chieftains were falling away from Egypt unto them. Only Rib-Addi of Gebal and Abdi-Khiba of Jerusalem remained unswervingly loyal to the Pharaoh.[1]

This historically demonstrated relation of the Habiru to the Hittites throws light upon a tradition preserved by Ezekiel. Three environmental cultural streams poured in upon the developing Israelites, Jerusalem, in Ezekiel's thought, being a symbol for the whole people.

Thine origin and thy birth is of the land of the Canaanite;
An Amorite[2] was thy father, and thy mother was a Hittite (Ezekiel 16. 3).

Upon a substratum of Canaanites in whose land the Hebrew nomads became a unified people, came the fructifying Amorite and the nurturing Hittite contributions. It was at this period that the Hittite contribution was the strongest.

The earliest discernible strand of the Habiru with which the Old Testament is concerned are the Hebrew Fathers Abraham, Isaac, and Jacob, the traditions concerning whom we have in three great cycles. Of basic importance for our discussion is the question as to their

---

[1] Kn. 126, 68. 12; 74. 19f.; 116. 37ff.; 286. 18ff.
[2] Omitting the definite article, with LXX.

existence as historical individuals. The view advocated
by Eduard Meyer that they were originally Canaanite
deities whom the Israelites came to revere as heroes
and ancestors, is no longer seriously held.[3] Of greater
importance is the interpretation of the names of the
Fathers as eponyms of the tribes wherein a tribe is represented by an imaginary personage bearing its name,
who is called into existence for the purpose of expressing its unity. From this point of view it would be natural to translate the seeming affinities of the various
tribes into the family relations of father, son, brother,
husband, wife, etc., of eponymous ancestors.[4] In this
view there is abiding value, for there is no question that
such genealogical treatment of tribal relationships
often was for the Hebrew historians a conventional
symbolism perhaps more transparent to them than to
us. But the exclusively eponymous interpretation
which denies to the Fathers historical reality must be
and has largely been surrendered.

The Fathers Abraham, Isaac, and Jacob are rightly
viewed not primarily as eponyms of tribes but as actual
historical individuals. This does not mean that the
narratives of the Fathers contain no traditions of tribal
movements or relationships. It was characteristic of the
Israelite conception of man and community that no
sharp distinction was made between the history of the
individual and that of the tribe. They were accordingly, as Pedersen suggests, "the Fathers who take part in
the life of the tribe." The tribe forms about a prom-

---

[3] Compare E. Meyer: *Israel und ihre Nachbarstämme*, pp. 249ff., and
R. Kittel: *Geschichte des Volkes Israels* (4th ed.), 1, pp. 442f.
[4] H. P. Smith: *Old Testament History*, p. 50; H. Guthe: *Geschichte
des Volkes Israels*, p. 4.

inent man and is called after him, and he exerts himself on their behalf. "He is not removed by death from his tribe, but continues to live in it and share its adventures. . . . He is at the same time the tribe and its Father, and to every one who joins the tribe he thus becomes a Father."[5]

The Abraham cycle of traditions (Genesis 11. 27–25. 11) begins with the migration of Chaldaean nomads represented by Terah, from Ur to Harran. At this latter ancient city, the most strategic point between the Tigris and Euphrates, they installed the worship of the god Sin and his divine family with characteristics such as they had possessed from time immemorial. Under the power of a profound religious impulse and stimulated by their nomadic instinct, a group of Aramaean nomads, led by Abraham, migrated to Canaan, the discernible Canaanite stations of their progress being Shechem, Bethel, and Hebron (Genesis 12). They adopted the language of Canaan and thus developed a barrier between themselves and the Aramaeans. In the account of the campaign of four eastern kings against five Canaanite kings, narrated in Genesis 14, one of many such expeditions into the Westland to assure to the eastern monarch political ascendancy over that region, "Abram the Hebrew" appears as a nomadic Habiru warrior with three hundred and eighteen troops under his control, bent on protecting the west from such an invasion. The sojourn in Egypt of Abraham nomads (Genesis 12. 10ff.) may, as Speiser thinks, have some relation to the early years of the domination of Egypt by the Semitic Hyksos (1788-1580 B. C.). This

[5] J. Pedersen: *Israel, Its Life and Culture*, p. 14.

would date Abraham somewhere within the epoch of Hyksos control, probably in the early part, c. 1700 B. C. Read in the light of our numerous extra-biblical sources for the nomadic Habiru, the account of "Abram the Hebrew," sketched in Genesis 14, is a correct portrait of an Aramaean nomadic warrior. He here appears as a vigorous warrior of flesh and blood, a confederate of local kings. But he is also portrayed as a man of religious faith, loyal worshiper of Yahweh El Elyon, and it is with this trait in his personality that the later idealized portraits of the Yahwist, Elohist, and Priestly traditions are most directly concerned.

In the first section of the cycle of the Jacob traditions (Genesis 25-30) it is possible that some relation exists between the history of the Aramaean Jacob tribes and the late years of the Hyksos domination of Egypt. Professor Breasted viewed them as Bedouin allies of the Hyksos rule. Among the scarab names of the Hyksos Bedouin chieftains is one which may represent a Semitic Jacob-el. The existence of Jacob-el as a place name in Canaan, as found in an inscription of Thutmose III on the Amon temple at Karnak, dating from c. 1479 B. C., suggests the possibility that a Bedouin tribe bearing the name of its leader Jacob had transferred its name to a place or district, a name which would naturally still be retained after the expulsion of the Hyksos from Egypt (c. 1580 B. C.). This would suggest that the Jacob tribes had been in Canaan at least as early as the late years of the Hyksos occupation of Egypt. It would seem from archaeological evidence that Jericho, Bethel, and Ai fell before invading nomads previous to the Tell el-Amarna period and, indeed, earlier than 1500 B. C. There may possibly be some relationship between the early Hebrew mastery of these important towns and the migration of the Jacob tribes into Palestine.

The Isaac cycle of traditions (Genesis 21ff.) embodies the historical reminiscence of fresh infusion of Aramaean stock (Rebekah) into the Hebrew nomads already settled in the Negeb with Beer-sheba as their center, probably shortly after the expulsion of the Hyksos (c. 1580 B. C.), but before the Tell el-Amarna period (c. 1400 B. C.).

The biblical record of the Tell el-Amarna phase of the Habiru penetration of Canaan seems to be mirrored in the second section of the Jacob traditions, those that narrate the re-entry of the Jacob tribes into Canaan enriched by fresh Aramaean elements (Genesis 31ff.). Genesis 34 (J) implies that the friendly relations which had formerly been established with the Canaanites of this region by the earliest Habiru nomads (Abraham) were broken by two clans of the new invaders (compare Genesis 49. 5-7). It was these Jacob tribes who mastered Shechem, wresting it from Amorite (that is, Canaanite) hands by the power of the sword (Genesis 48. 22 [E]). With this agrees perfectly the lament of Abdi-Khiba, loyal Canaanite chieftain of Jerusalem, to his Egyptian overlord, that Labaya, the leading figure of central Canaan, and Shechem (matu Sa-ak-mi) had surrendered to the Habiru. Upon its re-entrance into the land of Canaan (c. 1400 B. C.) the Jacob tribe united with the Habiru already there and took the name "Israel" (Genesis 32. 28), a name which was probably originally tribal, expressing a wish or prayer, "may God rule." About 1223 B. C. we meet this name as the designation of a group of nomads yet in the period of transition to settled existence, in the triumphal stele of Merneptah, which celebrated his quelling of a general rebellion of his dependencies in Canaan. This is the earliest appearance of "Israel" applied to a group of people, known to history. The reminiscence of the Aramaean origin of Israel is preserved in an important fragment of ancient High-Place ritual (Deuteronomy 26. 5), wherein the worshiper was accustomed to recite the cultic words, "A wandering [that is, nomad] Aramaean was my father."

It was probably a section of these "Israelites" who, still as nomads, entered Egypt (Genesis 46). They were tribes such as those which the Egyptian Sinuhe tells of meeting at the border when he was fleeing the country, and among whom he found protection, being recognized by one of their Bedouin sheiks "who had been in Egypt." They were probably driven to seek sustenance in Egypt and refuge from the turmoil of Canaan even as had been the case slightly earlier with certain "Asiatics" of the time of Amenhotep IV of whom Pharaoh's officer reports:

Their countries are starving, they live like goats of the mountain. A few of the Asiatics, who know not how they should live, have come (begging a home in the domain) of Pharaoh, after the manner of your father's fathers since the beginning.

Down into Merneptah's reign the same trek of Semitic nomads to the land of privilege is in evidence from the report of one of the Pharaoh's officers that

a tribe of Bedouins from the land of Edom have been allowed to pass the fortifications of Thuku to find sustenance for themselves and their flocks in the territory of the Pharaoh.[6]

In some such manner as this did the "Israelite" Bedouins find entrance into Goshen at the eastern edge of the Nile delta.

It is reasonable to expect that traditions which, thus interpreted, embody a kernel of historical reminiscence, should likewise retain a residuum of reliable data concerning ancient Hebrew religion. But to recover the dominant aspects of the religion of the Hebrew Fathers from these traditions is a delicate task. W. Graf von Baudissin, a master in the whole field of Semitic religion in general and of Old Testament religion in particular, maintains that "the reconstruction of the religion of the Hebrews before Moses belongs to the most difficult tasks of the history of Old Testament religion, and one may say, of the history of religion in general."[7] The chief reason for the difficulty is that the literary sources which deal with the Hebrews before Moses all date from a period centuries later than the epoch they purport to portray. The earliest collections of traditions, the Yahwist and Elohist documents, date from the tenth or ninth century and the eighth century B. C., respectively. These sources may embody, however, significant features from the earliest centuries of Hebrew life. But to find therein dependable data for the Hebrew religion of the period previous to the thirteenth century B. C. is manifestly difficult, so much so that many scholars hold that from these documents can be derived a picture of

---

[6] C. Noyes: *The Genius of Israel*, pp. 34f.
[7] W. von Baudissin: *Kyrios*, III, p. 159.

Hebrew religion only for the centuries in which the documents took shape. As von Baudissin has maintained: "In my opinion, we have no justification for seeking in the God and cult of the patriarchs the conscious and for the most part not incorrect delineation of a pre-Mosaic stage of the religion of the Hebrews. The picture of the worship of God seen in Genesis seems to me to be nothing other than an antedating of the folk religion as it existed at the time when the sagas were developing on Canaanite soil."[8] Such negative conclusions, however, are unwarranted, as will at once appear.

The most rewarding approach to the religion of the Hebrew Fathers is that suggested by Dr. Albrecht Alt, who takes his stand at the Yahweh religion, as introduced to the germinal unity of Israel by Moses, and asks a basic question. Can there be discerned in the religious situation of the tribes previous to their unity in the nation Israel a preparation for this Yahweh religion of the epoch of Moses so that the latter would represent no radical break with the past? The contribution of Alt's work lies in the affirmative answer to this question. The major features of his argument[9] are accepted by the present author and are embodied in this discussion.

Illuminating for the religion of the Aramaean Hebrews before 1200 B. C. is the religion of the Nabataean and Palmyrenian Aramaeans, who, in a manner similar to the Hebrews and scarcely a millennium later than they, made the transition from the nomadic state

---

[8] W. von Baudissin: *Kyrios,* III, p. 152.
[9] Albrecht Alt: *Der Gott der Väter,* 1929.

to the developed civilization of Palestine and Syria [10]
Good sources for the religion of these later Aramaeans
are available in inscriptions which date from the time
after the nomads had become settled in the culture
lands. And while much in them reflects the civilizations
they found at hand in the regions where they settled, a
residuum can be discerned of certain nomadic elements
which reach back to their earlier stage of civilization
and which have been retained with great tenacity. Certain specific features of this religion which these sources
contain may be distinguished:

1. The particular deity is designated by the name of
the individual who founded his cult. In a Nabataean
inscription from Simdsch, near Bostra, the god worshiped
by the whole group who view one Qasiu as their an-
cestor, is called El Qasiu, "The god of Qasiu." Similarly, a Palmyrenian inscription speaks of the patron
deity of Thaimi as "The fortune of Thaimi," who was
also worshiped by the clan of Thaimi (bene Thaimi).
Again, whole communities of the Nabataeans shared in
the worship of "the god of Aumos," and the spreading
advance of his cult can be traced from the second to
the fourth centuries A. D.[11]

2. This association of the deity with the founder of
his cult was the result of the driving, constraining
power of the revelation to that worshiper of a hitherto
unknown god. He who was deemed worthy of so great
a new revelation, as the pioneer worshiper of the deity
thus disclosed, won a unique relation to the god which
no other person shared.

[10] *Ibid.*, pp. 33ff.
[11] *Ibid.*, pp. 35-41.

3. The essence of this relationship established by the revelation of the god to the individual was personal. It was not bound to any locality. Indeed, we can trace the spreading advance of the worship of the god of Aumos from Ledscha to the foot of the Hauran highlands. The tie between the deity and the founder of his cult was one which united the deity to his personal life in special care for his welfare.

4. This personal orientation of the deity to his worshiper rather than his attachment to any particular locality was congenial to the changes of location characteristic of nomadic life.

5. The worship of the god established by the one to whom the original revelation came was participated in by the group more or less connected by blood kinship. This cultic group included the clan and descendants of the founder, the whole tribe, and, after settlement in the culture lands, the neighboring villages and communities.

6. In some instances we can trace the progress and spread of the cult and the tendency of the cult to identify its god with the deity of the region entered, without, however, losing the distinctive connection of the deity with the original founder.

With our minds sharpened by these characteristics of late Aramaean religion we shall now study the classic episode of the call of Moses, as narrated by the Yahwist, the Priestly writer, and the Elohist, in order to discern the relation to the later Yahweh worship of the God of the Hebrew Fathers.[12]

[12] Yahwist, Exodus 3. 2-4a, 5, 7-8, 16-18. Priestly writer, Exodus 6. 2-13; Elohist, Exodus 3. 1, 4b, 6, 9-14.

The Yahwist, whose work dates not later than 850 B. C., and possibly a century earlier, conceives Yahweh as having been known to the Hebrew Fathers from the beginning. Yahweh was the god of Abraham, Isaac, and Jacob. In other words, according to him, the God of Israel was identical with the God of the Hebrew Fathers. The Priestly narrator, however, whose work dates c. 500 B. C., maintains that the God worshiped by the Fathers, beginning with Abraham, was El Shadday. God was not known by the name "Yahweh" until the time of Moses, to whom he so revealed himself. The most penetrating and profound analysis, however, is given by the Elohist, whose work dates 750 B. C. Like the Priestly narrator, he interprets the revelation of God to Moses as having behind it a history. The conception of stages of development in Israel's worship of God, which in the Priestly account seems formal and theoretical, in the Elohist is penetrated with a vital sense of history. Before Abraham, the ancestors of the Hebrews (Terah) beyond the Euphrates worshiped other gods (*Elohim aherim*, Joshua 24. 2). Beginning with Abraham there opened a new epoch of the divine self-revelation: he was to the Fathers "the God (*Elohe*) of Abraham, the God of Isaac, and the God of Jacob" (Exodus 3. 6). Then with a climactic word of vital importance (Exodus 6. 14), the Elohist connects the new revelation God made of himself to Moses as Yahweh with the earlier revelation he had made to the Fathers, thus spanning the interval from the Fathers to Moses, and making the God of the Fathers identical with Yahweh.

While the Priestly writer designates the God of the

Fathers as "El Shadday," the Elohist designates him as "the God of Abraham, the God of Isaac, and the God of Jacob." Evidently, these two authors were bound by no fixed tradition. The Priestly writer seems to have chosen one of the existing "El" designations, Shadday, to the sacrifice of others because it best fitted his controlling theological concept, the idea of the sovereignty of god. On the other hand, the Elohist has as his major purpose to link together the era of the Fathers with the later era of Moses by showing the deep inner connection they had with one another through the worship of the same god. The Elohist, however, is not here creating independently, giving in *a priori* fashion his theory of the development of the religion of Israel. His concept of an inner unity between the god of the Fathers and the Yahweh of the time of Moses and Joshua embodies ancient and reliable tradition. For the religion of the Fathers played a significant rôle in preparing the ground for the worship of Yahweh and establishing certain features to which as contact points that later worship attached itself.

The Elohist's classic designation of the God of the Fathers as "the God of Abraham, the God of Isaac, and the God of Jacob" brings into a formal unity the resultant of great creative personal and social religious experiences that were originally distinct and separate from one another in time and space. To understand from our records what actually happened it is necessary, as J. Pedersen has maintained, to cut the thread which binds the different cycles of legends together and take them separately.[13] We find alongside of this formal

---

[13] J. Pedersen: *Israel*, p. 13.

designation of the God of the Fathers certain names of
individual deities with which the different personalities
of the Fathers were definitely related. The present
records, written in the light of late religious development, tend to neutralize these differences in favor of
an emergent monotheism. But these names, which owe
their very preservation in the records to the conservative nature of cultic terms and practices, are like
precious windows through which, taking our stand at
the time of Moses, we can peer into the religion of a
past epoch, for they antedate by centuries the traditions
that transmit them. These names are "The Fear of
Isaac" (*pahadh Yichaq*, Genesis 31. 53b [E]) and
"The Mighty One of Jacob" (*abhir Yaaqobh*, Genesis
49. 24; Isaiah 49. 26; 60. 16; Psalm 132. 5; Isaiah 1. 24,
where "Israel" replaces "Jacob"). Originally there was
also an individual deity associated with Abraham, as
we learn from the treaty between Laban and Jacob,
where in typical Oriental fashion, the deities of the two
participating groups, respectively, become the joint
guarantors of the treaty, Laban swearing by "the god
of Nahor," and Jacob by "the god of Abraham" (Genesis 31. 53a [J]), wherein the god of the one was different from the god of the other. This difference is not
expressed in the Elohist's account because his theological viewpoint would not admit the existence of the
god of Nahor alongside of the god of Abraham, so, according to him (Genesis 31. 53b [E]), Jacob swears by
"The Fear of Isaac." In another Elohist fragment
(Genesis 15. 1b), which impresses us as ancient, it is
possible that there has been preserved the otherwise
missing name of the deity connected with the founding

of the cult of the god of Abraham, the "Shield" of Abraham.[14]

To each of the three Fathers—Abraham, Isaac, and Jacob—while still in the nomadic period, there came a great moment of religious experience when a deity became a reality to him and was exalted to the place of exclusive veneration in the life of the individual. Moreover, the experience of each was so dynamic, so overwhelming and epoch-making, that from it there issued a cult which was permanently linked with the name of its founder. The phrase "The god of Abraham" is to be construed as the god, possibly to be designated "The Shield," whose first worshiper Abraham was and whose cult he founded. "Shield" emphasizes the deity as personally related to Abraham as protector. "The Fear of Isaac" means the deity, the revelation of whom to Isaac, set him in dread and established with him a personal relationship which expressed in primitive strength what Rudolph Otto has called the *"mysterium tremendum,"* and which was destined profoundly and permanently to influence Israelite religion (compare Isaiah 8. 13). "The Mighty One of Jacob" designated the deity who first revealed himself to Jacob in the personal relationship of power exercised on his behalf. And this relationship, of signal importance for Hebrew religion, was made permanent through the cult established by him, a cult destined to have an expanding influence.

Now, these deities of the Fathers were originally separate from one another and distinct both in nature

---

[14] A. Alt: *Der Gott der Väter,* pp. 26ff.

and in the cult which grew up around each. Yet, in the light of the analysis of the later expressions of Aramaean religion dealt with above, we may maintain that the religion of the Hebrew Fathers represents a single type. The distinctive points which mark it, may be summarized as follows:

1. The worship of the deity was in each case inaugurated by a personal revelation of the deity to the individual in which the characteristic nature of the god was made manifest.

2. This individual and personal revelation such as Abraham, Isaac, and Jacob each experienced, was so dynamic that there issued from each the founding of a cult of the particular deity by his pioneer worshiper which was limited to the tribe or group of the founder.

3. The deity thus revealed to the founder of his cult was designated by an expression which connected him in his characteristic nature in a unique sense with his pioneer worshiper, "The god (or Shield) of Abraham," "The Fear of Isaac," "The Mighty One of Jacob."

4. The deity thus worshiped was not bound to any locality but was united in personal relationship to the founder of his cult and those who shared in its rites.

5. The most decisive trait of this religion was the conviction that each of the gods of the Fathers, respectively, had by free choice entered into relationship with the founder of his cult and with the members of the tribe who participated in it.[15]

Although the worship of the deity of each of the

---

[15] *Ibid.*, p. 69.

Fathers was not bound to any particular locality, we
can distinguish certain centers where each cult was
particularly at home. The worship of "the god (or
Shield) of Abraham" had its chief center at the terebinth sanctuary at Mamre (Genesis 18), near Hebron.
It was just at the northern edge of the Negeb, a border sanctuary which was a common pilgrimage center
for neighboring tribes, especially for the Calebites and
the Judaeans. This deity came to be connected also
with the traditions of Beer-sheba (Genesis 21) by tribes
who shared in the veneration of that sanctuary. His
connection with Shechem and Bethel (Genesis 12)
would arise from contacts with the Joseph tribes experienced in the southernmost sanctuary at Beer-sheba.
The cult of "The Fear of Isaac" was concentrated at
Beer-sheba (Genesis 26). Its geographical situation in
the Negeb hindered its spread from place to place, but
led to the worship of this deity by the tribes of Simeon
(Joshua 19. 2ff.), and Judah (Joshua 15. 21ff.), and other
groups. For from early times, as Elijah's journey suggests (1 Kings 19. 3), it was a cherished pilgrimage
point and in the period of the Israelite and Judaean
Kingdoms its famous sanctuary drew hosts of devotees
(Amos 5. 5; 8. 14). The worship of "The Mighty One
of Jacob" came to have its center at the sanctuaries west
and east of the Jordan which the traditions associated
with Jacob. These are Bethel (Genesis 28. 11; 31. 13;
35. 7, 15), Shechem (Genesis 33. 18; 35. 2ff.), Dothan
(Genesis 37. 17ff.), Mahanaim (Genesis 32. 2f.), Penuel
(Genesis 32. 25ff.), and Succoth (Genesis 33. 17), all of
them ancient cultic centers from pre-Israelite times.

These locations imply that it was primarily the Joseph tribes which were the bearers of this worship, as likewise the ancient poetic source suggests (Genesis 49. 24).

> The arms of his [Joseph's] hands were made strong
> By the hands of The Mighty One of Jacob.

Vigorously from locality to locality, keeping step with the advancing movement, it spread over a vast region, its adherents being of the same tribal group.

These centers and concentration points for the worship of the several gods of the Fathers, especially Bethel, Shechem, Beer-sheba, and Mamre, came to have great attraction for the Israelites. They became famous and powerful sanctuaries, points of spiritual gravitation that drew pilgrims from long distances and from different tribal connections (Amos 4. 4; 5. 5; 8. 14; Hosea 4. 15; 6. 9; 2 Samuel 2. 1ff). It was customary, for example, as late as the middle of the eighth century, even after the division of the kingdom, for Israelites to "cross over" to Beer-sheba, although it was at the southern end of Judah.

Originally there were other cults of the Aramaean Hebrew Fathers, as the fleeting reference to "the god of Nahor" shows (Genesis 31. 53). The cults of "the god (or Shield) of Abraham," "The Fear of Isaac," and "The Mighty One of Jacob" represent the survival of the fittest, those wherein the worship best ministered to the various groups of devotees and consequently endured. The intermingling of the different cults of the gods of the Fathers through pilgrimage to the various sanctuaries led naturally to a process of interchange and interfiltration between the various surviving cults.

Moreover, this was made the more possible because there was in these Hebrew tribes a deep-seated drive toward national unity and toward religious unity. And this process of interrelation and mutual contact between the separate cults led normally to the crowning act which we can discern in the traditions. The several cults were eventually to be connected and concentrated into a single cult, the worship of "the God of Abraham, Isaac, and Jacob," and with him Yahweh was to be identified. But this did not take place until after the introduction of the worship of Yahweh as the national deity under Moses and Joshua.

The religion of the Fathers had its origin, as we have seen, in the nomadic pre-Palestinian period of the Hebrews. The traditions concerning the Fathers came into Palestine with the migration there of the worshipers of the several deities of the Fathers. They attached themselves to Canaanite sanctuaries already in existence in the period previous to Moses and Joshua. The original sagas dealing with each cult as first established in the nomadic period, having no relationship to the new home in Canaan, were forgotten, but elements of the cults and the names of three of their founders were preserved, due to the fixity and conservative nature of cultic traditions.

In the biblical traditions the fact of the appropriation by the Hebrew Fathers of the sanctuaries of Canaan is presented in the form of revelations to the Fathers as the inaugurators of the cults there found. The Canaanite cults had long been established and, indeed, threatened to take into their power the cults

of the gods of the Fathers. There was real danger that
the distinctive religion brought in by the Fathers from
their nomadic life would be lost. This religion met in
Canaan the strongly entrenched El deities of the
Canaanite religion with which we have already dealt,
El Shadday (Genesis 17. 1) and El Elyon (Genesis 14.
18ff.), El Roi at the spring Lahayroi, between Kadesh
and Bared, south of Beer-sheba, El Olam of Beer-sheba,
El Bethel of Bethel, and El Berith of Shechem. In our
present sources these various manifestations of the
Canaanite El are connected with Yahweh. But we must
keep in mind that these sources mirror the concluding
stage of a living process of development. Originally
the El gods, as we have seen, were manifestations of a
Canaanite deity, and, as is for the most part clearly
discernible, they were connected with specific localities
in Canaan, such as Beer-sheba, Bethel, and Shechem.
However, at points where promises of great progeny
and possession of land in Canaan are made to the
Fathers, and where, because of their connection with
definite localities, one would look for the mention of
such manifestations of El, they are not referred to at
all. There is here implied the consciousness on the part
of the narrator that the El deities belong to another
and lower category and are in essence to be differen-
tiated from the gods of the Fathers.[16]

These various manifestations of El were thus not an
original part of the cult of the Fathers in the nomadic
pre-Canaanite period. They were Canaanite deities,
localized manifestations of the great Canaanite deity El.

---

[16] *Ibid.,* p. 71.

Upon their migration into the culture land of Canaan the Hebrew Fathers encountered these El deities and absorbed them into their cults, relating them to "the god (or Shield) of Abraham," "The Fear of Isaac," and "The Mighty One of Jacob," which absorption marked a degeneracy in the religion of the Fathers. They had been thus absorbed when the Yahwist and Elohist began to give literary form to the existing religious traditions and cultic situations. But never did this worship of El in his various manifestations become fully acclimated in the religion of the Fathers. For each El was bound to a locality while a characteristic feature of the religion of the Fathers was that each deity was bound not to a place but to a person and persons. From the very beginning in the type of religion practiced by the Fathers there was a fundamental connection between the deity and man which brought the god into vital personal relation with the founder of his cult and with the community, clan, tribe, or social group to which such relationship with the deity was extended. This essentially personal relationship was the very heart of the religion of the Fathers.

The later Yahweh religion was destined to create new sanctuaries in Palestine, but, even as the religion of the Fathers had done before, it was in turn to take root in sanctuaries already in existence, in some of which the religion of the Fathers had been and was being practiced, and there the Yahweh worship was to find prepared soil. For central to this religion of the Fathers was the idea of divine choice and the divine concern for the tribe. The covenant idea which, as we shall later see, was to have its national application in

Yahwism, had its tribal expression in the religion of the Fathers. Accordingly, it is not secondary here, a dating back to the time of the Fathers of an idea that did not actually arise until Moses. In germ it was already present, within the limits of tribal application. It was already extant in the oral traditions from which the Yahwist and Elohist worked, for shimmering through these traditions, especially as shaped by the Elohist, is the ancient nomadic interest in the increase and maintenance of the tribe. In making legitimate the worship at the great sanctuaries thus appropriated by the Fathers, the sacred cultic words depict both divine choice and divine promise, and unite nomadic interests with those which could only arise in and apply to the Canaanite period. Where this nomadic interest appears it becomes likely that the narrator is working with ancient traditions that carry us back to the reli-gion of the Fathers.[17]

It is quite incorrect to view the religion of the Hebrew Fathers as at the stage of polydemonism. If they had merely worshiped locally fixed spiritual powers, the religion of Moses, spiritual genius that he was, could never have taken hold upon the soil of Canaan. Von Baudissin's thoroughgoing investigation of the whole field of Semitic religion has demonstrated that the Semites, in one form or another, all have the conception of God as Lord, which clearly gives expres-sion to his personal nature, a conception far in advance of polydemonism, although there remained from the earlier polydemonistic period a residue of a belief in spirits.

[17] *Ibid.*, p. 71.

Moreover, in the strictest sense of the term, the Hebrew Fathers were not polytheists. They used for deity the word Elohim, which is a plural form, but with it they did not designate a pantheon. By it they, rather, meant the plurality of tribal deities and the spiritual forces under their dominion. For the early Hebrews the tribal god was the pre-eminent god. For tribal deities they had different names but not for the spiritual forces. All the more remarkable becomes the later mighty work of Moses in steering the religious course of Israel toward monotheism rather than toward polytheism. And at this point the religion of the Hebrew Fathers served as a preparatory stage for the worship of Yahweh.

The new and driving passion, the feeling of nationality so deeply impregnated with a sense of Yahweh's choice of Israel and Yahweh's personal relation to his people which was to be introduced by Moses, had its preparation in the religion of the Fathers. "Within the narrow confines of smaller groups the fundamental relation between God and man was effective to which in the Yahweh religion of Israel the whole nation yielded. . . . The gods of the Fathers were the tutors (*paidagogoi*) for the greater God who later entirely took their place."[18]

Abraham, Isaac, and Jacob we rightly view as towering figures among the ancient Hebrews. Although shrouded with mystery they must have been personalities of great religious genius to have so permanently influenced Israel. And it is suggestive for their unique

---

[18] A. Alt: *Der Gott der Väter*, pp. 67f.

significance to note how Jesus referred to them as representative figures in the kingdom of God. In that universal kingdom,

Many from East and West shall come and sit down with Abraham, and Isaac, and Jacob, in the kingdom of the heavens (Matthew 8. 11).

CHAPTER III

THE RELIGION OF MOSES

A SECOND phase of the prelude to the drama of the evolution of Old Testament religion was that which took place in the wilderness. In this chapter we are concerned with the major and characteristic features of the religion of Moses. In him, the greatest Israelite before Christ, we meet the most creative personality in the history of Old Testament religion. He gave Israel its national consciousness, its distinctive religious bent, and its enduring religious passion. The great classic interpreters of Yahweh's nature and requirements of the eighth century B. C., either expressly or by inference, pointed back to the epoch of Moses and the wilderness as the normative period of Israelite religion (Hosea 11. 1f.; 13. 4f.). To it, as to a refreshing and purging fountain, the prophets were convinced that the Israel of their day must return. By the spirit of that epoch, Israel's religious trends must be checked and corrected.

For the sources of the religion of Moses, apart from a few important hints from the classical prophets, we are limited to the Yahwistic document (J), dating from a period not later than the ninth century, and possibly as early as the tenth century;[1] the Elohistic document, dating from the eighth century; Deuteronomy, dating in its milder sections from the time of Hezekiah and in its more aggressive sections from the reign of Manasseh in

---

[1] E. Sellin assigns J to the epoch of David-Solomon.

the seventh century;[2] and the Priestly document, dating from 500-400 B. C.

For the date of Moses the recent discoveries of Dr. Nelson Glueck in his explorations in eastern Palestine and the Negeb in 1933, and especially in Moab and Edom in 1934, have made it impossible to escape the conclusion that the Exodus of the Israelites through southern Transjordan could not have taken place before the thirteenth century B. C.[3] These Israelites were the Joseph tribes, probably a section of that "Israel" (Jacob) to which Merneptah later refers, who had migrated to Egypt and there had come under the leadership of Moses. If, as many historians have maintained, the Exodus through southern Transjordan had taken place earlier than the thirteenth century B. C., neither Edomites nor Moabites would have been found there. For archaeological investigation has made it clear that Edom and Moab, although occupied in the Late Early Bronze and Early Middle Bronze Ages (2200-1800 B. C.), were not again occupied until the thirteenth century B. C. Had the Exodus taken place before the thirteenth century, there would have been no Edomites to refuse Israel's request to pass through their territory. These researches, therefore, tend to confirm the interpretation of the results of Garstang's excavation at Jericho given by Père L. H. Vincent, who dates the destruction of the Late Bronze city of Jericho c. 1250-1200 B. C., thus rejecting Garstang's date of 1411-1375 B. C., and accepting the later date for the Exodus.

---

[2] J. E. McFadyen: *Introduction to the Old Testament* (New rev. ed.), p. 70.
[3] *Bulletin of the American Schools of Oriental Research*, No. 55, p. 16.

If this date be approximately correct, our earliest
source for the religion of Moses comes from a period at
least two and possibly three centuries later than the
experiences with which it deals. A history of the epoch
of Moses, therefore, in the strict sense of the term, we
do not have. Yet these early traditions unquestionably
contain valuable historical material. Moses, born as
his name (= Meshu, child) suggests, in Egypt, early
gave dramatic evidence of a vigorous social passion for
his fellow Israelites. From the peril to his life into
which his indignant resentment at an Egyptian task-
master's cruelty toward a fellow Israelite had placed
him, he had fled to Midian. Through Jethro (Reuel),
Kenite priest of Midian, whose daughter he married, he
was introduced to the worship of Yahweh. While resid-
ing in Midian as Jethro's shepherd, and naturally
imbibing from him the Yahweh religion, he had a
mighty religious experience in which this Midianite
inheritance was personalized and made creative and
unique. The earliest strand of tradition introduces us
to this moment in the inner experience of Moses. The
experience defies adequate analysis, and the potency of
it can only be rightly grasped in the light of the subsequent events to which it gave rise.

Certain aspects of Yahweh and his worship may be
deduced from the Yahwist's account of this creative
moment of religious experience (Exodus 3. 2-4a, 5, 7-8,
16-18).

1. Yahweh's worship in the life of Israel was inaugurated by a personal revelation to Moses (Exodus 3. 2ff.).
This gave the religion of Moses a significant point of
contact with the religion of the Fathers, the worship of

"The god (or Shield) of Abraham," "The Fear of
Isaac," and "The Mighty One of Jacob." This moment
of religious experience was supremely individual and
personal. In the last analysis all advance in religion is
dependent upon such a unique and in ultimate terms
incommunicable element in personal religious experience.

2. Yahweh identified himself with the Israelites. He
chose them to be his people. Their "cries" and their
"sorrows" moved him. He proposed to "deliver them"
from the cruel Egyptian domination and to provide
them a homeland (Exodus 3. 7-8). We have here the
beginnings of the covenant relation of Yahweh to Israel,
established by Moses, the divine side of that mutual
agreement which was destined to play so vital a rôle in
the Israelite conception of religion.

3. The worship of Yahweh implied social obligation.
The revelation to Moses came not to be enjoyed as a
personal mystical religious experience, but as a challenge to social action. "Go," "Gather the elders together," "say unto them" (Exodus 3. 16-18)—here was an
experience in the realm of vocation which transformed
Moses from a lighthearted shepherd into a deeply obligated social servant. The realities that shimmer through
this early account are as essential for understanding the
work of Moses as are the experiences of chapter six of
Isaiah for an insight into the career of that great
prophet.

The Priestly account views Moses as the pioneer
recipient of the revelation of Yahweh and the one who
introduced his worship to the Israelites (Exodus 6. 2ff.).
The Elohist's account shows that less than five centuries

later than Moses, by the middle of the eighth century
B. C., the gods of the Hebrew Fathers, having made their
preparatory contribution, had become merged into the
Yahweh worship which at that time was the possession
of all Israel. But the Elohist has the clear conviction
that for its beginnings this consummation went back to
Moses (Exodus 6. 6).

Under the soul-awakening power of this experience,
Moses returned to Egypt, and became, for his fellow
Israelites who were oppressed under the lash of the
great builder Pharaoh, their advocate, spokesman, and
dedicated leader. Under the initiative and magnetic
passion of his leadership the Israelite tribes made their
way out of Egypt, probably taking the Red-Sea route
stretching from Suez to Akaba. Drawing near to Akaba
in the Midianite region, they discovered the Egyptian
army in pursuit, and their hearts sank. Then the unexpected happened. The earth trembled under volcanic
action, the Gulf of Akaba, arm of the Red Sea, rose up
in a mighty wave and the pursuing Egyptians were en-
gulfed. As to the meaning and significance of this
event, the records of the Old Testament are a unit.
Marvelous was the deliverance of Israel. It had come
about through Yahweh, the God of that very region
to which Moses had led them, the God in whose name
he had come to them. In this historical deliverance
Yahweh had shown his power, and by so rescuing the
Israelites from imminent peril he had chosen Israel to
be his people and had offered himself unto them as
their God. Yahweh had cared for the Israelites and
on their behalf had revealed his mighty arm. The
Israelites were thus obligated to accept him as their god.

The tie between Israel and Yahweh was neither natural nor physical. It was historical.[4] It began at a particular time. It was introduced by a particular personality. It was authenticated and acknowledged by a particular episode. The Israelites sang at their dance of triumph one of the earliest songs retained in the sources of their national life:

> Sing ye to Yahweh,
> For he is highly exalted;
> Horse and its rider
> Hath he thrown into the sea (Exodus 15. 21).

The task of the interpreter of the religion of Moses is to discover in the fragmentary traditions the creative germ of the mighty religious development which eventually issued in the monotheism of Israelite prophecy. As we have seen, it was the tribe of Kenites, a section of the Aramaean Midianites, who mediated to Moses his initial conception of Yahweh. This creative Kenite influence upon Israel is supported by considerable evidence. Moses' father-in-law was a Kenite (Judges 1. 16). When Moses and the Israelites left Sinai and set out with their faces toward Canaan, his father-in-law (there called Hobab) acted as "eyes" for them through the wilderness, where he was at home (Numbers 10. 29f.). Jethro visited the camp of the Israelites under Moses after the Exodus had taken place, presided at a sacrifice of thanksgiving, and instigated the primitive organization by Moses for the distribution of justice, thus inaugurating precedents for the development of

[4] Compare the brilliant and suggestive portrayal of the events in H. Gressmann: *Mose und seine Zeit*, pp. 443-8.

Israelite law (Exodus 18). At the invasion of Canaan from the south the Kenites made common cause with Judah (Judges 1. 16). In the great battle of the Israelites under Barak against the Canaanites under Jabin, it was Jael, the brave Kenite Bedouin woman, who aided Israel by felling Sisera, the fleeing Canaanite military chieftain, in her tent (Judges 4. 17ff.; 5. 24ff.). In the days of Saul the consciousness of indebtedness of Israel to the Kenites was still strong (1 Samuel 15. 6), and David solidified the Kenite tribe with Judah (1 Samuel 30. 29; 27. 10). The Rechabites, who in the ninth century B. C. appeared in alliance with certain Israelite leaders fanatically working for a purer Yahweh worship, were Kenites (1 Chronicles 2. 55).[5] All this evidence, herewith assembled, argues for a strong Kenite element in Israelite religion.

Mount Sinai was the chief sanctuary of the Kenites. The Midianite territory in ancient times lay east of the Arabah and the Gulf of Akaba and extended from Moab as far south at least as Dedan (el-Ala). Phythian-Adams locates Mount Sinai at Tadra or Hala el-Bedr, southeast of the lower end of the Gulf of Akaba, in the Harras of the northern Hejas. Gressmann, however, with greater probability and in closer harmony with biblical tradition, locates it farther north, southeast of Akaba, the city which was at the northern end of the gulf bearing that name. This would place Mount Sinai in the volcanic region which extended along the eastern coast of the Red Sea from Aden in the south over Mecca and

---

[5] The best statement of the Kenite origins of Yahweh worship is given by K Budde in his *The Religion of Israel to the Exile*, pp. 14ff., a view maintained also by B. Stade and E. Meyer.

Medina to Edom in the north.[6] Mount Sinai, the
"mount of god," was most probably a volcanic mountain, and Yahweh, the Kenite god, was originally a volcanic deity, as the Israelite traditions suggest.

1. The mountain quaked (Exodus 19. 18), a feature
which is usually an accompaniment of volcanic eruption. At the eruption of Mount Pelée in modern times
the mountain fairly quivered under its work.

2. The mountain smoked, the smoke ascending like
that of a furnace (Exodus 19. 18).

3. Fire was visible at the top, burning "unto the
heart of heaven" (Deuteronomy 4. 11). These volcanic
phenomena are accountable for the classic Israelite
symbols of Yahweh's presence, the pillar of cloud by
day and the pillar of fire by night (Exodus 13. 21; 40.
36-38; Numbers 9. 15). The present author vividly
recalls the similar pillarlike formation of white smoke
ascending from the top of Mount Vesuvius. At night
such a column of ash smoke and steam issuing from
Mount Sinai would be colored from beneath by the
burning fires in the crater, giving the impression of a
pillar of fire. Thus was created the Israelite symbols
for the presence by day and by night of the awesome
Yahweh who "came" from Sinai.

4. The voice of the trumpet waxing louder and
louder (Exodus 19. 19) would be accounted for if
Mount Sinai were volcanic. Professor Heilprin's description of the eruption of Mount Pelée offers a close
parallel. "There were no accentuated detonations, but

---

[6] W. J. Phythian-Adams, in PEFQS, October, 1930, p. 209; biblical
data in Judges 5. 4-5; Deuteronomy 33. 2 (reading with most scholars
Meribath-Qadesh); Habakkuk 3. 3ff.; Deuteronomy 1. 2; Compare
Gressmann's *Mose*, p. 418.

a continuous roar that was simply appalling. . . . No words can describe it. Were it possible to unite all the furnaces of the globe into a single one, and to simultaneously let loose their blasts of steam, it does not seem to me that such a sound could be produced." And eyewitnesses of the eruption of Stromboli tell us that one of the several vents "blew off at intervals from twenty to forty minutes with a loud, startlingly sudden blast like a steam whistle from a gigantic locomotive."[7]

The earliest form of the Yahwistic tradition suggests that immediately after the Exodus Moses led the Israelites a three days' journey into the wilderness to Meribath-Kadesh (Exodus 15. 22-25; Exodus 5. 3). The Priestly document places the first encampment of Israel at Sinai in the third month after the Exodus (Exodus 19. 1). Most likely the stay at Sinai was brief, for the place of the greatest significance for the formative work of Moses was Kadesh. There most of the wilderness episodes are centered. A fragment of poetry which immediately continues the Elohist's account of what followed upon the Exodus, clearly suggests Massah (proving), that is, Kadesh, as the location of Moses' legislation:

> There he made for them a statute and an ordinance,
> And there he proved them.   (Exodus 15. 25b.)

Yahweh had his dwelling on Mount Sinai. The pilgrimage to Sinai was the culmination of the sojourn at Kadesh, although, as Lods maintains, it was probably made only by part of the tribes. In the earliest tradi-

---

[7] Quoted by W. J. Phythian-Adams: "The Volcanic Phenomena of the Exodus," in *Journal of the Palestine Oriental Society*, 1932, pp. 86-90.

tion there was a record of legislation promulgated by
Moses while the Israelites were at the foot of Sinai
(Exodus 34). Yet the most creative center of the work
of Moses was Kadesh. It is probable that a later genera-
tion, feeling it would be more fitting for the people
all to go to Sinai and there receive Yahweh's revelation,
transferred to Sinai what actually happened at Kadesh.[8]
It was from Sinai that Jethro came when he visited the
Israelite camp, evidently at Kadesh (Numbers 10. 30
[J]; Exodus 18. 27 [E]).

Yahweh, who had his dwelling at Mount Sinai,
"came," as the ancient poems suggest, from his holy
mount to the Israelites in Kadesh. Kadesh is now
identified with the country of Ain el Guderat, Kossaima,
Muweilleh, and Ain Kadeis. Only there are to be
found sufficient water and green growth to maintain a
large tribe for a long time. These four main springs,
from one to three hours' distant from one another,
watered a region suitable for a long sojourn. The most
abundant of these springs, the first mentioned, flows
from the rock in three streams each having the thickness of a man's arm.[9]

What was the nature of Yahweh? Since he was the
god of Midian it is through Arabic rather than Hebrew
etymology that we may possibly derive some hint as to
his nature. He was "the one who causes to fall," "the
destroyer." Volz has called attention to a certain
demonic element in Yahweh with which this etymology
is in harmony and which in some measure, indeed, is

---

[8] Compare A. Lods: *Israel,* pp. 178, 180; C. Noyes: *The Genius of Israel,* p. 60.
[9] C. L. Woolley and T. E. Lawrence: "The Wilderness of Zin," in PEFA, 1914, pp. 70f.; A. Lods: *Israel,* p. 176.

retained throughout the Old Testament view of God.[10]
As a volcanic deity, the destructive, fear-inspiring
aspects of Yahweh would fit well into the etymological
significance of his name.

Certain features of early Yahweh worship have led a
number of scholars[11] to maintain that Yahweh was a
moon god. If, as is likely, the Midianites were Aramaeans, this fact might well account for the inclusion
in the nature and worship of Yahweh of influences from
Harran, the outstanding Aramaean center of the moon
god. Moreover, the name "Sinai" most likely contains
the name of the moon god Sin. In addition, the Midianites of the Sinaitic region were nomads, and for the
nomadic Arabs the chief deity was the moon god. To
them the sun was not the promoter of growth and of life.
Rather did it burn up vegetation and hinder labor. It
was the moon which guided the caravan through the
desert, for in the steppes the caravans escape the ardu-
ous heat of the sun by traveling during the night by the
light of the moon. By the moon the days, weeks, and
months were determined. All Semitic nomads were
bound together in religion through their common worship under different names of the moon god, viewed as
a fertility deity. This could not have been without its
influence upon the religion of Moses as well as upon the
religion of the Aramaean Hebrew Fathers. But this
aspect of Yahweh was by no means central in Moses'
conception.

The most ancient and valuable tradition we possess

---

[10] P. Volz: *Das Dämonische in Jahwe*, p. 5.
[11] F. Hommel, H. Winckler, H. Zimmern, D. Nielsen. Compare also
G. A. Barton: "Yahweh Before Moses," in *Studies in the History of
Religion*, presented to C. H. Toy, pp. 187-204.

regarding the nature of the worship of Yahweh to which
Moses introduced the Israelites, is found in a collection
of summaries of tribal history preserved in the Blessing
of Moses and dating from not later than 850 B. C. (so E.
Meyer) and perhaps as early as 937 B. C. (so S. R.
Driver). Here (Deuteronomy 33. 8-11) the Levitical
priesthood is traced back to Moses, who was of the tribe
of Levi (Exodus 2. 1 [E]). We meet the tribe of Levi
with no cultic associations whatever in a yet earlier
source (Genesis 49. 5-7). It was evidently through Moses
that "Levi" received its spiritual significance. As a
tribal entity it vanished, the beginnings of its destruction being suggested in the old poem by the "dividing"
and "scattering" of Levi (Genesis 49. 7). But as a
priestly guild it was destined to have a great future. It
is likely that Moses' pioneer institution of the Israelite
priesthood developed under the influence of Jethro, the
Midianite priest of Yahweh (Exodus 18). The priesthood of the Mosaic epoch had a threefold function: 1.
The most primitive was that of giving oracles through
the instrumentality of the sacred lots, *thummim* and
urim, a primary function which survived down to the
time of the early kingdom. 2. The teaching of ordi-
nances (*mishpatim*) and the giving of directions
(*toroth*) which began in the utterance of oracles, but
developed into a separate function. 3. The ministra-
tions of the altar, such as the burning of incense and
the offerings of sacrifice (*kalil,* the whole burnt offering).

In a chapter of great historical significance (Exodus
18 [E]), we have a living picture of Moses in the very
act of giving directions (*toroth*). The people came to

him "to inquire of god," and Moses judged "between a man and his neighbor," and made them "to know the statutes (*huqqim*) of God and his laws" (*toroth,* that is, "directions"). Here are the beginnings of Israelite law. It was under Kenite influence that an organized development along this line was introduced.

The real sanctuary of the period of Moses was the tent of meeting.[12] It was the place where Yahweh revealed himself to Moses. There the individual Israelites came to him for the divine oracle (Exodus 33. 7b [E]; compare Exodus 18. 7, 13f.). The tent of meeting was viewed as the dwelling place of Yahweh, a most natural sanctuary for a nomadic people. It was, accordingly, the most significant cultic object. The sacred lots were there, and a servant stayed there continually (Exodus 33. 11). Parallel conceptions of such a sacred portable tent are widespread among the nomadic Arabs. The Qarmaten, for example, had such a tent and were accustomed to say, "The victory comes down from this tent." The sacred tent served among the Israelites as the place of assembly and illumination. It was the room where the deity revealed himself to his worshipers.[13]

The Festival of Pesach was essentially a nomadic festival and goes back to the pre-Canaanite period for its origin. It was evidently the chief festival among the Kenites and was introduced to Israel at Kadesh by Jethro (Exodus 18. 12). It was entirely distinct from the Feast of Unleavened Bread originally, for this latter festival was a Canaanite institution. Nor did it at first

---

[12] The present author views the ark as dating from the Canaanite period.

[13] R. Hartmann: "Zelt und Lade," in ZAW, 1917-18, pp. 217ff., 223ff.

have any connection with the Exodus. Four ancient features may be distinguished: 1. It was a nocturnal festival originally connected with the moon which followed the spring equinox, or which was nearest to the spring equinox. 2. An animal of the flock (sheep or goat) and of the herd (Deuteronomy 16. 2) was sacrificed. The age of the victim was probably one year, according to the requirement which persisted in Israelite law as late as the Priestly code (Exodus 12. 5). It was an offering to the moon deity conceived of as a fertility god. It was consumed before morning as the feast must take place in the presence of the deity, that is, before the moon departed. The sacrifice was a kind of primitive magic designed to secure increase in the flocks and the herds. The offering was probably made by each head of a family or clan before each respective nomad tent or before the chief tent of the clan. 3. The blood of the victim was smeared upon the outside of the tent. This is a persistent peasant practice in Palestine and was designed to ward off the sinister demons which were thought to be dangerous to men and animals in the time of the full moon. 4. A central feature was the dance which gave rise to the popular name of the feast, Pesach, a term which comes from a root (pasah) meaning "to limp," and probably refers to the limping dance that accompanied the sacrifice.[14]

This festival was distinct from that of nomads in general only in that it was consecrated to Yahweh. Its form of introduction by Jethro was probably in accordance with the way it was observed at Kadesh. Its purpose

[14] For Pesach compare Oesterley and Robinson: *Hebrew Religion*, pp. 98f.

was to secure protection from demonic powers and to assure fertility in the fields and fecundity in the flocks and herds. These fertility features formed an essential point of connection with the nature cults that the Israelites were to meet in Canaan and made easy the absorption into Israel of many Canaanite features and religious conceptions.

The Yahweh worship received by Moses from the Kenite Midianites was very primitive. As we have seen, in their conception of Yahweh there were moon-god elements. He was also a volcanic deity. Moreover, from the very first there were in his nature demonic traits. The major festival celebrated to him differed little from that of nomads generally. Yet Yahweh, God of Moses, was a far greater being than Yahweh, God of Jethro. The element of terrible destructive power, a conception inherent in his very name, remained. But as apprehended by Moses this terrible being was at work for moral ends. The element of power before which a human will was but a wisp of straw remained, but it was power directed toward an emancipating and constructive purpose.

In Moses' conception of Yahweh there was the profound enrichment that came fresh and unique from his own religious experience. The being so imperfectly and fragmentarily grasped by the nomadic Kenites found in the soul of Moses a channel of creative disclosure. To Israel he brought from his soul-stirring experience of Yahweh a conception of the divine nature that had in it the germ of ethical monotheism. Just what that distinctive germ was our sources do not permit us adequately to say. One element, however, is clearly present. To him we owe the conception of the covenant which is the germinal idea in the religion of Moses. In brief, it may be summed up in the words, Yahweh is the God of Israel, Israel is the people of Yahweh (compare Exodus 19. 5-6 [J]). The prophets clearly view this covenantal relationship as founded on an ethical basis. God's requirement of Israel was moral obedience. Jeremiah gives the clearest conception of this cove-nantal relationship as it was treasured in the deepest prophetic insight:

For I did not speak with your fathers,
Nor did I command them in the days when I brought
   them forth from the land of Egypt,
Concerning (so LXX) burnt offering and sacrifice.
But this word I commanded them, saying,
"Obey my voice, and I will be your God,
And ye shall be my people" (Jeremiah 7: 22-23).

The prophets did not create it but found it, ethically deepened it, and applied it. As Professor Cornill has maintained, the prophets put out at interest the pound they inherited from Moses. The idea itself was Mosaic, and it represents in germ the greatest religious concept of Israel.[15] Yet, as we have seen, the way for the devel-opment and spread of this fundamental concept of a covenantal God had already been prepared by the reli-gion of the Fathers.

Dean Knudson has suggestively said, "What was ethically significant in the work of Moses was not the establishment of a new voluntary relation between a people and its God, but the new and profound sense of gratitude and loyalty called forth by the marvelous

[15] Compare W. Robertson Smith: *The Religion of the Semites*, p. 319.

deliverance of the Israelites from Egypt."[16] The human side of the covenant was but a response in terms of moral obedience to what God had done for Israel, a response which was itself the outflow of gratitude and loyalty to Yahweh. The most abiding, fructifying, and creative contribution of the religion of Moses was his spiritual intensity. There was in his nature, as reflected particularly in the Elohist's traditions, the quality of identification with Israel. His was the most self-effacing leadership in Israelite history (Exodus 32. 30-33 [E]). But likewise written into the very warp and woof of the traditions that impress us as being most authentic, is his passionate devotion to Yahweh. This personal passion it was his great genius to communicate to the newly created Israel. That Yahweh was not simply absorbed by Canaanite Baalism was due in no small measure to the religious passion of Moses, that divine intensity with which he fired the soul of Israel.

---

[16] Albert C. Knudson: *The Religious Teaching of the Old Testament*, p. 159.

CHAPTER IV

CLASH AND TRANSITION

*T*HE twofold prelude has taken place. The first act upon the stage of Canaan is ready to begin. It portrays the career of Israel from the invasion and conquest of Canaan by the Israelite tribes to the achievement under David of a united nation. It describes the clash of the nomadic Israelites with the settled agricultural civilization of Canaan and their transition from nomads to agriculturalists. This meeting of Israelites with Canaanites resulted in one of the most deeply significant clashes in the history of human culture.

1. When Israelite Meets Canaanite

We turn first to the story of the Israelite tribes and how they first came in contact with the Canaanites. In the main our sources are of two kinds, those giving the narrative of the conquest itself, and those the center of interest of which is in the individual tribes, their history and spirit. For the invasion and conquest we have one account in Joshua 1–12, according to which the twelve tribes, working together under the leadership of Joshua, in four campaigns covering a period of seven years (Deuteronomy 2. 14; Joshua 14. 10), mastered Canaan. The other account, the more historical of the two and the earlier in date, is Judges 1. 1–2. 5, according to which the tribes acted singly, or in groups united by common interests. The conquest was only partial and extended over a long period of time. Ac-

cording to this source, the Canaanites were not extermi-
nated but kept their foothold among the Israelite
invaders, sometimes retaining the upper hand but more
often simply dwelling among the dominant Israelites.

The sources dealing with the spirit and career of the
individual tribes are fourfold. The Song of Deborah
(Judges 5), the earliest extant monument of Hebrew
literature, records the participation, or lack of it, on
the part of Israelite tribes, in the battle of Barak against
Sisera, the Canaanite chieftain. It is contemporary or
nearly so with the events described and may be dated
c. 1150 B. C. The Blessing of Jacob (Genesis 49. 1-28a)
reflects the period in which Hebrew nationality was
being consolidated. Some of the individual tribal
oracles of which it is composed originated previous to
the monarchy, perhaps all of them except the one concerning Judah, which presupposes the kingship of
David. The Blessing of Moses (Deuteronomy 33) con-
sists of eulogies of the tribes. It has the Israelite, as
distinct from the Judaean, point of view and probably
dates from shortly after the disruption of the monarchy,
c. 937 B. C. The traditions of the Yahwist and Elohist
in Genesis also preserve early tribal reminiscence. The
best possible way to grasp the significance of the dramatic meeting of Israelites with Canaanites is through a
study of the tribal experience as preserved in these
sources.

There were three groups of Israelite settlers in
Canaan: the southern tribes—Reuben, Judah, Simeon,
and Levi, with their major strength in Judah; the northern tribes—Asher, Gad, Dan, Naphtali, Zebulon, and
Issachar; and the central tribes—Ephraim, Manasseh,

and Benjamin. Reuben, the oldest tribe and the first in Canaan, was of vigorous, warring, Bedouin temper. It had its center east of the Dead Sea, in northern Moab (Numbers 32). It could not expel the indigenous population and never settled down to agriculture. Filled with internal dissensions, it had no consciousness of union with the other tribes (Judges 5. 15) and early lost its pre-eminence, falling at length into insignificance (Deuteronomy 33. 6). Judah, according to the oldest tradition (Genesis 29), entered from the east, being one of the earliest of the tribes to settle in Canaan, having established itself there long before the Exodus. In origin it is most likely Aramaean (Genesis 29. 35). But this tribe intermarried with the Canaanites (Genesis 38) and its recognition as part of Israel was quite late. It was in the Davidic era that Judah achieved greatness, becoming then the premier among the tribes, politically pre-eminent as the center of kingly authority, and religiously pre-eminent, inasmuch as David was viewed as the popularly expected ideal ruler (Genesis 49. 10).

Certain other tribal groups merged with Judah—Simeon, Levi, and clans of the Kenites. Simeon and Levi made an early and brutal attack upon Shechem in Central Canaan, as a result of which they were dispersed (Genesis 34; 49. 5-7). Possibly, as Burney thinks likely, the Tell el-Amarna mention of Shamhuna (Kn. 225. 4) refers to Simeon. Evidently a small tribe, it sought a home in close proximity to the clans of Judah, with which its fortunes were identified until it vanished as a tribal factor (Judges 1. 3, 17). The fate of Levi as a tribal entity was similar to that of Simeon.

It seems clear that after expulsion from central Canaan
(Genesis 49. 5-7) it settled in the far south in contact
with the clans of Judah and with north Arabian Kenite
clans as well. With these latter elements and with the
remnants of Simeon, it made common cause in the conquest of the Negeb, moving directly north from Kadesh
(Judges 1. 16-17). It is likely, however, that elements
of this tribe, Semitic Bedouins, had moved across the
Egyptian frontiers, and from this branch had come
Moses, born of Levitical parentage (Exodus 2. 1-2).
How the fierce, cruel, secular tribe became the Priestly
guild we do not know, but our oldest traditions (Deuteronomy 33. 8ff.), as we have already seen, represent the
Levite Moses in sole control of the Priestly functions.
These elements of Levi probably came to represent
the uncompromising worshipers of Yahweh, and they
date their Priestly prerogatives from the time of Moses.
The Kenites were leaders in the direct invasion of southern Canaan from Kadesh (Judges 1. 16). Advancing
northward, they conquered the territory of Arad (Numbers 21. 1-3), mastered Zephath (Hormah) (Judges 1.
16-17), and from this as a base, took Kiriath Arba (Hebron), and Kiriath-Sepher (Debir) (Joshua 15. 13-15).
Judah, probably conceived as including these tribal
groups that had now merged with it, mastered the hill
country of southern Canaan, but was unable to expel
from Jerusalem the Amorite-Hittite Jebusites (Joshua
15. 63).

Of the northern tribes the earliest mentioned is
Asher. The name (Asaru) occurs as a tribal district in
the hinterland of southern Phoenicia, in which region
Egypt had made conquests since Seti I (1300 B. C.) and

which had been conquered by Rameses II. This was a
fertile region rich in oil (Judges 1. 31; Deuteronomy
33. 24). Asherites were settled also on the Phoenician
seaboard (Judges 5. 17). The Canaanites were the
dominant people there and so remained, the Israelites
not driving them out but dwelling among them (Judges
1. 32). In the tribal scheme (Genesis 30) Asher is represented as being one of the remotest sections of Israel,
so far as national feeling was concerned. It took no
part in the great Israelite tribal muster against the
Canaanites but abode under Canaanite protection on
the shore of the Mediterranean (Judges 5. 17). The
tribal name, as Burney suggests, may have been derived
from a deity, "Asher," the masculine counterpart of the
Canaanite goddess, Asherah. In some sense closely
related to Asher, and likewise only remotely connected
with the dominant Israelite tribes, was Gad. It occupied the region of Gilead, east of the Jordan, where it
was exposed to the raids of Ammonite Bedouins. It
retained a fierce, nomadic, warlike temper (Deuteronomy 33. 20f.; 1 Chronicles 12. 8). It received its
name from the Aramaean deity, the god of Fortune.
Dan, also but loosely connected with normative Israel
(Genesis 30. 6), probably invaded Canaan previous to
the entrance of the Joseph tribes. The Danites had first
tried to establish a foothold in the Shephelah (Joshua
19. 41-46). The Canaanites in this territory, probably
themselves driven eastward toward the highlands by
the invading Philistines, pushed them back into the
region of Zorah and Eshtaol (Judges 13–16). Pressed
by such contraction of territory, at some time previous
to 1150 B. C., the greater part of the tribe of Dan

migrated northward (Judges 17–18) to Leshem (Laish = Tell el-Kadi), at the foot of Mount Hermon. There the tribe lived under the protection of the sea-faring Phoenicians (Judges 5. 17). It, however, retained its Bedouin character, being venomous and unexpected in attack upon caravans (Genesis 49. 17; Deuteronomy 33. 22). Dan received its tribal name from a Canaanite deity, possibly "the judge of heaven and earth." Naphtali, likewise in origin only remotely connected with Israel (Genesis 30. 8), had its prior seat near the early territory of the Danites in the vicinity of Beth Shemesh, a vantage point for conquering the maritime plain (Deuteronomy 33. 23). Although hard pressed, it was encouraged to master the Philistine coast and the adjoining foothills. Like Dan, Naphtali was forced northward and came to occupy the rich, productive region bounded by the Jordan on the east, Zebulun on the south, Asher on the west, and close under Lebanon on the north (Joshua 19. 32-39). Naphtali, however, made no real conquest, being unable to dislodge the Canaanites, but dwelt among them (Judges 1. 33). Along with all the northern tribes it was under the domination of Jabin, Canaanite king of Hazor (Judges 4. 2ff.), but with great valor hurled its strength into the struggle against the Canaanite forces under his general Sisera (Judges 5. 18b). Naphtali retained its foreign character down to the eighth century B. C. (Isaiah 9. 1). Zebulun (Joshua 19. 10-16), according to the account in Judges (1. 30), and Issachar (Joshua 19. 17-23), occupied northern Canaan, a region bounded on the north by Asher and Naphtali and on the south by the plain of Esdraelon. But hints from data concerning the minor Judges, probably derived from an ancient source (Judges 10. 1-2; 12. 11-12), suggest an earlier location in the central hill country along with other "Leah tribes," Reuben in the southeast, Simeon and Levi in the Shechem region, and Issachar, whose exact location is indefinite. As Burney thinks likely, this may be the way they were distributed centuries before the Joseph tribes (Benjamin, Ephraim, Manasseh) entered under Joshua's leadership. Eventually they found their way to the north, where Zebulun had access to the seat above Mount Carmel, and evidently were accustomed to participate in an ancient Canaanite festival on that famous mountain which was attended by peoples from surrounding regions (Deuteronomy 33. 19). This location gave Zebulun distinct commercial advantages, and it became increasingly involved in Phoenician maritime enterprises (Genesis 49. 13). In Issachar the nomadic temper early died out, and the tribe suffered the indignity of becoming a toiling labor gang (Genesis 49. 15). Probably later than this, however, in the battle against the Canaanites under Sisera, both Zebulun and Issachar played heroic parts (Judges 5. 14-15). Issachar furnished Deborah and Barak. Zebulun displayed unforgettable valor (Judges 5. 18).

The third or central group included the Joseph tribes—Benjamin, Ephraim, and Manasseh (Joshua 17. 17)—which occupied central Canaan (Judges 1. 22-29).[1] These tribes represented the most creative section of Israel. They had been in Egypt, had come under the direct influence of Moses, and had experienced the

---

[1] That Benjamin was reckoned to the Joseph tribes we may infer from 2 Samuel 19. 20.

mighty deliverance. They had been introduced to
Yahweh (Deuteronomy 33. 16b). Accordingly the
Joseph tribes, and to a unique degree Ephraim, the
strongest of them, represent the normative Israel. The
leader of this group of tribes in the invasion into
Canaan was Joshua.

Benjamin had an instinctive zest for conflict and was
famous for its bowmen and stone slingers (1 Chronicles
12. 2; Judges 20. 16). In its early history it had out-
witted Moab (Judges 3. 15-30). It was described as a
ravenous wolf (Genesis 49. 27). It participated in the
battle against Sisera (Judges 5. 14b), and it showed its
dauntless courage in the desperate stand it made against
the rest of Israel in defending its own tribal honor
(Judges 20–21). This tribe, which was to give Israel its
first king, was called "the darling of Yahweh" (Deuteronomy 33. 12) and was considered to be especially
favored because, as the Jews later maintained, the
Temple site was just within Benjamin's rocky borders.
Next to Joseph, Judah and Levi, as E. L. Curtiss suggests, no tribe is more prominent in the Old Testament
narratives than Benjamin. The Joseph tribes (Genesis
49. 22-26) are represented as hearty and fruitful. Although vigorously attacked by Midianite bowmen
(Judges 6–8) they remained steady and unmoved,
strengthened by "The Mighty One of Jacob," that God
of the Hebrew Fathers, whose worship they expanded
in Israel, identifying him with Yahweh, and whose
symbol at the time of writing was the sacred stone, the
maccebah (Genesis 49. 24a), probably located at
Shechem (Joshua 24. 26). The Joseph tribes were
blessed with fertility of soil, increase in population, and

the favor of Deity. These are the earliest data we have
concerning the Joseph section of the Israelites, and, as
yet, Ephraim and Manasseh are not viewed as separate
tribal entities. But in the later poem they are distinct (Deuteronomy 33. 13-17), the Joseph tribes including both "the ten thousands of Ephraim" and "the thousands of Manasseh." Their productive land, abundantly
fertilized by rain, dew, and underground springs,
yielded rich harvests and its mountains and hills were
fruitful to the very top. These tribes held pre-eminence
among the Israelite invaders. They are compared to a
vigorous young bull with formidable horns butting the
nations in his strength (Deuteronomy 33. 17). Both
tribes took part in the struggle with Sisera (Judges 5.
14a, c.). Yet strong as they were, neither tribe could
expel the Canaanites. Ephraim could not drive out the
Canaanites who were centered about Gezer, but among
the Israelites the Canaanites continued to dwell (Judges
1. 29). And Manasseh, while it could not dislodge
the Canaanites from their row of frontier cities, Beth
Shean, Taanach, Megiddo, and (on the coast) Dor,
nevertheless, eventually won the upper hand and sub-
mitted them to task work (Judges 1. 27–28).

2. ANTAGONISM

There was a deep-seated, instinctive antagonism at
first between the Israelite nomads and the agricultural
Canaanites. The Bedouin has always carried on a feud
with the settled population. At the root of his life is
the tribal organization, and this was not done away
with upon the capture of towns in Canaan. For a time
Israelites and Canaanites lived side by side. At certain

centers, such as Shechem, the Israelites concluded covenants with the Canaanites (Genesis 34. 1-24), as the invading Habiru of the fourteenth century had done in
relation with Gezer, Ashkelon, and Lachish. But in the
early period of invasion and settlement the Habiru-like
mood of proud antagonism to the settled Canaanites,
vigorously expressed by the Israelite tribes of Simeon
and Levi (Genesis 34. 25-31), was more characteristic.

The Canaanites and Israelites represented diametri-
cally opposite ideals. The former had already advanced
far beyond the stage of the desert clan. Land was to
them private property and they were in control of the
soil. To the nomad, however, land was common property. To be sure, the nomad's tribal group held certain
districts in common as their absolute property over
against regions similarly occupied by other nomadic
groups. But the Canaanite "bought, sold, and rented
that which the nomad looked upon as the common
foundation of life."[2] To make land the security for
mortgage loans, and on these loans to charge interest,
was to the nomad abhorrent. To take over property
because of debt, and sometimes to include the debtor
himself, aroused the vigorous resentment of the nomadic settlers. The horror of the Canaanite procedure
in disposing of their soil, such as we see the Canaanite
Araunah (2 Samuel 24) doing, never fully left the
Israelite mind. Even after the concept of common property of the tribal group had contracted to that of common property of family groups, the view later uttered
by the scandalized Naboth was characteristic of Israelite
feeling. Under no conditions would he sell the inheri-

---

[2] Louis Wallis: *The Sociological Study of the Bible*, p. 90.

tance of his fathers (1 Kings 21. 3), not even to a king.

The antagonism between the Israelite nomads and the agricultural Canaanites was at first most intense along religious lines. The Canaanite attitude toward the soil was part and parcel of their religion. The local Baalim of Canaan were the "lords" of the land. They were attached to particular regions, and their worship assured to those regions productivity of the soil. But the Yahweh of the Israelites was a being of an utterly different sort. He was a volcanic Deity, whose ancient seat was Sinai. But as God of war he fought the battles of Israel, coming from Sinai, beaming upon his people from Seir, shining forth from Paran and drawing near from the steppes of Kadesh (Deuteronomy 33. 2). He was Yahweh *Cebhaoth*, Yahweh the militant (Exodus 7. 4 [J]), congenial to the nomadic temper of Israel.

The most authentic glimpse of such passionate antagonism is given in the ancient poem of Judges 5. It tells the graphic story of the battle of certain Israelite tribes, united under Barak of Issachar, against the oppressive domination of the northern Canaanites commanded by Sisera of Harosheth, which took place in the Plain of Esdraelon. On the one hand were the Canaanites of the northern league, at whose head was Jabin, king of Hazor, the Canaanite capital north of the Sea of Galilee. United against him were certain Israelite tribes of the central and northern groups—Ephraim, Benjamin, Machir (Manasseh), Zebulun, and Naphtali, under Barak. Reuben, Gilead (Gad), Dan, and Asher failed to rally to the cause of Israel. Judah was not mentioned. From his ancient seat in Sinai, accompanied by earthquake and storm, came Yahweh (Judges

5. 4f.) to fight for the Israelite tribes. The Canaanites were utterly routed. The old Kenite loyalty to Israel, evident since the days of Moses, blazed forth afresh in the bold act of the Bedouin woman, Jael, who murdered the fleeing Sisera. Here was as yet no interpenetration of Israelites with Canaanites, but only enmity, fierce and uncompromising. Indeed, as Wallis has clearly shown, the outstanding principle which best interprets the early relation of Yahweh to the Canaanite Baalim is group antagonism. The late Deuteronomic editor gives the impression that in this early period Israel went over to Baal worship (Judges 3. 7f.; 3. 12f.; 4. 1f.; 6. 1f.; 8. 33f.; 10. 6f.; 13. 1f.; 1 Samuel 7. 4. The material is best analyzed and sociologically interpreted by Wallis). But a careful study of the sources themselves reveals that wherever there is mention of any connection of Israelites with Canaanites, an essential antagonism exists. The authentic sanctuaries of early Israel in Canaan were all in the highland regions where the Israelites vanquished the Canaanites. They are Shechem (Genesis 12. 6; 33. 18ff.), Bethel (Genesis 12. 8; 28. 18f.; 35. 1, 14f.), Hebron (Genesis 13. 18), Beersheba (Genesis 21. 3%; 26. 23ff.; 46. 1), and Penuel (Genesis 32. 30f.). Wallis has finely summed it up by saying: "First and last, the Baals are the divinities against which the champions of Yahweh spend their force. The local Baals of Canaan are, so to speak, the villains in the mighty drama of the Bible."[3]

3. TRANSITION AND MERGING

It was the external stimulus of common danger that

---

[3] Wallis: *The Sociological Study of the Bible*, p. 99.

forced the Canaanites and Israelites to drop their antagonism and enter into combined action. On one
hand it was the invasion of Canaan by the Midianite and
Ammonite Bedouin hordes. It mattered little whether
the leadership of the country directed toward the pun-
ishment and defeat of these Bedouin marauders was
Canaanite or Israelite. Whoever took the lead in resist-
ing these invading hordes fought the common enemies
of both. It happened that, at first, the Israelites, themselves still largely Bedouin, were able to furnish the
vigorous type of leadership demanded. This was one
element which went far toward welding the Israelites
and Canaanites into unity. The Israelite religion in
consequence began to merge with that of the Canaanites.

This first stimulus to the merging of Israelites with
Canaanites, the Bedouin invasions, appears earliest in
the narratives of Joash, Gideon, and Abimelech. Joash,
the father of Gideon, had a private sanctuary at Ophrah
near Dothan, which was clearly Canaanite in nature, although it had evidently been taken over by the Manas-
sites for Yahweh worship. It was an open-air sanctuary
under a terebinth at the summit of a hill (Judges 6.
11f.), where there was a smooth rock with cup-shaped
holes (Judges 6. 19f.). Part of it was an altar to Baal,
possibly originally, as Gressmann maintains, to Baal-
Shalem, a Canaanite deity. There was also a wooden
pole of considerable size beside the altar, an asherah.
By the name which Joash gave Gideon, "Jerubbaal"
("Let Baal contend"), we are probably to understand
that it was Yahweh who was viewed as Baal, that is,
Lord, owner, without at the time any conscious antagonism to the Canaanite Baal principle.

Gideon, called into action by the Midianite Bedouin
raids upon the plain of Esdraelon and the fertile area
around Dothan, became the champion of a purer
Yahweh worship, over against the Canaanized cult of
the community. He destroyed the altar of Baal and
built a new one to Yahweh. He cut down the asherah
and used the wood from it to offer a whole burnt offering as a dedicatory sacrifice (Judges 6. 25). Upon his
defeat of the Midianites, Gideon returned to Ophrah
and there set up an Ephod, an idol made of the gold
earrings taken from the Midianites. This was a portable object used by the priest when he consulted an
oracle, and it became the focus of an idolatrous Canaanized cult (Judges 8. 22ff.).

The interpenetration increased apace. Abimelech
was a half-breed Israelite, the son of Gideon by a
Canaanite concubine of Shechem, the principal city of
central Canaan. Shechem was within the region over
which the invasion of the Joseph tribes under Joshua
had spread. In Joshua's day there was a terebinth tree
at the sanctuary with a *maccebah* under it. It was then
clearly in Canaanite hands, although destined later to
become a rallying place for the northern tribes of Israel
(1 Kings 12. 1). In Abimelech's time the Canaanite
deity of Shechem was called Baal-Berith, and he had a
temple dedicated to his worship (Judges 8. 33; 9. 4).

Gideon's success against the Midianite marauders had
been as helpful to the Canaanites at Shechem as to the
Israelites of the region. Consequently, the Canaanites,
who had accepted his leadership, gave their allegiance
to his sons, until, playing on racial antipathy by stirring
up the Canaanites against the encroaching Israelites,

Abimelech rose to power, being buttressed by public funds from the temple of Baal-Berith. But after he had held the control for three years, the Shechemites evidently began to suspect that he was more the son of his Israelite father than of his Canaanite mother, more of an Israelite than a Shechemite in his sympathies and spirit.

Gaal, a Canaanite newcomer, brought this suspicion to a head and, at the psychological moment, when a Canaanite vintage festival was on, led a Shechemite revolt against Abimelech. The revolt was defeated by the strategy of Abimelech, who captured Shechem, desolated it, killed its inhabitants, and burned the citadel of the temple of Baal-Berith (= El Berith, compare Judges 9. 4 and 9. 46ff.) and with it the thousand Shechemites who had taken refuge there. His attempt to capture the near-at-hand Thebez led to his death. The soldiers in Abimelech's army were Israelites, being subjects of his (Judges 9. 22), and sided with him against the Shechemites (Judges 9. 55). This whole story is a living commentary on the statement that the Israelites did not drive out the Canaanites but the Canaanites dwelt among them (Judges 1. 27ff.). The interplay of the one group upon the other was steadily increasing. It is probable that the Israelite domination of Shechem dates from this destruction. We next hear of it as an Israelite town possessed by the tribes of the north, their rallying point at the time of the revolt under Jeroboam (1 Kings 12. 1).

It was the forays into the west Jordan region of the Bedouin Ammonites that compelled the Israelite Gileadites to summon the exiled, illegitimate, but coura-

geous Jephthah to be their dictator chief (Judges 11. 5).
They swore him loyalty at the sanctuary of Mizpah in
Gilead. Returning from a triumphant campaign against
the marauders, in fulfillment of his vow to offer to Yahweh, in case of victory, the first human being coming
from his house to meet him, he sacrificed his own daughter (Judges 11. 39). The story is cited as the origin of a
ceremony consisting of an annual festival of mourning
carried out by the women of Gilead (Judges 11. 39f.).
The original significance of the yearly lamentation
which this Israelite myth grew up to explain, was an
annual mourning for the death of a deity, with which
human sacrifice was connected. Such a deity was originally a fertility, vegetation deity, whose annual death,
as we have seen, was celebrated throughout the Near
East with lamentations and festival rites. It is likely
that we have here a new Israelite motivation for a festival of lamentation carried out by women, which was
found already in existence among the Canaanites by the
Gileadites upon their occupation of Transjordania,
which they adopted and to it gave new significance.

In the closing chapter of Judges we have a brief description of an annual "Feast of Yahweh" at Shiloh,
where the young women of Shiloh "come out to dance
in the dances." It was, as Julius Morgenstern suggests,
the festival which was held, according to the Talmud,
on the fifteenth of Ab (Mishnah, Taanit, IV, 8). It was
similar to the Canaanite vintage festival described at
Shechem, which was there accompanied by festal eating, drinking, and noisy hilarity in the temple of Baal-
Berith (Judges 9. 27f.). Here at Shiloh it had become
a feast of Yahweh. It is clearly another illustration of

the merging of Yahweh worship with a Canaanite agricultural festival.

4. THE PHILISTINE STIMULUS

A second impulse toward the merging of the Israelites and Canaanites came from the Philistines. By presenting to them a common peril, the migration of the "northerners," or "sea peoples," into Canaan, of whom the chief were the Philistines (Peleset), gave a great stimulus from without to that merging. They had first appeared in Canaan in the Tell el-Amarna age (Kn. 123. 15; 151. 52), and Sir William Flinders Petrie found archaeological evidence for their presence in southern Canaan, at Tell el-Fara (Beth Pelet), as early as c. 1240 B. C. Originally they had come from the Balkans and had poured forth over the shores and islands of the Aegean Sea, ending the Minoan, and developing the Mycenaean culture. By 1200 B. C. they had swept across Asia Minor, putting the New Hittite empire to an end. Under Rameses III, shortly after the Israelites had invaded Canaan, they came in a comprehensive migration from Asia Minor by land and sea, bent upon finding new homes in the Asiatic provinces of Egypt. Repulsed by Rameses III from settling in Egypt, they had established themselves on the maritime plain of Canaan. They were a vigorous people and their empire was soon widespread over the land. They had swept across the plain of Esdraelon and had established a stronghold as far east as Beth Shean (1 Samuel 31). Their entrance into Canaan was of outstanding cultural significance, for it marks the end of the great Bronze Ages and the beginning of the more common use of iron. They gave their name to Palestine, which is a corruption of "Philistia." They dominated the Israelites, as the narratives in Judges and Samuel testify. They shoved the Canaanites eastward and mastered their great cities—Gaza, Ashdod, Ashkelon, Ekron, and Gath. Zephaniah expressed what was once, practically speaking, a fact, when he called Canaan "the land of the Philistines" (Zephaniah 2. 5). Macalister maintains that Palestine and Philistia are far more nearly synonymous than the current maps would lead us to suppose. Their command of all the seaports of southern Canaan gave them a great advantage. The author stood one spring morning on the top of Tell Jezar (Gezer), just at the western edge of the Shephelah, and saw spread out before him like a carpet in variegated green, the rich territory of the plain leading down to the Sea, which they held at the time of the Israelite invasion. It was not hard to understand the resentment with which the Israelites regarded them through centuries of time.

It was the menacing pressure of the Philistines that brought into being the Israelite kingdom. The establishment of Saul's kingdom differed fundamentally from the abortive attempt of Abimelech, which had aimed at bringing together the two races, Canaanites and Israelites. Saul's kingdom was distinctly Israelite and was limited to the hill country clans. He was not of a temper capable of welding into a unity Canaanite and Israelite, as his shortsighted dealing with the "Amorite" Gibeonites clearly implies (2 Samuel 21. 2). The interpenetration of Israelites and Canaanites, which by the end of the period of the Judges had evidently reached a positive stage (1 Samuel 7. 14), was destined to be halted during his reign. He was a religious zealot,[4] and it was under the pioneering leadership of Samuel, and with the sympathy and co-operation of the ecstatic nationalistic religious enthusiasts, the prophetic bands, that he became Israel's first king (1 Samuel 9. 1–10. 16).

Unquestionably, Saul was a leader of real ability. Our records of his primitive kingdom are told with a Judaean bias and present in unfavorable light this bitterest enemy of David, the latter being Judah's most beloved hero. The whole coastland, and not merely the Philistine Pentapolis, evidently opposed the attempt at a monarchy on the part of the Israelite tribes. Saul's efforts to hold the two great salients running from the coast to Jerusalem and to Beth Shean show the wisdom of his military strategy.[5] In physical form, and no doubt originally in mental and spiritual caliber—for the far-seeing Samuel had approved his choice—Saul towered head and shoulders above his contemporaries. He took the first steps that had to be taken to weaken the domination of the Philistines, but was only able to lay the foundations for their ultimate defeat. He was vanquished by the Philistine forces at Mount Gilboa, where he fell. A. B. Davidson, who had deep insight into his greatness, has finely described his fall:

Here was a great mind knowing its failure, conscious of its incapacity, yet resenting it, mad against circumstances and men and Providence, not going out like a slowly smoldering fire, but burning out like a volcano.[6]

[4] 1 Samuel 28. 9. We also learn in the earliest strand of narrative of his "first altar," 1 Samuel 14. 35.

[5] Compare S. A. Cook, in "The Rise of Israel," in CAH, Vol II, pp. 381, 391.

[6] A. B. Davidson, The Called of God, p. 153.

Truer to an adequate estimate of his greatness than the prose traditions offer, is the precious fragment of early poetry, David's dirge to which the fall of Saul and Jonathan gave rise (2 Samuel 1. 19-27). According to this, Saul was "the beauty" of Israel. He was a brave and successful warrior. The news of his death, tragic for Israel, would mean triumphant joy for the Philistine women of the cities of the Pentapolis, as they went out to meet their warriors returning victorious from Mount Gilboa. "Swifter than eagles," were Saul and Jonathan, "stronger than lions," yet they were "lovely and pleasant in their lives." New delights and new luxuries their first king had introduced to the people of his primitive kingdom.

How are the mighty fallen,
And the weapons of war perished!   (2 Samuel 1. 27.)

5. SAMUEL AND ECSTATIC GROUP PROPHECY

Contemporary with the beginnings of the Israelite monarchy and in close relation to its establishment, there had emerged in Israel a prophetic movement called the "Sons of the Prophets." It was already in full swing, the earliest mention of it (1 Samuel 10. 5ff.) being quite incidental, for the narrator's interest is not centered so much upon the phenomenon itself as upon the fact of the newly anointed young king's participation in it. It was to appear in clearer light a century later when Elijah and Elisha were its outstanding leaders. However, by the time it first appears in the Israelite records in the time of Samuel, it had already received its distinctive bent and its characterizing spirit. These "Sons of the Prophets" were very numerous.

They moved about the land in "bands" or "companies," but were also associated with certain famous sanctuaries, such as Gibeah, Ramah, Bethel, Jericho, and Gilgal. The term which describes their characteristic activity was (ecstatic) "prophesying" (*mithnabbeim*). To induce the ecstatic state, at the head of the bands were musicians playing upon the psaltery, timbrel, pipe, and harp. The object of the ecstatic activity was to achieve unity with deity. In a state of high emotional tension, a spokesman of the group or the group as a whole might utter a prophetic oracle (1 Kings 22. 11-12). Moreover, this ecstasy was contagious, and as was the case with the ecstatic devotees (Galli) at the temple of Atargatis in Hieropolis, onlookers or bystanders might be seized by the ecstatic passion and forcibly drawn under its control (1 Samuel 10. 10; 19. 20-24). These bands had leaders such as Samuel, who appeared "standing as one appointed over them" (so S. R. Driver, 1 Samuel 19. 20). The members of the bands called such leaders by the designations "man of God" (2 Kings 4. 40), or "master" (2 Kings 6. 5), or "father" (2 Kings 2. 12). The "Sons of the Prophets" were often married (2 Kings 4. 1). They lived together (2 Kings 6. 1f.) and ate together (2 Kings 4. 38ff.), often supported by the charity of Israelite citizens (2 Kings 4. 42f.). Dr. Hermann Gunkel, with keen insight into the positive religious values of the movement, maintains that the members of these prophetic bands were not just ordinary men, but were strong, enthusiastic personalities, men of powerful, passionate natures, and young men with warm blood in their veins. Three things met in them —stirring nationalistic enthusiasm, noble religious thoughts, and powerful religious excitation. Whence came this remarkable phenomenon?

Although this ecstatic group prophecy is somewhat similar to what we may still see today among the nomadic dervishes of the Arabian desert, it was not brought into Canaan by the Israelites from their nomadic period. The only evidence of prophetic frenzy in the wilderness is the Elohist's story (Numbers 11. 16-17a, 24b-25), wherein Yahweh placed his spirit upon the seventy elders. "When the spirit rested upon them they prophesied, but they did so no more." This was but a momentary experience and had no abiding effect upon them. Moreover, such ecstasy as we see among the "Sons of the Prophets" did not obtain among the ancient Arabs. It was not the latter's desert possession, but came about through contact with settled culture under Christian, Persian, and Indian influence.[7]

The unique home of this ecstatic religion was Thrace, from whence it spread in two directions. On the one hand, it spread west and south into Greece, and there in the form of Dionysiac frenzy, as Otto Kern affirms, stimulated a profound ethical and religious reform. On the other hand, it spread east and south into Asia Minor, Syria, and Canaan. As C. P. Tiele has maintained, it was a constituent and permanent part of the cults of the Near East such as those of Attis, Eshmun, and Adonis. The Phrygians, who in 1600-1400 B. C. (so J. B. Bury) came from Thrace into Asia Minor, brought with them these powerful emotional elements in the worship of their deities whom they identified with the indigenous Ma (Cybele) and Attis. The orgiastic ele-

---

[7] So C. Snouck Hurgronje: *Mekka,* Vol. II, pp. 160-62, 203.

ments in this vigorous Thracian worship were intensified in the Phrygian region, where the extremes of climate stimulated emotional excesses in religion. We are well informed concerning features of this Attis fertility cult, as practiced at its chief center in Pessinus in Asia Minor, on the shores of the Gallos River. Nocturnal celebrations were held, carried out by torchlight, which accompanied the sacrifice of a steer. Dull-toned kettle-drums, sharp-toned hollow brass cymbals, rattles, Phrygian flutes, and horns worked into a frenzy the devotees of the goddess, the Great Mother.

Southward it spread into northern Syria, where Lucian gives us our best glimpse of this group ecstasy as experienced by the devotees (Galli) of Atargatis (= Astarte) at the famous Aramaean-Phoenician holy city of Hieropolis. On into Canaan (Phoenicia and Palestine) it spread. From the narrative of the Egyptian Wen Amon's adventures we get a vivid picture of it at Byblos in the period of the Judges, in the account of the ecstatic seizure by the Baal of a noble youth during a sacrifice. The most adequate authentic picture of it in Canaan, however, is the account of the ecstatic prophets of Baal at Mount Carmel, as given by the biblical narrator (1 Kings 18. 21-29). Here is an authentic fragment of the group ecstasy of the Canaanite-Phoenician prophets of Melqarth, Baal of Tyre.

There were four hundred and fifty of them. The center of the cult and its climactic act was the sacrifice unto the Baal. We hear the long-continued and oft-repeated cultic cry, "O Baal, hear us." We see the limping dance about the altar. We get just a hint of the Adonis nature of the Baal who perhaps "sleepeth and

must be awaked." We feel the rising tide of emotion and
the setting in of the ecstatic state, as with knives and
lances the devotees gashed themselves, the blood spurt-
ing forth upon them. This is our earliest evidence for
self-laceration in the ecstatic prophecy of Canaanite'
religion.

Long before the Israelites entered upon the conquest
of Canaan this type of prophetic activity had been acclimated in the land. The Israelites took it over along
with other features of the Canaanite culture, and, even
as they did with the Canaanite festivals and sagas,
"Israelized" it.[8]

This, however, they did in no mechanical way. In
spite of the elemental power and contagious passion of
this Thracian-Anatolian-Syrian ecstasy, thus mediated
to Israel by Canaan, it never took Israel into mastery.
It was at this point that Samuel made a great contribution. He had the wisdom not to oppose this wild ecstasy,
but to utilize it, give it guidance (1 Samuel 19. 20), and
link it to great Israelite objectives. Under his hands it
became an expression of devotion to Yahweh and a
fountain of nationalistic enthusiasm. There was a creative, germinal concept in Israel, deposited in its soul by
Moses, which made it possible for Israelite religion to
absorb without either being itself absorbed or becoming a mere religious syncretism. This concept was the
covenant, that sense of mutual obligation between Yahweh and Israel, with its deep, ethical urge. This Israel
retained, but Canaanite ecstatic prophecy thrilled it
with fire and intensity. In the noblest prophetic spirits
of Israel the native Israelite drive toward righteousness

---

[8] Compare G. Hölscher: *Die Profeten*, pp. 142f.

was heightened into a passion, and Canaanite ecstasy made its contribution to this.

Moreover, when we penetrate to the heart of this ecstasy, we find it to be, as R. Kittel suggests, a form of mystical apprehension of the divine. Its unattractive excesses should not blind our eyes to the longing for deliverance from carnal instincts and for union with deity, which this orgiastic group-worship so passionately expresses. This hunger for union with God was to find increasing satisfaction as Israelite prophecy progressed. For, as John Skinner maintains, there was no discontinuity between the "Sons of the Prophets" of Samuel's day and the great prophetic figures of the eighth and succeeding centuries.

6. COALESCENCE

It was under the kingship of David that the merging of Israelite and Canaanite cultures reached its climax. He built upon the pioneering foundations laid by Saul, but he was a far greater statesman than his predecessor. His political genius brought to successful accomplishment what Saul had never attempted and what Abimelech had earlier tried to achieve and failed—the unified political control of the two peoples. As Wallis with penetrating sociological insight has revealed, the Israelite nation came into being under David "at the point of coalescence" between Israelites and Canaanites. The main feature of the cultural development of Israel was this conflict between and fusion of the two peoples, and the Davidic empire had a great part to play in furthering that fusion.

Up to the time of David the tribe remained the center of gravity among the Israelites. David, however, broke through the tribal order and established in its place the idea of the monarchy. He introduced the West-Asiatic social idea of a king, a concept which was far more Canaanite than Israelite and to which Israel never fully accommodated itself. The late narrative of the founding of the monarchy (1 Samuel 8) shows clearly how the old Israelite order of things, with its concept of family or tribal rights, resented the monarchy, with its emphasis upon the right of kings. The large cities, the centers of politics and trade, felt the change the most keenly. Here new dominant classes arose associated with the king, which appropriated the property and gained control of the cities. The consequent degenerating of the small landholders into a proletariat of the oppressed and poor created strategic problems in Israel. The cities best adapted themselves to the Canaanite spirit.[9]

David's empire was Israelite in its political control and Yahweh was the national god, but the empire included the Canaanites. With great political astuteness, David made a famous old Canaanite fortress, Zion (Jerusalem), the capital of his empire. This city, which had first emerged in Egyptian sources c. 2100 B. C. as a center of revolt against Egypt, had next appeared in the clear light of history in the Tell el-Amarna correspondence, when it was a loyal Canaanite principality of Egypt. The Canaanite "Jebusites" remained after David's mastery as a part of the population of Zion (Joshua 15. 63). With some of them he contracted state marriages (2 Samuel 5. 13). Canaanite cities helped to

---

[9] Compare J. Pedersen: *Israel*, pp. 22-25.

man his army (2 Samuel 23. 32, 37). The census which
he took of his empire included the Canaanite population (2 Samuel 24. 5-7). Araunah, the Canaanite, is
represented as rendering fealty to him as "my lord, the
king" (2 Samuel 24. 21). Merging into Israel the
Canaanites disappeared as a political entity, yet, culturally speaking, their influence continued strong. It may
be said that the Canaanites lost their life only to find it
in a Canaanized Israel. The laws of the Code of the
Covenant (Exodus 20. 23 to 23. 33), which date from the
time of the Judges or the United Monarchy, and which
prevailed more or less widely in Israelite city communities, are rooted in an agricultural social life and, as
Pedersen maintains, are almost completely Canaanite.

Another influence that aided in the coalescence of the
Israelites and Canaanites under David was the new importance given by him to the ark of Yahweh. It was
formerly held that the ark dates from the Mosaic period.
E. Meyer interpreted it as a wilderness institution
appropriate to Israel's nomadic nature. He explained it
as a wooden chest containing a stone fetish of the deity,
or perhaps, as G. F. Moore has conjectured, a stone
from Sinai. In the earliest traditions of the wilderness
wanderings, however, the ark appears with certainty but
once, in connection with a ritual (Numbers 10. 35-36).

Arise, Yahweh,
And let thine enemies be dispersed;
And let those hating thee flee from before thee.

Return, Yahweh,
To the ten thousand families of Israel.[10]

[10] Author's translation. For "families," compare G. B. Gray: *Numbers,* pp. 9 [on 1. 16] and 97.

This early fragment of ritual with which the ark was connected, while it carries with it the stamp of ancient origin, probably dates not from the nomadic, but from the Canaanite period of Israel, and is best interpreted, not as connected with the breaking up and establishing of the camp in the wilderness, but as the setting forth of the Israelite forces to battle in Canaan, with the ark as their war palladium (1 Samuel 4. 17), and the returning of the sacred object to its resting place victorious from the fray. Particularly, as G. B. Gray suggests, does the second bit of the ritual imply that settled life in Canaan already exists. The richest traditions concerning the ark which we possess (1 Samuel 1–6) all have reference to the history of Israel after the settlement in Canaan had occurred. The rôle which the ark seems to play in the invasion of Canaan (Joshua 3ff.) does not appear in the earliest account (Judges 1) and represents a process which Dr. J. E. McFadyen has suggestively called a "telescoping" of history, a throwing back into the earlier period of that which in reality was a later development. It is part and parcel of the unhistorical conception of a single, unified invasion of Canaan under the common command of Joshua.

While it is becoming increasingly clear that the ark of Yahweh dates from the Canaanite period of Israel,[11] no unanimity has been reached by authorities who support this view, concerning the nature of the ark. Dibelius proceeds from W. Reichel's hypothesis suggested in 1897, that the ark, the classic description of which (Exodus 25. 8ff.) comes from the Priestly writer, was a

---

[11] This is argued among others by M. Dibelius, R. Hartmann, H. Gressmann, W. R. Arnold, G. Hölscher, and S. Mowinckel.

portable throne. Dibelius views it as the chief cultic symbol of the imageless worship of Yahweh and interprets it as a primitive throne but an empty throne for Yahweh, who although present was invisible. Under Babylonian influence this empty throne represents the cosmic throne of Yahweh. Meinhold also views it as a portable throne of Yahweh, the proper sanctuary of Israel, but places its origin at Sinai.

Attractive as this theory is, neither Dibelius nor Meinhold have answered the trenchant arguments of Budde that the word for ark (*aron*) does not and cannot mean "throne," but does and must mean a "box" or "chest" which is intended to contain something. Richard Hartmann, by approaching the question from the standpoint of comparative religions, leads us a step closer to the correct understanding. He views it as a transportable sanctuary carried in cultic processions, the closest parallels being the Egyptian processional barges. It was not a nomadic sanctuary, for its abiding place, as we note at Shiloh, was a Temple (1 Samuel 3. 3). He inclines, however, toward an Egyptian origin for the ark, but views it as mediated to Israel through the Osiris (= Adonis) cult. He sees original connection between the ark of Yahweh and the coffin of Osiris, the fertility deity who dies but to rise again into vitality and power. "The coffin of the god," he maintains, "is at the same time his seat."

An important view concerning the nature of the ark is that advanced by W. R. Arnold. He interprets it as a sacred box which held the sacred lots. It was a "miniature temple" which actually housed the spirit of the divinity at the moment when the disposition of the sacred lots was being effected—a sort of shrine or refuge within which the Numen could work its mysterious spell upon the lots while shielded from the scrutiny of the human eye. He contends that the reading "ephod," wherever in the Old Testament it stands for a solid object, has been deliberately substituted by Jewish scribes for a more troublesome word, the word "ark" (*aron*), "the specific instrument of Priestly divination among the ancient Hebrews." At every sanctuary of Yahweh which was in the custody of a consecrated priesthood such an ark existed. By the middle of the ninth century B. C., in official circles the institution of Priestly divination (1 Samuel 30. 7-8) had given place to the instrumentality of inspired human speech, or prophecy. The early association of the Priestly prerogative with the ark, however, continued (Deuteronomy 10. 8; 31. 9, 25, 26), and the institution was projected back into Moses' and Joshua's times. The Deuteronomists of the seventh century, who were concerned with making legitimate the sole sanctuary of the Jerusalem Temple, represented the two tables of the law as having been the content of the ark (Deuteronomy 10. 1-5; 1 Kings 8. 9, 21) and the Priestly document carried on the development by calling it "the ark of the testimony" (Joshua 4. 15), likewise setting it back into the Mosaic days.

Formerly an advocate of the view that the ark was the empty throne of Yahweh, Dr. H. Gressmann at length surrendered it for a more adequate view which makes a vital contribution to our understanding of its nature and significance. He starts with the suggestion of R. Hartmann that the ark was a processional sanctuary, not of the wilderness but of Canaan, and presupposes as its resting place not a tent but a temple. He maintains that it originally contained an image of Yahweh, as is suggested by the references to the "presence" of Yahweh, which will go with Israel (Exodus 33. 13, 14), probably, as the later records of the religious institutions of Jeroboam II may imply, in the form of a young steer (Psalm 132. 5).[12] The ark comes from the Baal religion of Canaan. With W. R. Arnold he believes that it was not a single but a manifold object, every Temple having its own ark and priesthood. The theory of a single ark corresponds to the Deuteronomic idea of a single legitimate sanctuary and represents, as we have noted above, a telescoping of history, a reflection back to earlier times of a later development.

The "sacred box" which was most significant in Israel's history was the one at the Temple of Shiloh, where we have already encountered an early Canaanite vintage festival (Judges 21. 19). It was called, as Arnold renders it, "the box of Yahweh militant." We first meet it when the Philistines were threatening to control Canaan. It was captured by the Philistines (1 Samuel 4. 17), restored to the Israelites, taken to Kiriath-jearim, and from there in two expeditions, both of religious, processional character, to Jerusalem, where it was placed in a tent specially prepared for it (2 Samuel 6). In David's day it had already achieved the position of

---

[12] H. Gressmann, *Die Lade Jahves*, pp. 27-29. Compare G. Hoffmann: "Versuche zu Amos," in ZAW III (1883), p. 124; B. Stade: *Biblische Theologie des Alten Testaments*, p. 121; E. Meyer, *Die Israeliten*, p. 284, and H. Gunkel: Genesis⁴, p. 486. That this Psalm dates from the period of the kingdoms, compare R. Kittel: *Die Psalmen*⁵, ⁶, p. 404.

being the nation's most sacred religious symbol. Yahweh had then been practically identified with the Baal of which the image was the bull. Yahweh was conceived as being uniquely present in it. To bring it in dignified religious processional to his newly captured capital shows in David the union of political and religious insight. It was a climactic act in the coalescence of the Israelites and the Canaanites.

Into that population, rapidly merging under David's dominant hand, as the result of his masterful victories over surrounding peoples, came the beginnings of a new cosmopolitanism in Israel. His expanding dominion over the Philistines, the largely Hittite Aramaeans of Coele-Syria, the purer Aramaeans of Damascus, and the Edomites, brought with it inevitably, through the unrestricted entrance of foreign cultural streams, an "expansion of Yahweh." Suggestively hinting at this evolution, the prophet of a later time, looking back toward the earlier days of Yahweh's dealing with Israel, says, "Israel was holiness unto Yahweh, the first fruits of his increase" (Jeremiah 2. 3). David began the process whereby Yahweh became the God of gods (Deuteronomy 10. 17). Moreover, the strength of his political control provided the foundation for Israel's religious development. Studying his contribution to Israel from the sociological angle, Wallis has rightly said that David "constructed the stage on which alone was possible the Yahweh-Baal conflict over the problem of mishpat" or social justice.[13]

The first act of the drama closes. The tribes are settled in Canaan. They have made the transition from

---

[13] Louis Wallis: *God and the Social Process*, p. 141.

nomads to agriculturalists. They have established a
monarchical form of government and David has fused
together Israelites and Canaanites in a strong, unified
rule. The way has been prepared for the second act
of the drama, the struggle between Yahweh and Baal.

CHAPTER V

YAHWEH OR BAAL

𝕿HE second act in the drama of Israel's religious development, as seen in the light of its Canaanite background, traces the pendulum-like swing back and forth between the two modes of religion in Palestine represented in the worship of Yahweh on the one hand and of Baal on the other. It follows the process of passionate action and reaction between these two basically antagonistic types of religion from the reign of Solomon to the eighth century B. C.

1. THE INFLUENCE OF SOLOMON

As early as the reign of David commercial relations between Phoenicia and Israel had already been established. Hiram, king of Tyre, "ever a lover of David" (1 Kings 5. 1), had then sent Phoenician ambassadors to Jerusalem. For the building of David's palace timber from the Lebanon had been used, and Phoenician masons and carpenters had begun to pour into the capital (2 Samuel 5. 11). Under Solomon these commercial relations with Phoenicia were greatly extended and sealed by treaties (1 Kings 5. 12). He proceeded upon a vast building program, including the Temple, the palace, the Millo, the wall of Jerusalem, and the formerly Canaanite cities of Hazor, Megiddo, Gezer, Bethhoron, Baalath, and Tamar. He built store cities, chariot cities, and cities for his horsemen. He also built a navy (1 Kings 9). The corvee, or labor gangs, necessary for this building program were, as Pedersen maintains, "the reduced Canaanites," the so-called *gerim* or sojourners (1 Kings 9. 21), but Israelites were certainly not spared. For Israelite religion the most significant of his building enterprises was the Temple.

The ultimate pattern for the Solomonic Temple was Egyptian, but it came to Israel through Phoenician (= Late Canaanite) mediation. The immediate pattern, as Gressmann says, was the temple of Melqarth, Baal of Tyre, there conceived as god of heaven and the sun god. Phoenician architecture was a mixed art with both Egyptian and Babylonian-Assyrian motifs. Many Phoenicians were employed in cutting the Lebanon cedars, and in shaping the stones and timbers, artisans from Sidon and Gebal (= Byblos) being particularly mentioned (1 Kings 5. 6, 9, 18). The brass work was under the direction of a Tyrian, a highly skilled artificer who knew intimately features of the Phoenician cult and was at home in the characteristic Phoenician religious symbolism (1 Kings 7. 13-14).

From the data furnished by the Temple records (1 Kings 6–7), supplemented by inferences from the plan of the new Temple given by Ezekiel, who had been familiar with the first temple, we can obtain a tentative reconstruction of the Temple of Solomon. The Temple area was surrounded by an outer fore-court enclosed by a wall. The Temple was oriented toward the east. Entering the east gate one stepped up to the middle fore-court on a higher level which, on all four sides, like the outer fore-court, surrounded the Temple and was enclosed by a wall. Steps leading up from the west end of this middle fore-court led through an entrance door into the inner fore-court which extended in front of but did not surround the Temple. This was the place of assembly of the congregation. Here stood the brazen sea, ten cubits in diameter, supported by twelve oxen arranged in threes, each triad facing toward one of the four cardinal points of the compass; and ten lavers of brass, large bowls placed on wheeled carriages, to convey water for ablution, five on the right side and five on the left. One crossed the inner fore-court and was at the entrance to the Temple proper. Here stood two lofty brass pillars eighteen cubits high and twelve cubits in circumference, one on each side of the entrance. This feature is further evidenced by a gilded glass found beneath the ruins of a burial chamber three miles from Rome, which contains a representation of the Jerusalem Temple as it lived in the memory of a pious Jew of 250-350 A. D., and which portrays two such pillars of dark metallic hue, thus reflecting the vitality of the ancient tradition. These twin pillars were similar to those already noted as present at the Temple of Melqarth at Tyre, and at Byblos, Shechem, Taanach, Hieropolis, Paphos, Sardes, and Idalion. In the Temple of Solomon the pillars were named Yakhin (= Jachin) and Boaz. As suggested by S. A. Cook, W. E. Barnes, and H. Gressmann, it is likely that the latter name, which in Lucian's recension of the Septuagint appears as Baaz, is a corruption of "Baal." Taken together the two pillars may mean, "Baal establishes." To the Tyrian artificer the "Baal" would refer to Melqarth, Baal of Tyre. The walls were decorated with carved figures of cherubim, palm trees, and open flowers.

From the fore-court ten steps led up to the vestibule (Ezekiel 40. 49 LXX), which was twenty cubits wide and ten cubits deep. The Temple proper was entered from this vestibule. The sanctuary was first entered. Here stood ten candlesticks, five on the right side and five on the left. Here also was the altar, with the twelve loaves of shewbread. The walls were lined with wood and the doors were ornamented with carved representations of cherubim, palms, and flower wreaths. The sanctuary was a long room forty by twenty cubits in area and thirty cubits high. To half its height it was surrounded on three sides by a three-story lateral structure forming in each story thirty small chambers (Ezekiel 41. 6). The walls of these rooms reduced in thickness from below upward so that the upper rooms were larger than the lower. These rooms were reached by a single door in the south side which led by winding stairs from one story to the other. They were intended for storage rooms, treasure receptacles, or clothing chambers for the priests. Some of them were probably cells for the qedheshim, or male prostitutes, "where the women wove hangings (or garments) for the Asherah" (2 Kings 23. 7).

The holy of holies (debhir) was cubical in shape, twenty cubits in each measurement. It was separated from the sanctuary by a wall of cedar and was entered by a door finished in olive wood. While the sanctuary was lighted by windows which were above the lateral structures, the holy of holies was completely dark. It was overlaid with gold. Within it stood two cherubim made of olive wood, each ten cubits high. Their wings, which measured five cubits, "were stretched forth, so that the wing of the one touched the one wall, and the wing of the other cherub touched the other wall; and their wings touched one another in the midst of the house" (1 Kings 6. 27).

In solemn processional and in festal celebration Solomon brought the ark from the sacred tent where David had installed it, and placed it in the holy of holies under the wings of the cherubim (1 Kings 8. 6f.). In an ancient literary fragment preserved, according to the Septuagint, in the book of Jashar (1 Kings 8. 12f.), is given Solomon's dedicatory address at the installation of Yahweh in the holy of holies of the newly erected Temple.[1]

The Lord [=*Baal*] in the Heavens establishes [=*yakhin*]
    the Sun,
Yahweh says he would dwell in the darkness.
I have surely built a house of habitation for thee,
A place for thy dwelling forever.

"The Lord [=Baal] in the Heavens" is here identical with Yahweh. It is Yahweh conceived, however, as Baal, the sun god. This is a conception quite foreign to the ancient Israelite view of Yahweh, but exactly in harmony with the Canaanite conception of Baal from the time of Ikhnaton on, and particularly of the Tyrian Baal, as we learn from Abi Milki of Tyre, who speaks of "the sun" as Hadad (that is, Baal) in heaven (Kn. 149. 7).

The appearance of the Hebrew proper names compounded with Baal from the time of the monarchy—Esh-Baal, Baal-Yadha, Baal-Ya, Baal-hanan—and earlier, Jerub-Baal, becomes intelligible in the light of this

---

[1] 1 Kings 8. 12f., following H. Gressmann's reconstruction; compare *Die Lade Jahves und das Allerheiligste der Salomonischen Tempels*, pp. 62f.

virtual identification. We see in this period, under the
influence of Solomon, the climax of a development
which began with the entry of the Israelite tribes into
Canaan, wherein, under cultural and political influence,
practically all the qualities of the Canaanite Baal *par
excellence,* the great solar deity and at the same time
the god of war, storm, and fertility, were attributed to
Yahweh. The total influence of Solomon's rule was
opposed to the stern simplicity of the ancestral nomadic
religion and congenial to the absorption of the Canaanite ideal.

It was the Deuteronomic historian, writing from the
sixth century B. C., who describes the policy of Solomon
toward foreign deities (1 Kings 11. 1-8). But the Deuteronomist is here manifestly working from dependable
historical sources and gives a reliable picture of the
situation for the tenth century B. C. Under the direct
patronage of the State, Solomon introduced foreign
cults, the worship of the Phoenician-Canaanite Ashtart,
here called the Sidonian Ashtoreth, the old Canaanite
and Ammonite King deity Milcom (=Malk or Milk),
more familiarly called Molech, to whom human beings
were sacrificed, and the Moabite Chemosh. While the
present text locates this foreign worship on the Mount
of Olives, the Septuagint, which here presents a superior
text, lacks that clause. It is likely that the Israelite
historian's location of these cults on Mount Olivet grew
out of the late Jewish horror at the thought that such
cults would ever have been tolerated in close proximity to the Temple. Solomon's policy, however, was
more than mere toleration. The evidence points
toward participation in these cults on the part of Sol-

omon himself (1 Kings 11. 5), with the inevitable influence that it would have upon the popular mind of
Israel.

It was probably from the era of Solomon, especially
under the development of the Temple with strong
influx of the Phoenician cultural contribution, that a
unique Canaanite influence began to be felt in Israel.
It was "Canaanite Psalmody." Winckler was the first
to call attention to a number of the Tell el-Amarna
letters which contain sections to which certain Psalms
of Israel and other like productions of the Old Testament are very similar. These letters were addressed to
the Egyptian Pharaoh, who was viewed in Egyptian
religion as a god or his representative. F. Böhl and A.
Jirku have demonstrated it to be probable that these
appeals to "my lord, the king," or "the king, my lord,"
were originally current forms of address to native masculine Canaanite deities. Consequently, in these letters,
as S. A. Cook rightly suggests, we are enabled to see
how Canaanites and Amorites thought of their sacred
beings. We see here a religious phraseology rich in
feeling and in the mood of devotion, already well established by 1400 B. C. We encounter in them a profound
sense of divine leadership (Kn. 288. 13-15). It was the
king (that is, the god) who had placed Abdi Khiba in
control of Jerusalem. The people of the city Irkata
pray, "May not the breath of the king forsake us"
(Kn. 100. 36ff.), wherein "breath" is equivalent to the
Hebrew "spirit" (ruah), a life-giving principle, a usage
of which we are forcibly reminded in Psalm 51. 11:

"Take not thy holy spirit [ruah] from me."

With this Canaanite thought Ezekiel's conception of
the reanimating "breath" or "spirit" of Yahweh is in
intimate harmony (Ezekiel 37. 14). The breath of the
king (that is, the deity) brings peace to the troubled
heart of Yaphi of Gezer (Kn. 299. 17-21). The king,
viewed as deity or his representative, is addressed as
"father" and "lord" by Rib Addi (Kn. 73. 35-38). The
mood of lamentation and weeping, so prominent in the
Psalter and finely expressed in the imaginative portrayal of Jerusalem weeping as a solitary widow (Lamentations 1. 1-2), finds an interesting prototype in the
lamentation of the city of Tunip (Kn. 59. 39-42):

> But now weeps
> Tunip thy city,
> And her tears flow,
> And there is no grasping of our hand.

In the Tell el-Amarna letters there are fragments of
"Canaanite Psalmody" which seem like prototypes of
specific Israelite Psalms. Abi Milki of Tyre writes
(Kn. 147. 13-15),

He makes his voice [lit., "sound"] resound in the heavens,
So that the whole land trembles before his voice.

Of this we are forcibly reminded when we read in the
majestic twenty-ninth Psalm:

> The voice of Yahweh is upon the waters:
> The God of glory thundereth (verse 3).

His address to his "lord" as the "sun" is recalled when
we read the beautiful hymn to the sun embodied in
Psalm 19:

His going forth is from the end of the heaven,
And his circuit unto the ends of it:
And there is nothing hid from the heat thereof (verse 6).

Writes Abi Milki:

> My lord is the sun who rises
> Over the land by day;
> According to the intention of his gracious father,
> He animates by his good. . . .
> He transfers the whole land into rest
> By the might of his hand (Kn. 147. 5-12).

Psalm 139. 8 reminds us of a letter from Tagi, in north Syria:

> If we ascend to the heavens,
> If we descend to the earth,
> Our head is in thy hands (Kn. 264. 15-19).

Three writers from different localities and independently of one another, quote with almost word-for-word identity from what must have been a common, beloved, and familiar Canaanite source:

> I have looked this way and I have looked that way,
> But it did not become light.
> Then I looked up to the king, my lord,
> And it became light.
> Yea a brick may forsake its (surrounding wall)
> But I retreat not from the feet of the king my lord.
> (Kn. 266. 9-25; 296. 11-22; 292. 8-12.)

We are reminded of this "Psalm fragment" when, in Psalm 139. 11-12, we read of God's presence manifest alike in the darkness and the light, and when in Psalm 80 we hear Yahweh's lamenting worshiper praying, "Cause thy face to shine" (verse 19).

Other "Psalm fragments," while not revealing such identity, show marked similarity and most likely go back in origin to a single source. Aziru of Amurru prays,

The face of the king, my lord,
The beautiful (face), I seek (Kn. 165. 6-7; 166. 7-8).

His son confesses,

> To thy face I look up,
> Thou art indeed my lord (Kn. 169. 9-10).

Abi Milki of Tyre laments,

> When shall I see
> The face of the king, my lord?   (Kn. 147. 59-60.)

And Abdi Khiba of Jerusalem affirms,

I will come in to the presence of the king, my lord,
And I will see the two eyes of the king, my lord (Kn. 286.
   39-41).

The striking phrases of these "Psalm fragments" are
recalled when we read,

As for me, I shall behold thy face in righteousness;
I shall be satisfied, when I awake, with thy likeness (Psalm
   17. 15).

> When thou saidst, Seek ye my face;
> My heart said unto thee,
> Thy face, Lord, will I seek (Psalm 27. 8).

Moreover, in some of these fragments of "Canaanite
Psalms" we see that the principal of parallelism, the
most outstanding feature of later Hebrew poetry, is
already present. (Compare Kn. 127.)

Immersion in these "Psalm fragments" helps us see
how vitally the religious concepts, expressions, and style
of such "Canaanite Psalms" indirectly influenced biblical psalmists and prophets by creating literary forms
for the expression of religious faith. Here is a religious
vocabulary centuries before the Israelite psalmists and

prophets began to write. And these "Psalm fragments" show us, as F. Böhl has suggested, the "rich treasure of hymn literature which pre-Israelite Canaan must have possessed and which Israel received from Canaan as an inheritance." We have no means of knowing when such influences began to be effective in Israel. But, in view of the close linkage of the Israelite Psalms with the public worship of Israel, which the recent studies of S. Mowinckel and H. Gunkel have established, it seems likely that their influence began to be felt in the period of Solomon from the time of the building of the Temple.

Yet, more thoroughly than David had done, Solomon sought to unify his dominion and to eradicate tribal and family loyalties. His economic organization of the whole nation into twelve administrative districts as a basis for taxation (1 Kings 4. 7ff.) struck right across tribal divisions. The Yahweh of nomadic days, who came from Sinai and led his people through the wilderness by pillar of cloud and fire, now had settled existence in Jerusalem in a Temple, built according to Egyptian ideals which were mediated to Israel through the Canaanite Phoenicians. And Yahweh had become practically identical with Baal. The epoch of Solomon thus marks a great transition, political, cultural, and religious, in the development of Israel.

2. THE PROPHETIC PROTEST

It was inevitable that the old nomadic temper in Israel, which best preserved the Mosaic ideal, would assert itself in vigorous opposition to the Canaanite influence so strongly expressed in the total trend of

Solomon's reign. The source of the protest was Shiloh, where "the ark of Yahweh militant," now housed in the Temple at Jerusalem, had formerly rested. It was voiced by Ahijah of Shiloh. In a prophetic oracle, accompanied by dramatic symbolism, he instigated the division of the monarchy, arousing the ten northern tribes to revolt from the house of David to form a new kingdom, with Jeroboam, Solomon's skilled superintendent of labor, at its head. Tearing his own new garment into twelve pieces he handed ten of them to Jeroboam (1 Kings 11. 29ff.). Thus fired by the prophetic word, upon the death of Solomon, when the same autocratic, syncretistic policy which the latter had inaugurated seemed to be promised under his son, Jeroboam led the revolt of the northern section of the nation and became the first king of Israel (933-912 B. C.), with his capital at Shechem in the beginning, and later at Penuel (1 Kings 12).

There is no doubt that the prophetic party, whose agent and spokesman Ahijah was, had hoped that the revolt of the north would open the way to a purer religion (1 Kings 14. 7-8). But they were soon to be disillusioned. While Jeroboam was nominally an adherent of Yahweh worship, as the name of his son Abijah (Yahweh is father) implies, to him religion was but an instrument of political quietus. He set up at each of two already famous sanctuaries, now Israelite, but with centuries of Canaanite religious tradition behind them, Bethel in the south and Dan in the north, a golden bull image, conceiving them, however, as images of Yahweh, God of the Exodus (1 Kings 12. 28-29). This bull worship was ultimately derived from Canaanite religion, the bull being the symbol of Hadad, Baal *par excellence,* and already a familiar image to the Israelites. However, the Canaanite bull cult had been enriched by the influence of the Osiris bull worship of Egypt as this had been mediated to Canaan through Phoenicia. It had probably already been absorbed in large measure into the cult of Yahweh, although the golden bull of the E narrative from the time of Moses (Exodus 32) represents a telescoping of history, a rooting back into the wilderness period of a tendency which actually developed in Canaan. What Jeroboam I really did was to dignify by official recognition what had already become a factor in the Canaanized cult of Israel, and thus carry into yet greater effectiveness that Canaanizing development in the religion which had steadily increased since the conquest and which had reached its high point in Solomon.

Ahijah, who had stimulated the revolt of the northern tribes, lived long enough to experience the disillusionment of the prophetic party and to rebuke Jeroboam I sharply for his Canaanizing influence (1 Kings 14. 7-16). As was the case a century later, when the Judaean Amos appeared with his prophetic invective at the sanctuary of Bethel, so now the judgment proclaimed by Ahijah was re-enforced by an anonymous prophet of Judah, who appeared at the sanctuary at Bethel, and, from the angle of pure religion, bravely inveighed against the policy of the king (1 Kings 13. 1-9). Moreover, he in turn won the admiration and aroused the conscience of an anonymous prophet of Bethel, who, until the preaching of his fearless Judaean prophetic colleague, had apparently acquiesced in the religious policy of Jeroboam without opposition (1 Kings 13. 11ff., esp. 31-32).

This Canaanizing tendency of Jeroboam I, with its idolatry, in the hands of the Deuteronomic historians three centuries later, became the touchstone by which the reigns of succeeding monarchs in Israel were judged (1 Kings 16. 19, etc.). It was viewed as the root sin in Israel, and created one of the most crucial religious problems for the eighth-century prophets.

3. The Influence of the Dynasty of Omri

Omri, vigorous military chieftain, captain of the army under Elah, was lifted to the throne and inaugurated a dynasty which was destined to have weighty significance for the religious development of Israel. With keen military strategy he selected Samaria as his new capital, a site of strategic advantage in case of attack. He mastered Mesha of Moab, as we learn from the famous Moabite stone. Long after his death the Assyrians called Israel "the land of Omri." Yet, from the religious angle, the most significant thing he did was to give to Israel Ahab, his son and successor, who ruled for twenty-two years in Samaria (876-854 B. C.).

Ahab was another Solomon. He brought Israel into the world stream. But it was in the field of religion that his reign was most influential. He allied his kingdom with Phoenicia and married the brilliant and forceful Jezebel, daughter of Ethbaal (Itto baal, so Menander), king of Tyre, and priest of Astarte. Up to the time of Ahab the religion of Israel had been strongly Canaanized but it was still the worship of Yahweh. Now, however, under the influence of the fanatical

religious zeal of the daughter of the Phoenician priest-
king, by whose strong hand Ahab, her husband, was
largely controlled, came the purposed introduction of
the Tyrian cult of the Phoenician Baal, Melqarth. This
cult included the *macceboth* and the *asherim*, which we
meet in Canaanite religion in general. But it also contained wild and dissolute elements which, up to this
time, Israel had experienced only in isolated instances
(Numbers 25. 1-3 [JE]). These were sacred prostitution, along with the magical practices associated with
it, as the numerous small Astarte figurine amulets reveal, and the wild ecstatic dance, orgiastic in nature,
with self-mutilation. Not only did Jezebel introduce
the cult of the Tyrian Baal Melqarth into Israel, and
by brilliant court example lead the adherents of it, but
she also forced it upon Israel. She launched a persecu-
tion of the prophets of Yahweh which lingered in the
memory of the prophetic circles as a reign of terror.
Ahab himself became an adherent of the Tyrian Baal.
He built a temple for Melqarth in Samaria and installed an altar for his worship, setting up an asherah
beside it (1 Kings 16. 30-33). The historian views his
introduction of the contemporary Phoenician cult as
the resurgence and intensification of the Old Amorite
(= Canaanite) influence in Israel (1 Kings 21. 26).

Vivid contemporary evidence of this vigorous introduction of the cult of Baal is given from certain Israelite
proper names regularly and beautifully written on
potsherds, in black ink, with the use of a reed pen.
Aside from the Gezer Agricultural Tablet (ninth century B. C., so Lidzbarski), these ostraca are our earliest
examples of Hebrew writing. They consist of tempo-

rary notes, accounts of wine and oil for palace use, and
may be dated c. 862 B. C. They were found by the
Harvard excavators of Samaria in a palace treasure
chamber, a room thirteen and one half by nineteen and
one half by twelve feet in size, in an inner part of
Ahab's palace. Most of the personal names inscribed
on them occur in the Old Testament. A few are compounded with El—Elisha, Elmattan, and Eliba. A considerable number are compounded with "Yau" (=Yah-
weh), such as Bedyau, Gaddiyau, Shemaryau, Yedayau,
Abedyau, Abiyau, Yauyosheb, Marnayau, Egelyau, and
Yauyada. Six names are compounded with Baal: Baal-
zamar, Baalazkar, Baalmeoni, Meribaal, Abibaal, and
Baala. We have already seen that even from pre-
Davidic times the title "Baal" was applied to Yahweh.
And it is instructive to see the name "Yahweh" compounded with "Egel" ("calf"), an indication of the bull
cult which, in a derogatory sense, the Israelites later
dubbed "calf" worship (Hosea 8. 5). But it is quite
likely that the names compounded with "Baal" are
rightly viewed as evidences of the effectiveness with
which the worship of Baal of Tyre had been introduced
under Ahab.

During Ahab's reign new cultural streams of influence poured in upon Israel. The excavators of Samaria
have found a number of beautiful ivories, such as were
used in abundance in the courts of the Near East to
ornament cabinets, couches, tables, and stools. They
throw vivid light upon the Israelite historian's reference to Ahab's ivory palace (1 Kings 22. 39), and make
concrete the bitter criticism hurled a century later by
Amos against the "houses of ivory" and the beautiful

"beds of ivory" of the "notable men" of Israel (Amos 3. 15; 6. 4). They date from the ninth and eighth centuries B. C., and fall into two groups, the one primarily Egyptian in conception, though not in craftsmanship, the other primarily Aramaean. The influence of Egyptian religious motifs is especially strong, and it is the fertility deities that predominate in the artistic portrayals carved in the ivories. Very popular is the representation of Harpocrates, or Horus the child. A winged goddess (Isis) is shown in adoration of a *tet* column, the raising of which symbolized the resurrection of Osiris. From the hands of the goddess spring lotus flowers, symbols of resurrection. A robed figure, identified by Fitzgerald with Osiris (corn deity), carries a flail in his right hand and an *ankh*, symbol of life, in his left. Maat, goddess of justice, holds a lotus scepter, symbol of fertility. Harpocrates, as Horus the child, wears a solar disc. These ivories have their origin in the region where the fertility cults were very strong, and they show vividly how all the allies against Assyria—Damascus, Hamath, Cilicia, Egypt, Phoenicia, and Israel—were culturally influencing one another.

These Canaanite-Phoenician tendencies fostered by Ahab and Jezebel by no means died out with them but lasted until the house of Omri was utterly rooted out of Israel. Ahaziah, son of Ahab and Jezebel, consulted Baal-Zebub (=Zebul, so T. K. Cheyne) at Ekron, a Canaanite deity which, like Baal Dagon, had been absorbed into the Philistine pantheon. And Jehoram, his successor, another son of Ahab and Jezebel, although he evidently instituted a slight reformation in the worship (2 Kings 3. 2), yet continued, in the main, the

Canaanizing tendencies of his mother and father (2
Kings 3. 3; 9. 22).

The Southern Kingdom of Judah was also affected by
the influences of the House of Omri. Jehoram of Judah, son and successor of Jehoshaphat, came under the
influence of the Canaanite-Phoenician ideals of Jezebel
and Ahab chiefly through his marriage to their daughter
Athaliah. She was a true daughter of her mother and
profoundly influenced Judah along the lines that Israel under Ahab had pursued (2 Kings 8. 18). Ahaziah
of Judah, son of Jehoram and Athaliah, carried on the
same Canaanite-Phoenician tendency (2 Kings 8. 27).
At Ahaziah's death his mother usurped the throne and
in high-handed, fanatical fashion, in which we feel the
powerful mind of her mother living on, did away, as
she thought, with all claimants to the throne. However, the infant Joash was secretly rescued by his aunt
Jehosheba, the wife of Jehoiada the priest, and kept in
hiding. Athaliah reigned in her own right for six
years, during which time she was patroness of the
Canaanite-Phoenician cult in Judah (1 Kings 11. 18).

4. The Prophetic Revolution

Again the prophets of Yahweh voiced their protest
in words and deeds that shook all Palestine and left
upon Israel an ineradicable impression. The creative
mind and most brilliant spokesman of the prophetic
party of the ninth century B. C. was Elijah. He was one
of the most dynamic personalities in Israel's religious
history, and the dramatic unexpectedness of his ap-
pearances and exits is in perfect accord with the volcanic quality of his spirit. As Sellin says, "He went

through history like a meteor." The objective of the prophetic revolution which now set in was the complete destruction, root and branch, of the Canaanite-Phoenician Baal influence in Israel. The program of the prophetic party, as clearly conceived in the mind of Elijah, was threefold (1 Kings 19. 15-18). 1. To displace Benhadad II of Damascus, king of Syria, and ally of Ahab (1 Kings 20. 34), by the ruthless Hazael, whose pitiless raids upon Israel would decimate Ahab's power. 2. To displace the dynasty of Ahab with that of Jehu, a soldier of fearless dispatch, commander of the Israelite army at Ramoth-Gilead, whose fanatical antagonism to the Canaanite-Phoenician influence of Ahab and Jezebel was well known. 3. To provide for the continuity of the spirit and program of the prophetic party by appointing Elisha as his disciple and prophetic successor. Within Elijah's lifetime only the third item of this program was carried out, but it was his personal contribution to be the mind of the revolution, and to grasp with unparalleled clarity and interpret with sharp simplicity the Yahweh-or-Baal issue which was of paramount importance. Who was the god of Israel? Was it Yahweh or was it Baal? Was it Yahweh worshiped as Baal? Or were both Yahweh and Baal to be worshiped? No one, as yet, had seen into the heart of the issue with which these questions are concerned, with the profundity of Elijah.

The story of the contest on Mount Carmel between Elijah and the prophets of Baal (1 Kings 18. 20-46) is an idealized account of a historical, intellectual-spiritual triumph of Elijah on behalf of Yahweh over the prophets of Baal. We must keep in mind how Yah-

weh, under the influence of Canaanite religion, had
gradually assimilated the characteristics of the Baalim
without any effective prophetic protest having been
voiced. But the vigorous, determined policies inaugurated by Ahab and Jezebel had brought the religion of
Israel to a crisis. The psychological hour of decision
had struck. The Israelites were summoned by Elijah to
Mount Carmel, where not far from the altar of the
Israelite High Place, now in ruins from the destructive
hand of Jezebel, was the High Place of Melqarth, the
Tyrian Baal. To its altar were summoned by Ahab
the four hundred and fifty prophets of Baal. The ultimate purpose of the sacrifice was to break a severe
drought (verse 45) which, as we learn from Menander
(Josephus' *Antiquities*, VII, 13. 2), occurred in Ahab's
reign. The story of the contest gives a vivid picture of
the limping dance (mg.) of the devotees of Melqarth,
such as Heliodorus describes for the Tyrian seamen,
whose cultic dance he had seen in Egypt. It was similar
also to the limping dance carried on at Penuel, which
gave rise to the legend according to which Jacob limped
because he had been wounded in a struggle with the
deity (El) of that place. There it was performed at
sunrise (Genesis 32. 31). The name of Saul's ancestral
home (Cela), as Oesterley suggests, may have been
another ancient sanctuary where such a dance was customary. And at Deir el-Kala, near Beirut, an inscription refers to a "Baal of dancing" (Baal-Marqodh). The
devotees of Baal Melqarth were accustomed to perform
such a limping dance about the altar at Mount Carmel,
the purpose of which was to arouse the pity of the
Baal, and, as Pietschmann suggests, magically coerce

from his hand rainfall and fruitfulness. Seizing upon this most characteristic feature of the worship, Elijah hurled his challenge in a fashion derogatory to the Baal cult, and in an ironical spirit:

> How long will ye go limping upon the two knees?
> If Yahweh be God, follow him;
> But if Baal, then follow him (1 Kings 18. 21).[2]

The Israelite narrator gives a vivid picture of this cult of Baal. The prophets of Baal dance about the altar in characteristic limping movements which steadily grow in intensity and abandon. The orgiastic character native to the cult gradually increases. The devotees cry aloud in piercing and oft repeated cultic cries, "O Baal, hear us." In frenzied fury they cut themselves, "according to their custom," with knives and lances until the blood gushes forth upon them and the climax of their passion is reached. But the Baal does not respond.

In contrast with the Canaanized temper of this cult of Melqarth, the narrative portrays the calm of Elijah, the approved prophet of Yahweh. The motivation of his sacrifice seems likewise to be coercive magic. Israel sorely needed rain, and one feels the element of venture inspired by faith in the all-potent Yahweh, which leads him to order poured upon his bullock twelve precious jars of the hoarded water. We feel his instinctive resort to the past for normative guidance, as, ignoring the

---

[2] Author's translation, following LXX, *tais ignuais* which interprets the Hebrew *hasseippim*, the root idea of which is "divide," as referring to the "knee cavities," ʒhe place where the leg is divided. Compare O. Thenius: *Die Bücher der Könige*², pp. 223f.; I. Benzinger: *Die Bücher der Könige*, pp. 109f.

historically accomplished division of the monarchy, with twelve altar stones symbolizing the unified Israel ideally called into being by Moses, he rebuilds the Israelite altar of pre-Jezebel days. At the hour of sacrifice he calls upon the God of Israel's mighty past, the God of Abraham, of Isaac, and of Israel (=Jacob), not in orgiastic cultic cries but in reasoned speech, not by ecstatic dance but in the attitude of prayer.

The outcome, however the contest was actually carried out, was a general, popular recognition of Yahweh's power. Yahweh and he alone was Israel's God (1 Kings 18. 39). Clearly, in Elijah's thought it was Yahweh who brought the rain as well as the fire. Before the storm broke he was certain that rain would come and that it was Yahweh who would send it. So he called upon Ahab to offer a sacrifice of thanksgiving (1 Kings 18. 41-42) and to proceed to Jezreel before the storm should break. Then came the storm that ended the drought, sent not by Baal but by Yahweh. The heavens grew black with clouds and wind, and there was a great rain (1 Kings 18. 45).

Moreover, Elijah made a contribution to the development of Israelite religion by his emphasis upon the essential inwardness and individuality of the revelation of Yahweh. He takes us a step away from the external, naturalistic evidences of Yahweh's presence and a step toward his inner revelation in the reason and conscience of men. Under the alternating mood of profound spiritual dejection which followed swiftly upon his triumph at Carmel, he made a pilgrimage to Horeb—Sinai, where Yahweh's true nature had been revealed to Moses (Exodus 34. 6), with whose prophetic spirit Elijah had closest

kinship.   A religious experience of creative significance came to him there.   Yahweh manifested himself
to Elijah, but not in wind, nor in earthquake, nor in
(volcanic) fire.   These were ways in which ancient
Israel had been accustomed to recognize the certainty
and reality of Yahweh's presence (Judges 5. 4-5; Deuteronomy 33. 2; Micah 1. 3f.; Habakkuk 3. 3-6).   But now
his presence and oracle is revealed in "a voice of gentle
stillness" (1 Kings 19. 12).   We thus take a significant
step toward the way to the apprehension of Yahweh
which is trod by the teachers of the eighth century B. C.

Elijah made yet another contribution in the realm
of justice for the common man which shows Israelite
religion moving into a new ethical stage.   Naboth,
owner of a vineyard at Jezreel near the palace of Ahab,
refused to sell his family inheritance to the king. Jezebel, indignant at this thwarting of Ahab's wish, plotted
Naboth's brutal murder in the king's name and suc-
cessfully accomplished this ruthless injustice.   Ahab,
who had just gone to Jezreel to take possession of the
murdered vine dresser's property, suddenly found himself confronted by Elijah.   "Hast thou found me, O
mine enemy?" the king exclaimed.   "I have found
thee," was Elijah's tense and solemn answer.   Then
followed his prophecy of the utter destruction of Ahab's
dynasty.   From this time down into the days of Hosea,
"Jezreel" was a symbol of prophetic judgment (1 Kings
21; 2 Kings 9. 36f.; Hosea 1. 4).   With Elijah, as Wellhausen with true insight has maintained,[3] we enter
upon a new stage in the history of Israelite religion.

A like protest against the policy of Ahab was that

---

[3] J. Wellhausen: *Israelitische und jüdische Geschichte* (3d. ed.), p. 74.

raised by Micaiah ben-Imlah, in connection with Ahab's Syrian war which was destined to cost the king his life. Ahab had summoned Jehoshaphat of Judah with his forces to support him in the campaign. Now Jehoshaphat had something of the puritan in his blood, for he was the true son of Asa (1 Kings 22. 43), Judah's greatest reformer king before Hezekiah and Josiah (1 Kings 15. 9ff.). Accordingly, he suggested consulting the prophets (1 Kings 22. 5), and when in ecstatic national religious frenzy the four hundred Baal phophets at Ahab's court urged the campaign, he insisted upon the independent consultation of "a prophet of Yahweh besides." Of these but one was available, Micaiah ben-Imlah, then in confinement under the governor of Samaria and one of the royal princes (1 Kings 22. 26f.), because he had previously stirred up the wrath of the king by his fearless teaching of the will of Yahweh as it concerned Ahab. While the monarchs sat in kingly style awaiting the appearance of Micaiah, the four hundred prophets staged an ecstatic manifestation of group enthusiasm in which their leader Zedekiah prophesied in symbolic manner (1 Kings 22. 11) the ultimate defeat of the Syrians and the triumph of Ahab. In the meantime the messenger dispatched for Micaiah tried to win his acquiescence in the prophetic counsel already declared (1 Kings 22. 13), only to call forth from Micaiah one of the finest statements of the spiritual freedom of the true prophet contained in the Old Testament: "As Yahweh liveth, what Yahweh saith unto me that will I speak" (1 Kings 22. 14). In prophetic irony he began as though he approved the counsel of the four hundred, only to be indignantly commanded by Ahab

to speak in Yahweh's name "nothing but the truth."
Then he described to Ahab his true prophetic vision of
the scattering of Israel's forces and the death of Israel's
king. All Israel would be dispersed on the mountains
shepherdless (that is, kingless). He explained the
counsel of the four hundred as the result of a spirit
sent by Yahweh into the ecstatics to lure Ahab to the
war that would eventuate in his death. His prophetic
independence in daring to withstand the king's chosen
policy resulted in his yet stricter confinement. But the
subsequent events proved his insight as a true prophet,
for Ahab met his death in that fatal campaign. The
protest of Micaiah not only implied opposition to the
Canaanized prophecy of Ahab's court, but was itself in
striking harmony with Elijah's insistence upon the inwardness of Yahweh's revelation and an evidence of
the growing development of a nobler type of prophecy
in Israel.

Elisha, called by Elijah from the plow to be his disciple and prophetic successor (1 Kings 19. 19-20), carried into political effect the first two items of the prophetic program outlined by his master. In the hope
that a new leadership on the throne of Damascus might
break the political power of Ahab's dynasty, Elisha
fired the ambition of the ruthless Hazael and set in
motion the influences that made him king of Syria as
successor to Benhadad II (2 Kings 8. 13). Throughout
the remaining control of the family of Ahab, Hazael
fulfilled the hopes of the prophetic party, decimating
the Israelite territory east of the Jordan and materially
weakening the power of the throne (2 Kings 8. 28).

Elisha carried out the second item in the program of

the prophetic party by instigating at the hands of a member of one of the guilds of the "Sons of the Prophets," the usurpation of the throne of Israel by Jehu, captain of the Israelite forces at Ramoth-Gilead. There began under his fanatical leadership an Israelite reign of terror, the most bloody chapter in Israelite history (2 Kings 9–10). It gives us, however, a solemn sense of the deep-seated and passionate prophetic resentment against Ahab's house.

Jehu was a leader of ruthless dispatch. Immediately, ere word of his anointing at prophetic hands could reach Jehoram, son of Ahab and Jezebel, he proceeded, "driving like Jehu," to Jezreel, where lay Israel's wounded king recovering from Syrian wounds inflicted at Hazael's hands, and where was Ahaziah also, the king of Judah, grandson of Jezebel, paying his Israelite relative a visit. When Jehoram and Ahaziah came out in their chariots to meet Jehu, who was already hurling his bitter taunts at the Israelite king because of the "whoredoms" of his mother Jezebel and her "witch-crafts," Jehu killed Jehoram. And as an act of poetic justice he ordered him buried in the territory from which his father had ruthlessly dispossessed Naboth. Then pursuing Ahaziah to Megiddo, he put to death the already wounded Judaean king. Going on to Jezreel, he saw the undaunted Jezebel looking down at him in proud disdain from an upstairs palace window. He ordered her brutally hurled down by the eunuchs. By letter he demanded the murder by the elders of Samaria of Ahab's seventy sons, and at Jezreel he did away with every person who showed any inkling of loyalty to Ahab's house. On the way to Samaria, he met and murdered forty-two of the family of Ahaziah of Judah who were on their way to see the king (2 Kings 9–10). As he continued on his way toward Samaria, he encountered Jehonadab, the Rechabite, coming to meet him (2 Kings 10. 15ff.). He was the leader of the Rechabites, a group who embodied a nomadic protest against the Canaanite agricultural civilization and expressed a passionate and ascetic devotion to Yahweh of the wilderness (Jeremiah 35. 2ff.). The Rechabite leader threw in his energies behind Jehu's "zeal for Yahweh" and rode with the usurper into Samaria. On a pretext of sacrificing to Baal in the Temple of Baal, he ordered, on threat of death to anyone found missing, a solemn assembly of all the prophets, priests, and worshipers of Baal to offer sacrifices and burnt offerings. At the psychological moment eighty soldiers, following his orders, set upon the entrapped Baal worshipers and murdered them. They burned the *macceboth* and destroyed the altar (so read with R. Kittel) and the Temple of Baal (2 Kings 10. 27).

There was an aftermath in Judah to this bloody reform. At the instigation of Jehoiada, loyal priest of Yahweh, and with the co-operation of officers of the army, the seven-year-old prince, son of Ahaziah, and rightful heir to the throne, whom Jehosheba had rescued from his grandmother's murderous intent, was anointed and proclaimed king. The usurper, Athaliah, was killed at the entry to the palace in Jerusalem. There followed immediately under Jehoiada's leadership the destruction of the Temple of Baal, its altars, and its images and the murder of "Mattan priest of Baal before the altars" (2 Kings 11. 17ff.). We get no surer evidence of the terrible, fanatical earnestness of the prophetic antagonism to the Baal influence in the religion of Israel than this brutal revolution. It is little wonder that a prophet of the next century criticized sharply the bloody, ruthless achievement of Jehu and gave his criticism permanence by the prophetic naming of his first child (Hosea 1. 4). Thus did a nobler prophecy condemn the violence of the earlier prophetic movement.

The Syrian forces inspired by the prophetic party to weaken the house of Ahab now turned upon the usurping dynasty. Hazael and Benhadad III of Syria drastically reduced Israel under Jehu (2 Kings 10. 32) and Jehoahaz, Jehu's son (816-800 B. C.) (2 Kings 13. 3, 7, 22). And Jehoash of Judah turned Hazael back from Jerusalem, only by paying heavy tribute of Temple treasure (2 Kings 12. 17ff.). It was not until the reigns of Jeroboam II of Israel (785-745 B. C.) and Azariah of Judah (780-740 B. C.). that the religion of Israel entered upon a new stage.

5. THE CANAANIZING OF THE ISRAELITE CULT

Long after the prophetic religion, as it became articulate in Elijah, had reached the stage of henotheism, the influence of the Canaanite cult of the Baalim stubbornly persisted in the public worship of Yahweh as practiced by the Israelites generally. These rites, as we have seen, had been taken over by the Israelites along with the agricultural processes of Canaan with which they were so vitally associated. The Israelites, to be sure, connected them with the worship of Yahweh, but their nature was such that they practically Canaanized the Israelite cult. These cultic rites, as absorbed and

practiced by Israel, come before us most fully in the
Priestly code (500-400 B. C.). This, however, was already
in process of formation as early as the first half of the
sixth century B. C., as the Code of Holiness (Leviticus
17–26, c. 560 B. C.) and the closing chapters of Ezekiel
(Ezekiel 40–48, c. 570 B. C.) show. Moreover, the
Priestly code, as was the case still later with the Talmud, contains many rites which were ancient features of
Israelite ritual. These considerations, studied in the
light of the conservative nature of cultic practices, and
the concrete details of the classic prophetic criticism of
the Israelite cult, warrant us in maintaining that by the
eighth century B. C. the public worship of Yahweh had
practically become Canaanized.

Although in Israelite usage the Festivals of New
Moon and Sabbath were customary times for consulting
a prophet (2 Kings 4. 23), and although the Sabbath
had been transformed by Israel from a festival of a
negative, magical character, such as it had originally in
Babylonia, to that of a day of rest for man (Exodus 23.
12), so far as actual observance was concerned both festivals had practically become Canaanite institutions
(Amos 8. 5; Hosea 2. 11; Isaiah 1. 13f.).

The Feast of Unleavened Bread was absorbed by the
Israelites from the Canaanites. The Israelites, however,
viewed the eating of the unleavened bread (*maccoth*),
the most distinctive rite of the feast, as intended
to recall the nation to the nomadic simplicity of the
pre-Canaanite days, and thus there was established a
natural link with Israel's own nomadic Pesach (Passover)
with which, by at least as early as the seventh century
B. C. (Deuteronomy 16. 1-3) and probably much earlier,

the Feast of Unleavened Bread had been merged. The
motivation by which Israel had connected the Pesach
with the deliverance from Egypt, was also extended to
the Feast of Unleavened Bread (Exodus 34. 18; 23. 15).
Its original nature as a sun festival, as Oesterley has
pointed out, still shimmers through the late Jewish
ritual in which Psalm eighty was used. In this Psalm,
however, it is no longer Baal as sun god to whom appeal
is made to shine (lit., "give light"), that is, "pour down
his rays," but Yahweh, that he might cause his face to
shine upon the congregation (verses 3, 7, 14, 19).

Israel likewise took over from the Canaanites the midsummer Harvest Festival (Weeks). Its original connection with Baal as sun god still shines through the later
Jewish ritual for it, wherein the readings connected
with this festival (Ezekiel 1; Habakkuk 3; Psalms 29,
68) portray a theophany in a thunderstorm with the
center of interest the midsummer sun:

And his brightness is as the light;
Rays from his hand had he:
And there was the hiding of his power.
Before him goes *Deber* (=Dibarra, Babylonian pest god),
And *Resheph* (Canaanite god of storm) goes forth at
    his feet (Habakkuk 3. 4-5).

The Canaanite autumnal Festival of Ingathering was
absorbed by the Israelites, who called it by the pre-
ferred name "Booths" (Leviticus 23. 42) or "Tabernacles" (*Sukkoth,* Deuteronomy 31. 10), a designation
which owed its origin to the vegetation, fertility booths.
In their original Canaanite significance, as Oesterley has
suggested, the booth stood for the sacred grove in which
the divine marriage was celebrated between Adonis-

Baal and Astarte. The first day of the Feast of Booths
was the Israelite New Year Festival, celebrated "at the
going forth of the year" (Exodus 23. 16 [E]), or yet more
accurately, "at the turn of the year" (Exodus 34. 22
[J]), the Israelite year of pre-exilic times beginning in
the autumn. In the old Canaanite ritual of nature religion, as was the case in Babylonia and Egypt, the king
was the incarnation of the immediate group. The
religio-economic ritual of expelling decay at the end of
the year and of releasing new life at the beginning of
the year was portrayed by an annual ritual to eject the
"old" king and install the "new" king. Israel did not
abrogate this ritual but adapted it, spiritualized it, and
made it the model for certain Psalms of the Ascension
of Yahweh to the Throne (Psalms 47, 93, 96-99) which
contain the cultic cry rightly rendered, "Yahweh hath
become king!" Moreover, Israel retained certain features that were mediated probably through the Canaanite observance of the Festival, but are seen most clearly
in the Babylonian and Egyptian New Year Festivals,
chief among these being the processional (Psalm 68. 24-
27; Psalm 47. 1, 2, 5-8) with the ark (Psalm 24. 7ff.) containing its image of Yahweh as the central focus of
interest. And, as was likewise the case in Babylonia
and Egypt, certain psalms (65; 74. 12-17) indicate that
the Israelites associated the idea of creation with the
New Year's Festival, emphasizing the creative power of
Yahweh and his mastery of the chaotic forces of the
deep (*Tehom = Tiamat*) which made creation possible.

The Canaanite-Phoenician sacrificial system was absorbed by Israel. This fact, which the early Ras
Shamra tablets have clearly demonstrated, rightly orients

us for understanding the characteristic prophetic attitude toward the Israelite sacrificial cult. Corresponding
to the Phoenician and North-Canaanite expiatory sacrifice (*kalil*), as M. J. Lagrange has made clear, there were
in Israelite ritual two types of such sacrifice—the offering
for the sin of error (*hattath*, Leviticus 4. 13), and for
the sin of transgression (*asham*, Leviticus 5. 6). This
distinction in Israelite practice, as G. B. Gray has shown,
existed as early as the end of the ninth century B. C.
They both belong in the same category so far as the
disposition of the sacrificial victim is concerned. Exactly corresponding to the Phoenician (*cewath*), and
the North Canaanite (*shelamim*), sacrifice of communion, in Israelite ritual were the peace offerings
(*zebah shelamim*, Leviticus 3. 1; Amos 5. 22), where the
flesh of the animal was eaten by the worshipers, except
choice portions which went to the priests, the blood
and fat being burned upon the altar unto Yahweh.
This was the sacrifice of alliance or friendship.

Corresponding perfectly to the Phoenician whole
burnt offering (*shelem kalil*) and the North-Canaanite
holocaust (*srp*), in Israelite ritual was the whole burnt
offering (*olah*, Amos 5. 22), for which a more accurate
designation would be "holocaust." Just as in Phoenician so in Israelite ritual there were also offerings of
less importance, such as birds, which probably served
as substitutes for the greater bloody sacrifices. The Israelite offering of that which is "perfect," "without
blemish" (*tamim*, Exodus 12. 5), corresponds to the
North-Canaanite perfect offering (*mtn tm*), and just as
in Phoenician practice, so in Israel, the term "*zebah*,"
"slaughtering," was applied to nonbloody as well as to

bloody sacrifices. To the Canaanite offering of sacred
first fruits (*qdmth qdshth*) in the Phoenician ritual,
correspond the Israelite first fruits (*reshith, minhath
bikkurim,* Leviticus 2. 12, 14). In Micah 6. 7 reference
is made to offerings of oil (*shemen*) such as existed in the
Phoenician system. With the Phoenician meal offering
(*zebah minhath*) the Israelite meal offering (*minhah*)
was identical. And the Phoenician term "grain mixed
with oil" (*bll*) is reflected in the Israelite "fine flour
mingled with oil" (*beluloth bashshemen,* Leviticus 2.
4), in the account of the meal offering.

The Israelite shewbread and the libations reproduce
such offerings as we meet in the North-Canaanite cult
of Ras Shamra, the bread placed upon the tables of
offering, and wine, "the blood of trees," which was
poured out in pots as food and drink for the gods. The
Israelite offering made by fire (*ishshe,* Leviticus 1. 9),
corresponds to the North-Canaanite sacrifice of fire
(*est*). The Israelite special votive offerings (*niphlaoth,*
compare *palle nedher,* Leviticus 22. 21), were similar
to the North-Canaanite sacrifice of communion (*nblat*),
an exceptional sacrifice having to do with the erection
of the Temple. Such likenesses grew out of the dependence of the Israelite sacrificial cult upon the
Canaanite, as the similarity in conception, and in several instances the virtual identity in terminology between the two systems, demonstrate.

There is clear evidence that human sacrifice, as at
least an occasional practice, was adopted by the Israelites
from the Canaanites, and to some extent, either directly
or through Canaanite mediation, from the Aramaeans.
In the earliest codes, the so-called J Decalogue (Ex-

odus 34. 19-20), and the Code of the Covenant (Exodus
22. 29), the form of the law at least goes back to the
time of the actual sacrifice of children, viewed as the
first fresh fruits of fertilizing powers.[4] The J Decalogue, however, provides for the redemption of the
first born.

Human sacrifice was practiced in the ninth century
B. C., as shown by Hiel of Bethel, who, at his re-
building of Jericho, offered up his oldest and his young-
est sons as foundation sacrifices (1 Kings 16. 34). And
when the eighth-century prophets began to prophesy,
while it was most likely an exceptional practice, nevertheless, child sacrifice existed in Israel. It was practiced by the Israelites in Hosea's day (Hosea 13. 2), and
Ahaz of Judah in the eighth century B. C. sacrificed his
own son (2 Kings 16. 3).

These indications confirm the conclusion that so far
as the public worship of Israel was concerned, by the
middle of the eighth century it had become largely
Canaanite worship. Israel had practically lost its theo-
cratic mission and had become "like all the nations"
(1 Samuel 8. 20), her Yahweh worship being scarcely
distinguishable from the fertility cults of the Baalim.
Only through such an approach to the era of the literary prophets are we in position to realize how des-

[4] So George Harford: Exodus (Peake's *Commentary*), p. 187, col. 2.
R. H. Pfeiffer argues cogently for the earliest extant edition of an
ancient ritual decalogue of Canaanite origin appropriated by the
Israelites not later than 800 B. C. in Exodus 22. 27-30 and 23. 10-19.
The requirement under consideration would then be the first of the
second section of laws which concerns the presentation of offerings
and sacrifices. Pfeiffer dates it tentatively c. 1200 B. C. Compare "The
Oldest Decalogue," in JBL XLVIII (1924), pp. 294-310, and "The
Transmission of the Book of the Covenant," in HTR., XXIII (1931),
pp. 99-109, esp. 102f.

perate was Israel's need for the penetrating, decisive, and clarifying work of the towering spiritual teachers of the eighth century B. C.

The second act closes with the issue, Yahweh or Baal, settled in principle, but the true nature of Yahweh and what he required of Israel remained yet to be clarified.

CHAPTER VI

THE PROPHETIC CLARIFICATION

THE third act of the drama of the development of Israelite religion is concerned with the contributions of the eighth-century prophets. That was the most creative single century in Israelite religious development and one of the most significant in the moral and spiritual progress of mankind. It was profound insight into the importance of this period which led the late Eduard Meyer, outstanding historian of the ancient Near East, to say: "The step forward which Amos, Hosea, and Isaiah took denotes one of the most momentous changes in the history of mankind. The all-subduing force of conscience or, more exactly, of the conscience of a single individual in opposition to the whole surrounding world, came into action and made itself felt for the first time. The consequences of the struggle fought out in the eighth and seventh century B. C. within the small area of Palestine are still felt throughout the whole range of our civilization."[1] The prophets of this strategic century, against the background of the religious conceptions and practices of the Canaanized public worship of Israel and Judah, and in contrast with it, stated with unapproached clarity the nature and requirements of Yahweh.

1. The Historical Background

We turn first to sketch in swift strokes the historical

[1] E. Meyer: *Kleine Schriften zur Geschichtstheorie und zur wirtschaftlichen und politschen Geschichte des Altertums,* p. 213.

background of the four prophetic pioneers of the eighth century, Amos, Hosea, Isaiah, and Micah.

Under the instigation of a prophet Jonah, son of Amittai, Israel recovered practically her Davidic limits (2 Kings 14. 25) during the long reign of Jeroboam II (785-745 B. C.), son of Jehoash, king of Israel, and entered upon a brilliant period of external development. This, however, because of its pagan character, as the prophets clearly saw, already carried within it the cancer of decay. After Jeroboam II the Northern Kingdom rapidly tottered to its fall. Jehu's dynasty came to an end with the murder of Zechariah (744 B. C.), son of Jeroboam II, by the conspiracy of Shallum, and he in turn, after the reign of a single month, was conspired against by Menahem, who became his successor (743-737 B. C.). For some six years he maintained the throne of Israel solely by the expensive policy of paying heavy tribute to Tiglath Pileser III (Pul) of Assyria (2 Kings 15. 19f.). The reign of Pekahiah, his son, was cut short (737 B. C.) by a conspiracy led by his captain, Pekah, son of Remaliah, who killed him and succeeded him on the throne (2 Kings 15. 25).

The attempt of Rezon of Damascus and Pekah of Israel (736-734 B. C.) to dethrone the weak Ahaz of Judah and to replace him by the Syrian Tabeel (Isaiah 7. 6), a mere tool in their scheming hands, hastened the invasion of the west by Tiglath Pileser III (733-732 B. C.). At his expedition against the west, Damascus fell (732 B. C.). Pekah of Israel was murdered by Hoshea, Assyria's tool, and Hoshea was himself established in the kingship (2 Kings 15. 30). Ahaz's tribute paid to Assyria (2 Kings 16. 7ff.) for the time being saved Judah

from Tiglath Pileser's attack. Hoshea's revolt to Egypt,
which was then emerging into fresh vigor in the new
Ethiopian kingdom (2 Kings 17. 4), led to the Assyrian
Shalmaneser's three years' siege of Samaria and the
city's fall at length to Sargon in 722 B. C. (2 Kings 17.
3ff.). Israelites were deported to Assyrian-controlled
regions (2 Kings 17. 6) and replaced in Samaria by
other captives. This gave rise to a religious syncretism
which represents the beginning of the Samaritan schism
(2 Kings 17. 24ff., 27ff.).

In the meantime, during Israel's expansion under
Jeroboam II, Judah, under Azariah (Uzziah) (780-740
B. C.), had been achieving a remarkable external and
internal development (2 Chronicles 26). A vigorous
military policy made Azariah master of Judah's neigh-
bors, the remnants of the Philistines and the Ammonites. He developed facilities for cattle raising in the
wilderness and greatly increased the yield of the fields
and vineyards. He likewise advanced the military
strength and equipment of Judah. His son Jotham
(740-735 B. C.) continued these constructive policies (2
Chronicles 27). Jotham's son, Ahaz (735-720 B. C.), a
timid and powerless young ruler, as we have seen,
cowered before the news of the invasion of Pekah and
Rezon, and sought Assyrian aid in the crisis.

Hezekiah, son of Ahaz (720-692 B. C.), was one of the
noblest of Judaean monarchs. He began a reform to
uproot the Canaanite elements from Judaean worship
(2 Kings 18. 4), evidently under the inspiration of
Micah (Jeremiah 26. 18f.) and Isaiah. He threw off the
Assyrian yoke (2 Kings 18. 7), and Judah, under him,
assumed the leadership of the small western states

against Assyria, turning for help to the new Ethiopian power, only thus to win the sharp criticism of Isaiah (Isaiah 20). As a security against attack, Hezekiah constructed the pool of Siloam and built the tunnel which brought the water supply into the city from the spring of Gihon. He faltered in his policy of political independence and paid tribute to Assyria. But he was responsive to the passionate preaching of Isaiah (Isaiah 36-37) that Jerusalem was inviolable, and, in the last analysis, refused to yield to Assyria at the invasion of Sennacherib in 701 B. C. The great Assyrian monarch took forty-six Judaean strongholds and shut Hezekiah up "like a caged bird" in Jerusalem.[2] Nevertheless, he could not bring about the submission of Hezekiah, but in time was forced to withdraw and the capital was saved (2 Kings 19. 35f.).

Hezekiah, toward the close of his reign, showed friendly response to the Babylonian Merodach Baladan (2 Kings 20. 12ff.), who, with the help of Elam, had defeated Sargon of Assyria. For this the king won the sharp criticism of Isaiah (2 Kings 20. 16ff.), who evidently felt the same about Babylon as he had felt earlier about Assyria—that alliance with her would be a peril and a snare to Judah rather than an asset.

Manasseh, Hezekiah's son (692-638 B. C.), was a ruler of quite a different stamp. As a vassal of Esarhaddon of Assyria[3] he retained his throne for fifty-four years. But he introduced a period of grave religious reaction into Judah, which brought the most characteristic features of the Canaanite cult, with specifically Assyrian

---

[2] G. A. Barton: *Archaeology and the Bible* (6th ed.), p. 471.
[3] *Ibid.*, p. 476.

increments, into Judaean religion. The High Places which had been destroyed by Hezekiah were repaired; altars for the worship of Baal were introduced; the *asherah* was erected; the host of heaven was worshiped; magic, necromancy, and child sacrifice came sweeping back (2 Kings 21. 1-9). Amon followed his father's religious policy (2 Kings 21. 19ff.), and after a brief reign (638 B. C.), was conspired against and killed by his servants.

2. Amos: Religion as Righteousness

It was in the roaring of a storm (Amos 1. 2) in the wilds of Tekoa that Amos received his call to the prophetic office, c. 760 B. C. Something of the quality of his environment was in the soul of the man, for truly, as George Adam Smith has said, he "haunted heights and lived in the face of very wide horizons." From his life at Tekoa as a herdsman and pruner of sycamore figs (7. 14), Yahweh forcibly "took" him, a man utterly unrelated to the ecstatic guilds of prophets, and made him a prophet to Israel (7. 14-15). He represented the nomadic, wilderness spirit in Israelite life. From Judah, the southern section of the Israelite people, which ever retained something of the old Bedouin temper, he went northward to Bethel, Israel, where the agricultural civilization of Canaan had largely smothered the stern desert spirit of the religion of Sinai. He criticized sharply the storing up of wealth—"violence and robbery" he frankly called it—in palaces (3. 9-10), in utter disregard of the principle of the right (*nekhohah*). Once Yahweh had been leader of Israel. That was in the epoch of the Exodus from Egypt and the wilderness

(2. 9-10). Yahweh's chosen instruments of influence in the past were the Nazarites and prophets, the former with their "dedicated" lives, their long, unkempt hair, and their abstinence from wine, representing a protest against the civilization of Canaan, and the latter, honorable agents of his guidance, whom the Israelites had silenced and cheapened (2. 11-12).

With revulsion in his soul Amos criticizes the prevailing rites of cultic prostitution in the name of religion, wherein Israelites, even father and son, as an accepted religious practice, held intercourse with a sacred prostitute (naarah), thus profaning, rather than honoring, Yahweh (2. 7). It was something new in Israel for this time-honored, originally Canaanite practice to be thus directly condemned.

Against the basic Canaanite conception that the fertility of the soil depends upon the cult of the Baalim, Amos portrays Yahweh as Lord of nature, creating, withholding, and destroying vegetation, according to his own will (4. 6-9; 7. 1-6). And this sovereignty over nature becomes one avenue of approach to Amos's practical monotheism. The God who is thus in universal control of nature is also regnant over the nations (9. 7).

Amos's picture of "the lamentation for an only son" (yahidh) probably refers implicitly to the annual ritual lamentation for Adonis. It recalls the legend of Philo of Byblos and of Porphyry that El-Kronos, the god of Byblos, sacrificed his only son (Ieoud), who probably is to be identified with Adonis.

He takes up certain popular oath formulae which often fell from the lips of Israelites of Samaria and

Beer-sheba, in which dependence upon particular Canaanite deities is implied (Amos 8. 14):

> They that swear by Ashimath[4] of Samaria, and say,
> "As lives thy god, O Dan;"
> "As lives thy Dod,[5] Beer-sheba."

Ashimath, as Lidzbarski maintains, is identical with Ashima (LXX Aseimath) of Hamath (2 Kings 17. 30), and is clearly a feminine Canaanite deity. She was worshiped, as Lods informs us, at Beirut, Emesa, and probably at Hieropolis as well as at Samaria. Dod (Duda), an ancient Canaanite god of the Tammuz-Adonis character, known from the Tell el-Amarna times (KAT[3], p. 224), as T. J. Meek maintains, was the name of Hadad (Adad) in Amurru (Syria and Palestine). According to the inscription of Mesha of Moab (the Moabite stone), the Israelites at Ataroth (Ashtaroth) worshiped Duda (Dod), whose altar hearth Mesha had captured. He was worshiped at Beer-sheba in the eighth century B. C. Amos maintains that these deities are powerless and cannot keep their devotees from falling. "They shall fall and never rise up again."

But sharpest and most penetrating of all was Amos's indictment of the sacrificial cult as it was practiced at the three most famous sanctuaries of Israelite antiquity—Bethel, Gilgal, and Beer-sheba. Amos maintained that the Israelites who brought their sacrifices, their tithes, their thank offerings of leavened bread, which, in contrast to the unleavened Bedouin loaves, represented the bread of the Canaanites, and who made

---

[4] So read for Ashemath. Ashimath is identical with Sima, daughter of Hadad (so Melito), compare M. Lidzbarski: *Ephemeris* III, p. 264.

[5] Reading with most authorities Dodhekha, compare LXX, "Thy God."

a public show of their free-will offerings (4. 5), were
really "transgressing" Yahweh, not worshiping him.
The more meticulous they were in their scrupulous
cult, the more they multiplied their sin against Yahweh (4. 4). When they seek Yahweh in such cultic
rites as were customary at the great normative sanctuaries of Bethel, Gilgal, and Beer-sheba, they will not
find him. For Yahweh "hates" the sacrificial worship
of Israel with its feasts and solemn assemblies, its
whole-burnt offerings (*oloth*), its meal offerings (*mine-
hoth*), and its peace offerings (*shalme*) of fat beasts.
Away with the songs and music that accompany the
sacrifices! Yahweh abhors them. What he does want
is justice, righteousness in social expression.

> Let roll along like the waters, justice,
> And righteousness like a perpetual wady (5. 24).

By rhetorical question Amos implies that sacrifices
(*zebhahim*) and offering (*minhah*) were not a part of the
Mosaic religion (5. 25). For justice (*mishpat*) and
righteousness (*cedhaqah*) in social conduct, the Israelites worshiping at these famous and representative religious centers have substituted ritualistic religious processionals, a beloved practice of the Near-East religions.
In such rites (so Gressmann) images of Sakkuth, "your
king," and Kewan, "the Star of your God," Babylonian
deities, manifestations of the Babylonian Ninurta, were
carried in impressive ceremonial.[6] Ninurta (=Ninib)
was a vegetation deity, the god of the morning sun, the
god of spring.

Now, this emphasis upon God's demand for right-

---

[6] Compare A. Zimmern: *Die Beschwörungstäfel Surpu*, No. 2. 1. 179f.,
"May Sakkut and Kaiwan . . . break the spell."

eousness, over against and in strict opposition to the whole Israelite sacrificial system, is arresting in Old Testament prophecy and runs like a golden thread of unique brilliancy through the warp and woof of Israelite prophetic teaching (Hosea 6. 6; Isaiah 1. 11ff.; Micah 6. 6-8; Jeremiah 7. 21ff., etc.). It represents the central and unique prophetic attitude, and it first appears clearly in the thinking of Amos. It was in this prophetic reaction to the purpose and practices of the public sacrificial cult that the distinctive nature of the Israelite prophetic message emerges.

We have already seen that the object of the public sacrificial cult in Canaanite religion was to control, in the interests of life, the mysterious fertility powers possessed by the deities. And we have further noted that the sacrificial system as practiced in eighth-century Israel was essentially a Canaanite institution. This conclusion was first forcibly argued by René Dussaud in his *Les origines cananéennes du sacrifice israélite,* and it has been unquestionably confirmed by the Ras Shamra tablets. The cultic myths there uncovered show that the whole sacrificial system of offerings was designed on the principle of gifts to the fertility deities, so as magically to secure, one might say coerce, their favor in guaranteeing fertility to the soil and fecundity in animal and human life.

Now, to this concept of magical control the concentrated essence of Old Testament prophecy was unalterably opposed. Against it, as it was expressed in Canaanized Israel, the prophets hurled the full weight of their genius. And among the most clarifying of prophetic minds at this point was Amos. He saw

clearly that such practices did not reach or influence
Yahweh. He was a moral being. He must be sought
by moral means. As W. C. Graham has finely said:
"Hebrew prophetic religion in its technique placed
emphasis on the revelation of the divine will by oracle
rather than on the magical control of it so prominent
in the nature cults. . . . It did not seek to placate
him so much as to understand and obey him. Thus it
becomes clear that the psychological basis of this religion is not fear but faith." Yahweh reveals his will
unto his servants the prophets (3. 7). To seek him
means to seek "the good" (5. 14), and what that "good"
is, Amos makes explicit. To seek the good means to
seek justice and righteousness in Israelite life. Moreover, this is a basically social conception. Righteousness, as Stanley A. Cook has expounded it, means
"conformity to the obligations which bind together not
merely the social unit (that is, Israel) but that organic
unit of which the deity formed a part." The cognate
root of the word in Arabic is used of what is congruent,
of what conforms to its proper nature. Hence the fundamental concept "what is due or just," "what should
be," is at the heart of the term "righteousness." Dean
Knudson reveals profound insight into this cosmic quality of righteousness as Amos conceived it, when he says
that Amos "identifies religion absolutely with the moral
law." Justice (*mishpat*) means that which in such an
organic social unity is the rightful due; it is righteousness in action. Righteousness is the basic, perpetual,
creative fountain expressing itself in justice—rightful
acts which are owed the social unity that Israel and
Yahweh together compose. Nowhere does Amos deal

abstractly with Yahweh's nature. But he who "knows" Israel in a unique sense (3. 2), and who judges the nations on moral grounds (1. 3, 6, 9, 11, 13; 2. 1, 4, 6ff.), and who can be found only through moral conduct (5. 14), must be a moral being. This mysterious, powerful being cannot be coerced or controlled, but he is friendly (5. 15b; 7. 3, 6) and can be trusted and cooperated with.

We stand here at a watershed in the history of religion. The prophets were against sacrifice, for it involved a magical conception of deity and left men trembling in uncertainty and fear. They were for moral, rational conduct because that involved intelligent and growing insight into the nature of a being who made known to man's intelligence and his moral nature his character and requirements. As Dean Knudson maintains, "Magic is selfish; it says, 'My will be done'; but religion in its essential nature is unselfish; it says, 'Thy will be done.'" Magic seeks to bend the deity to the worshiper's will. The prophetic religion of Amos seeks to know and to do the will of God.

3. HOSEA: RELIGION AS ETHICAL UNION WITH GOD

Hosea, son of Beeri, married Gomer, daughter of Diblaim, who, up to the time of her marriage, had apparently been connected with one of the Israelite sanctuaries as a votary in the service of Astarte, a service to which, from the popular point of view, there was no stigma attached. Hosea married her in the conviction that he was fulfilling the summons of Yahweh (Hosea 1. 2). That Gomer would leave her life of a votary was no doubt due to her conviction that Hosea,

who evidently had something of the ecstatic in him
(Hosea 9. 7), was god-inspired. For her, Hosea, the
tenderest soul of all the prophets, had a deep affection,
and it was simultaneously with his marriage that his
prophetic career began.

To them[7] was born a male child, to whom was given
a characteristic prophetic name, "Jezreel" (*Yicreel*). It
was a name bearing a message of judgment upon Israel,
"God sows"—that is, judgment, upon the still existing
dynasty of Jehu because of the bloody revolution which
that usurper had inaugurated, with its center of horror
at the town bearing the same name (2 Kings 9–10).

The second child, a daughter, was given the name
"Lo Ruhamah," meaning "unpitied"—that is, by Yahweh, because of the persistence of Israel's sin against
him. The third, a son, was named "Lo Ammi," meaning "not my people," which taught that Israel no longer
had any claim to be called the people of Yahweh.

But behind these last two names stalks the gaunt
visage of tragedy. Hosea here does not cease to be a
prophet, for the names are clearly meant to bear a
message to Israel. Yet they give equally poignant expression to the tragic revelation which, since Jezreel's
babyhood, had been forced upon him, that the second
and the third child were not his. They had been born
out of wedlock (2. 4b). Gomer had been disloyal to
him and had back-slidden into the old life which she
had known as a votary, a *qedeshah*, of the sanctuary.
In a yet more intimate and personal sense than in its

---

[7] We infer this from the fact that "she bare *him* a son" (or daughter)
is stated only for Jezreel, and from Hosea 2. 1 (LXX), where Hosea
speaks to Jezreel concerning the other two children.

application to Israel, Lo Ruhamah was "unloved," and
Lo Ammi "no kin" of his. Was it some lack in Hosea's
provision that had led her to seek what she had before
known, the "hire" of her lovers, her paramours, who,
at the sanctuary for the services of her person, had given
her bread and water, wool and flax, oil and wine
(2. 5c)? In the sad wail of his broken heart we feel his
world crashing about him. We infer that in solemn
sternness he turned her out of his home and that she
went back to the old life, that of a sacred prostitute.[8]

But Hosea's love for Gomer is a great love, and it
persists in the very face of her disloyalty.[9] He becomes
conscious of a deep-seated impulse to win her back to
his home and to his heart. He buys her from her
"friend" (*rea*) for fifteen pieces of silver and a homer
and a half of barley. Conscious of the mighty lure she
will still inevitably feel to surrender to the seductions
of her paramours, he surrounds her with a discipline
of restraint and negation (3. 3; 2. 6) in the hope that
at length when she cannot satisfy her illicit desires, her
loyalty and exclusive devotion to him will awaken (3.
3; 2. 7). Of the outcome of this domestic experience
he does not inform us. This he leaves his readers to
infer from the tremendous strength, drawing power,
and persistence of his great love, for his sole reason for
telling the awful experience was to interpret to Israel
the deep, creative insight which was born through it.

---

[8] The inference is based primarily on 3. 1. "Go, still love a woman
loving (so LXX) a friend, even an adulteress."

[9] Hosea 3. 1. I follow Wm. Robertson Smith in his judgment that
odh in 3. 1 should be rendered not "again" but "still," and that it
modifies not "go" which is the secondary verb of the sentence, but
"love" which is the primary verb: "Go, still love."

As he was the husband of Gomer, so Yahweh was the husband of Israel. As he had found Gomer and had fallen in love with her, so Yahweh, in the period of the wilderness wanderings, had found Israel "like grapes in the wilderness," "as the first-ripe in the fig tree at her first season" (9. 10). As Gomer had responded to him, so Israel had then tremblingly, sensitively responded to Yahweh (13. 1; 2. 15) and she had become his "wife." But just as Gomer had been lured away from loyalty to him by the seductive gifts of her "lovers," the harlots' "hire" of food and clothing, oils, drinks, and jewelry (2. 5, 13), so Israel had been lured away from Yahweh, her true husband, by the attraction of the Baalim, the Canaanite gods of fertility, thinking that thus to serve them coerced their favor. For the Canaanites had taught Israel that fertility in crops, in animal and human life, depended upon the practice of the cult of the Baalim. It was the Baalim who were the lords of fertility. They provided the rain and made the soil productive. And it was the time-honored service of the sacred prostitutes, the *qedheshoth*, which coerced these gifts. Israel, whose very existence in the agricultural land of Canaan now depended upon the yield of the soil, had participated in the cult which had fertility as its object. As Gomer forgot her true husband under the lure of her lovers, so Israel "went after" the cult of the Baalim and had forgotten Yahweh (2. 13).

It was at this point that Hosea made a distinct advance in Israelite religion. We see the conception of Yahweh expanding under the stimulus of contact with Canaanite Baalism. All that the Canaanites claimed

to be dependent upon the Baalim as lords of the soil,
gods of fertility and productivity, and assured by the
cultic acts that magically coerced their help, Hosea
claims for Yahweh, and takes it up into his sphere.
Speaking for Yahweh, he says:

> For she [Israel] did not know that I gave her
> The grain, and the new wine, and the oil,
> And multiplied unto her silver
> And gold, [which] they made into the Baal (2. 8).

At a single stroke he has brought into pioneering, explicit, and germinal statement the conception that
Yahweh is "the giver of every good and perfect gift" in
the realm of nature.   Later the Deuteronomist, with
more developed thought, also attributes this same fertility and productivity to Yahweh:

And he [Yahweh] will love thee, and bless thee, and
  multiply thee;
He will also bless the fruit of thy body and the fruit of
  thy ground,
Thy corn, and thy new wine, and thine oil,
The increase of thy cattle and the young of thy flock,
In the land which he sware unto thy fathers to give thee
  (Deuteronomy 7. 13; compare also Deuteronomy 28.
  4, 18, 51).

But the Deuteronomist is here dependent upon Hosea,
who is the pioneer in associating such productivity with
Yahweh.   And one feels instinctively the Canaanite
background of such words.   To Canaanized Israel,
however, Hosea says: that which your worship implies to be dependent upon the Canaanite fertility
deities, in whose cult you participate, is in reality
dependent upon Yahweh.   Just as Hosea had stripped
Gomer naked and thrust her from her home, so as a

disciplinary judgment upon disloyal Israel, Yahweh, who is lord of the fertility of the soil, will lay waste her vineyards and fig trees (2. 12; 13. 15), and by withholding the growth of grain, new wine, and the production of wool and flax (2. 9), will reduce the nation to desperate straits. Through captivity, also viewed by Hosea as a discipline of Yahweh, Israel will be wrested from the land of Canaan and its Baalistic agricultural life, and will be reduced to the stern simplicity of nomadic existence (12. 9), as in the wilderness days when Israel was sensitively responsive to Yahweh. And even as Hosea, with unabating love, in spite of Gomer's disloyalty, went after her, took her from her paramours, and held her in restraint where she could not have relations with her lovers, until her old love should awaken for her husband (3. 1-3; 2. 6-7), so there in the wilderness to which Yahweh will have reduced Israel, he will "allure her," and "speak to her heart," until, with the very names of the Canaanite Baalim forgotten, she will once more say the words Yahweh longs to hear, "my man!", "my husband!" (2. 14, 16). When she has thus repented, Yahweh will "return" from his "place" to which he had gone when he abandoned Israel to her disloyalty (5. 15), and will again live for his people in power and in blessing. Then, with moral repentance accomplished, He who alone controls fertility, will send the rain, the latter rain that will water and fertilize the earth (6. 3b).

A characteristic concept of the Canaanite religion was the sacred marriage of Adonis and Ashtart (or Anath). In connection with this annually enacted celebration the festal rites of sacred prostitution were practiced.

We view them more adequately when we understand
their representative and substitutional features. Every
woman, designated by Hosea as Israelite "daughter"
and "bride" (Hosea 4. 13-14), represented Ashtart, and
every foreigner who appeared and held union with
her, as W. Mannhardt maintains, represented Adonis
come from the foreign region, the land of the dead.
The sacred harlots sought by sympathetic magic to
secure the blessings of fertility. That practices of this
sort existed in Israelite worship at the High Places is
certain. Indeed, unique in Hosea is his penetrating,
detailed criticism of this phase of the Canaanized worship (Hosea 4. 11-14). These High Places were situated "upon the tops of the mountains," and "upon the
hills." Here were sacred trees—oaks, poplars, and terebinths. And under the shade of these trees the licentious Baal cult was carried on in the name of Yahweh,
one phase of which was sacred prostitution. Both sexes
prostituted themselves in the service of the deity, the
official male prostitutes being called *qedheshim,* and
the official female prostitutes called *qedheshoth.* The
gains of this prostitution carried on by these temple
servants with Israelite worshipers, both male and
female, were dedicated to the deity (Deuteronomy 23.
18. "the hire of the harlot" and "the price of a dog").
The Israelite fathers "go apart" and practice this immorality in the immediate precincts of the High Place.
It seems from the context that such practices were common at Gilgal, Bethel (Beth-aven), and Beer-sheba
(Hosea 4. 15).[10] This is the earliest clear indication

---

[10] I so read, inserting (compare Amos 5. 5) with the tentative suggestion of W. Nowack, "at Beer-sheba" after "swear."

from the prophets of how complete had been the Israelite absorption of this aspect of the Canaanite cult.

Now, against this immorality in the name of Yahweh worship, which already had upon it the sanction of the centuries of accepted practice, Hosea uttered his profound and penetrating criticism. He saw the utter inconsistency of sacred prostitution—which he, for the first time in Israel, dared to brand common "harlotry" and "adultery"—with the worship of Yahweh, who required goodness and the knowledge of God (4. 1, 13f). The major blame he placed at the door of the corrupt, Canaanized priesthood, a body both numerous and of great prestige (4. 7). They had rejected the knowledge of God. They who should have been leaders in insight as to the nature and requirements of Yahweh, were themselves victims of the Canaanized cult and had become immoral drunkards, irresponsible interpreters of Yahweh's will (4. 6). Indeed, they thrived on the unhealthy enormity of the sin offerings of the Israelite worshipers (4. 8). The road to Shechem, a famous pilgrimage point, was beset by bands of marauding priests. At Mizpah (of Gilead), Tabor (on the borders of Issachar and Zebulun), and Shittim,[11] this degenerate priesthood insulted the dignity of Yahweh. But with the priests the Israelite laymen shared the blame. When the leaders of Israel consort with "lewd women" and sacrifice with "harlots"—for such he dared to call the sacred prostitutes—the "daughters," one of whom was Gomer, and "daughters-in-law" cannot be blamed (Hosea 4. 14).

---

[11] So Hosea 5. 2, which is corrected to read, "and the pit of Shittim they have made deep." Compare Numbers 25; Hosea 9. 10; compare also S. L. Brown: *The Book of Hosea,* pp. 49f.

The stubborn persistence of this practice of sacred prostitution in the Near East, even into the time of Constantine, shows how deeply entrenched it was in the life and religion of the people. All the more significant becomes the daring grapple of Hosea and others who followed him with this characteristic feature of Canaanite religion.

Most creative in its influence was the daring thought of Hosea in venturing to use the Canaanite conception of the sacred marriage, purged of its materialistic and sensual associations, as a medium for interpreting his view of the nature of religion. The marriage of Yahweh with Israel suggests his concept of religion, as in essence, union with God. Professor R. Kittel rightly suggests that this profound aspect of religion, which in turn was to affect Christianity creatively, came largely from the stimulus of Canaanite thought. This is the case also with the related concept of the indwelling of the deity in men. But these concepts of union and indwelling, which in Canaanite religion had sensual and materialistic connotations, by Hosea are lifted to the high plain of ethical fellowship. One of the profoundest utterances of Hosea starts with the concept of "betrothal," where we see most fully this characteristic ethical emphasis:

And I will betroth thee to me for ever;
Yea, I will betroth thee to me in righteousness [cedheq],
    and in justice [mishpat], and in loving kindness
    [hesedh], and in compassion [rahamin];
And I will even betroth thee unto me in faithfulness
    [emunah]; and thou shalt know Yahweh (2. 19).

Religion starts in the love of God expressing itself in

these deeply ethical directions. To this mighty passion
of the primal, persistent, and unchanging love of God,
religion is the response of Israel. Religion, then, is
exclusive loyalty to Yahweh, a loyalty that is called into
being by his love, which Israel's wrongdoing does not
destroy. As Dean Knudson says, "His love is constant.
It is not canceled by human sin."[12]

Among the tenderest and deepest chapters of all
prophetic writing is chapter eleven of Hosea. Here, to
be sure, the figure changes. Instead of being the husband of Israel the bride, Yahweh is viewed as the father
of Israel the son. But we read Hosea's words aright
only when behind the figure of the father dealing ten-
derly and compassionately with the immature son, we
keep in mind his prior concept, the husband dealing
with his fickle bride. We feel the love of Hosea that
could not let Gomer go, for suddenly the pensive mood
of recall changes to passionate lament. We feel the very
heart of Yahweh speaking:

> How can I give thee [up] Ephraim?
>   can I reject thee Israel?
> How can I deliver thee [up] like Admah?
>   can I make thee like Zeboiim?

Although Israel deserves to be cast away from the
divine concern and delivered up to destruction as were
Admah and Zeboiim, in the ancient Hebrew story of
the catastrophe that destroyed Sodom and Gomorrah
(Genesis 14. 8; Deuteronomy 29. 23), Yahweh cannot
surrender his people to such a consummation. His
redemptive love is yet greater than the heat of his
wrath:

---

[12] Albert C. Knudson: *Beacon Lights of Prophecy*, p. 119.

> Turned upon me is my heart,
> Together are my compassions kindled.
> Not shall I perform the heat of my anger,
> Not shall I turn back to destroy Ephraim.
> For God am I, and not man;
> In the midst of thee the Holy One;
> And I shall not come in wrath (11. 8, 9).[13]

Religion is thus ethical union with God; God united to man with an indissoluble bond of love, man united to God in piety, in leal love. To take a conception which in Canaanite religion was so intimately associated with immorality, and to cleanse it of all its sensual associations, but to preserve its warmth and hunger for union with deity, is an evidence of a daring, receptive, and original mind. F. Cumont has shown how the Canaanite way to the good life, in common with all the cults of the ancient Near East, fed the thirst for emotion. Hosea thus brought into Israelite religion an emotional content which made the love of God the fountain of conduct.

The alliances with Assyria and Egypt, with all the cultural and religious interchange involved in them, are but Gomer surrendering to the seductions of her paramours. Religion is exclusive, passionate, ethical union with Yahweh, finding utterance in kindness, in justice, in waiting continually for God (Hosea 12. 6; 10. 12; 6. 6).

Hosea takes for granted as familiar to his hearers many practices and conceptions of the Canaanite cult with which Israelite religion had become so permeated. With the true instincts of a great teacher he deals with

---

[13] Author's translation. This literal rendering preserves the order of emphasis of the original.

them freely and creatively, now absorbing them into his conception of Yahweh, now rejecting them and setting into vivid contrast with them his own view of the nature and requirements of God.

Of illuminating interest is such use of the cult and myth of Adonis which, as we have seen, already had long been in vogue in Canaan.[14] As in the widespread Adonis myth the vegetation deity Adonis was torn by a wild boar, so Yahweh is represented by Hosea as "a lion" (5. 14; 13. 7), "a lioness" (13. 8), "a leopard," "a bear" (13. 7-8), or other "wild beast" (13. 8), tearing Israel (6. 1). Ephraim's moral "death" (13. 1) he compares to the ruin wrought when the deity—upon whose power all vegetation (13. 15) and all fecundity in animal and human life depend (9. 11)—departs, or dies (5. 15; compare 1 Kings 18. 27). The death of all animal life (4. 3) and the dearth of crops, familiar in the Adonis myth, he interprets as the mourning of the land for the dead deity (7. 14). Such lamentation was ritually performed by women who, as J. P. Peters maintains, represented Ashtart sorrowing for Adonis, "womankind, the womb of nature seeking fertilization."

Hosea gives a vivid picture of the wailing and the orgiastic character of the lamentations in these essentially Canaanite rites (Hosea 7. 14):

> And they have not cried unto me with their heart,
> Though they wail upon their beds;
> For grain and for new wine they lacerate[15] themselves;
> They rebel against me.

---

[14] In this section I am indebted to H. G. May: "The Fertility Cult in Hosea," in AJSL XLVIII (1932), 73-98.

[15] Reading with the LXX (katetemnonto) and 12 MSS. yithgodhadhu for yithgoraru. Compare also 1 Kings 18. 28. "They cut themselves after their manner with knives and lances."

Probably similar to those rites is the popular lamentation connected with the predicted "departure" from
Canaan of the bull god of Bethel as spoil to Assyria
(10. 5-6). In the Adonis festival this ritual mourning,
as we learn from Plutarch, continued two days, and was
followed on the third day by rites of rejoicing signifying
the resurrection of the fertility god. It is an implicit
reference to this which Hosea gives when he criticizes
the nation's presumptuous confidence that her sad
estate will be transformed into health and healing by
Yahweh. The superficial nation is saying (6. 2):

> After two days will he revive us;
> On the third day he will raise us up,
> And we shall live before him.

Their lamentations, so they think, will bring him back
in healing to Israel, and with him the productive rains
(6. 1-3). But their expectations of Yahweh's turning
unto them in response to such magical practices, Hosea
sharply condemns. What Yahweh wants and what
alone will make possible his help, is goodness (*hesedh*),
substantial and dependable, not like an ephemeral
morning cloud or the dew, which before the burning
sun swiftly evaporates (6. 4, 6).

This demand of Hosea for "goodness" (*hesedh*, 4. 1;
6. 4-6; 10. 12; 12. 6) places before us his most characteristic summons and at once takes us more deeply into the
roots of conduct than does Amos. The term *hesedh* is
one of the richest in prophetic thought. It expresses
the virtue which knits society together. It involves in
its expression toward men considerate and brotherly
conduct. An illuminating use of the Arabic expression

of the concept is the joint exercise of hospitality to a
guest (*hashadu lahu*). Perhaps, as Nelson Glueck suggests, the best single term to give it adequate rendering
is the Latin *pietas,* "piety." A number of English words
are needed, however, to give utterance to the fullness
of the prophetic meaning, such as goodness, love, mercy,
loyalty, and courtesy. Always the concept is social.
And in Hosea it is clearly implied that the social conduct is the outflow of this basic relationship to Yahweh
which the term expresses.

An outstanding motif in the Adonis cult and myth
was the seeking of the departed fertility deity by his
partner, viewed now as lover, now as sister, and now
as mother. This "seeking" of the departed deity took
place in the springtime, the time of seed sowing. This
aspect of the Adonis cult made upon Hosea a profound
impression. He knew the Canaanite practice of planting the Adonis gardens. This was a form of primitive
magic, the purpose of which was to bring the dead
Adonis, the corn and fertility god, to life, and to restore
to the earth the fructifying waters.

Hosea implies that it is not by the sowing of such
seed in the Adonis gardens that the presence of Yahweh
in salvation and fruitfulness will be secured. Such
sowings do not influence him. Here again we feel
the watershed quality of prophetic thought. Yahweh
requires a sowing of an entirely different order.

Sow to yourselves in righteousness,
Harvest in proportion to piety;
Freshly till your untilled ground;
For it is time to seek Yahweh,
Until he come and rain righteousness upon you (10. 12).

The coming of the spring rains gave evidence in Canaan that the search of the fertility goddess Astarte for the dead fertility god Adonis had been successful and his resurrection accomplished (6. 3). The productive processes of nature would then again be effective. But, maintains Hosea, unless Israel ethically seeks Yahweh in terms of piety and righteous conduct her search will be unavailing (10. 12).

Connected with the seeking of the dead or departed fertility deity, is the sacrificial system. It was the chief cultic resort of Canaanized Israel for assuring fertility to the soil and to animal and human life. But Hosea, like Amos, was set solidly against it as a way of finding Yahweh. He is a different kind of being. Sacrificial animals from flock and herd will not avail to find him. He must be sought in another way:

With their flocks and their herds they shall go to seek
    Yahweh;
But they will not find him:
He hath withdrawn from them (5. 6).

A less common type of sacrifice, which was connected with the fertility cult and under Canaanite influence widely practiced in Israel, was human sacrifice (2 Kings 16. 3; 21. 6). It had as its motive the securing of fecundity from the deity who controlled it. Hosea makes a derisive reference to it, designating by this single practice, the Canaanized worshipers: "Sacrificers of men, let them kiss calves" (13. 2).

The stubborn persistence of these various rites of the fertility cult makes all the more significant the prophet's courageous grapple with this aspect of Canaanite religion. We have in Hosea one of the profoundest spirits of Israel and one of the greatest of the pioneering, trailblazing minds which this people gave to the world.

4. ISAIAH: RELIGION AS TRUST IN THE SOVEREIGN GOD

Isaiah is the most majestic of all the prophets. He was no doubt familiar with Malk, the king deity of Canaanite religion. The great autobiographical account of his inaugural vision in the temple is colored by the Canaanite conception of El-Kronos, "the King," as presented by Philo. The seraphim, each with six wings, strikingly recall Philo's description of El-Kronos with six wings, "two pairs in the act of flying and one pair at rest." "Whilst he rested he was flying, yet rested while he flew." The two upper wings represent intelligence and feeling (Frag. 26). The coins of Byblos confirm and supplement this description. Yet the being of Yahweh, as Isaiah conceives him, is "high and lifted up" above the Baalim, for he is a moral being and his chief characteristic is moral holiness (6. 1-8).

Of all the prophets, Isaiah has most kinship in spirit to Amos. In principle, Amos had shattered the conception of religion as cult religion and folk religion and had made it supremely ethical. Isaiah shared with him this basic conception. More in detail than either Amos or Hosea had done, however, he hurls his criticism at the Canaanized sacrificial cult (1. 11-15). Incidentally we get from his words a vivid picture of the popular Judaean worship of his day.

Isaiah inveighs against the various types of offering. The "sacrifices" (zebhahim), offered in great numbers, wherein the fat and blood were brought to the altar and the rest of the bullocks, lambs, or he-goats were eaten by the worshipers in a sacrificial feast; the whole-burnt offerings (*oloth*) of rams, slaughtered on (Genesis 22. 9f.) or beside (Leviticus 1. 4f.) the altar, and then entirely burned; and the daily cereal offering (*minhah*). These all meant nothing to Yahweh. He had no delight in the portions given unto him. The aroma of incense accompanying the offering, instead of being a "sweet savor" unto him, was a detested odor. The sacrificial worshipers were but irreverent "tramplers" of the temple courts.

Their congregational worship, their celebration of the Sabbaths, their New-Moon festivals, the great annual harvest festivals with their processionals, the occasional assemblies for penitence, prayer, and thanksgiving, he views as worthless dissipation. The prayers connected with such ceremonies are incompatible with the true requirements of Yahweh.

Over against this Canaanized cult, in the spirit of Amos, but with more concreteness, he states what Yahweh does require of his worshipers (1. 16-17). Moral cleanness, the cessation of evil deeds, and education in right conduct, are his demands. They must seek justice, relieve the oppressed, help the fatherless, and support the cause of the widow.

But Isaiah went far beyond Amos in his insight into the nature of religion. That which was new in Amos's teaching, pre-eminently the ethical note, he grasped more profoundly. And he interpreted more creatively the positive quality of the religion of Yahweh. Conceived in its essence it was faith, dependence upon Yahweh. To be sure, his contemporaries knew and expressed a kind of faith—confidence in magic and idolatry (2. 6, 8), in fortifications and military power (2. 7, 15; 31. 1), in commerce (2. 16), in statecraft and diplomacy (3. 1-3; 30. 1ff.; 20. 5f.) in human shrewdness (5. 21; 29. 14f.; 31. 2), in acts of oppression and distortion (30. 12). But such faith, in the ultimate analysis, is dependence upon human power, skill, and ingenuity. Isaiah's religion is dominated by the feeling of distance between God and man.[16] God is "the Holy One." There is but one sin against him—pride (28. 9-13, 22; 30. 9ff.). Religion rises in awe before the Holy God (8. 12f.). Religion is belief in God (7. 9), trust (28. 16), quietude, confidence, and dependence (30. 15) in him. He thus reduces "the moral and religious lifte to one underlying principle. This principle in Isaiah is faith."[17]

Canaanite nature worship with its fertility cults was nearly as prominent in eighth-century Judah as in Israel. And it is clear that Isaiah felt keenly the degenerative influence of these cults upon Judaean religion. He inveighs against the sacred trees of the High Places (1. 29, reading second person with 3 MSS. and Targum):

"Ye shall be ashamed of the oaks which ye have desired." He also gives our clearest biblical data for the Canaanite-Phoenician Adonis cult as practiced by Judaeans of his century. He refers to "the gardens which ye have chosen" (1. 29), by which he means the Adonis gardens, and in a passage of great importance, after charging the Judaeans that they had forgotten the god of their salvation, he continues:

[16] G. Hölscher: *Geschichte der israelitischen und jüdischen Religion,* p. 108.
[17] Albert C. Knudson: *Beacon Lights of Prophecy,* p. 150.

Therefore thou plantest pleasant plants [lit., "the plantings
   of Naaman," a by-name of Adonis]
And dost seed it with vine slips of an alien [god].
In the day of thy planting thou didst make it grow,
And in the morning thou didst make thy seed to sprout
   (17. 10-11a).

But Isaiah maintains that such magical ceremonies are
fruitless so far as the bringing of salvation of Yahweh
is concerned, for

> . . . the harvest fleeth away[18]
>   in the day of woe
> And of pain incurable (17. 11b).

At Byblos and Alexandria, as we learn from Plutarch,
Adonis was identified with Osiris, to whose cult it is
likely that Isaiah makes reference (10. 4a). Following
the conjecture of Lagarde the verse should probably
be read:

> Beltis (=Baalath) is sinking,
> Osiris has been broken,
> Under the slain they fall.

Beltis or Baalath here is Isis, who is equivalent to Astarte. In a period when Judah had begun to turn for
help to Egypt, the deities to whom they would be fleeing
were those viewed as life-giving deities—Osiris and his
consort Baalath, or Isis. But Isaiah is clear that no
help may be expected from that quarter, for those
deities are powerless. They will themselves fall under
the slain.

The cultural background of Isaiah's vineyard song in
5. 1-7 is the cult of Dod[19] (= Hadad), clearly the god

---

[18] Reading with O. Procksch, *nadh* for *nedh*.

[19] I am indebted in this section to the penetrating insight of W. C.
Graham in his "Notes on the Interpretation of Isaiah 5. 1-14," in
AJSL, Vol. XLV (1929), especially pp. 167-171.

of fertility.   Isaiah's reference to "the song of my Dod"
(*shirath Dodhi*) is not correctly translated "the song of
my beloved," but, as Waterman maintains, the reference is to a proper name, that of the Canaanite god
Dod.   In these opening words of the song,

Let me sing for "my darling" (*yedhidhi*)
A song of "my Dod" (*shirath Dodhi*) about his vineyard,

Isaiah makes satirical reference to the fertility cult of
Dod, applying ironically to Yahweh concepts of deity
quite foreign to his true nature, but which were at
home in the fertility cult.   He had reference to fertility
rites which were being practiced in Jerusalem.   He
uses the term "my darling" as expressive of a relationship which the adherents of Yahweh consider themselves to have with him, a relation that inclines toward
magic and which is part and parcel of the underlying
concepts of the nature cult of Dod.   The worship which
applies such terms to Yahweh is a magical worship, its
sensual, licentious nature being implied in the attitude
toward deity which the terms suggest.

So by terms familiar in Canaanite fertility rites, since
they viewed Yahweh as a deity of the Dod type, he pictures him preparing his vineyard for a gracious yield
for "his darlings," his devotees.   Then, when the ex-
pectation is strong in the minds of the prophet's hearers
that he will assure them of Yahweh's care for his people, just as Amos did with his ominous "therefore"
(Amos 3. 2), Isaiah turns the tables and emphasizes
Israel's moral responsibility to God.   It is at this point
(5. 2d) that the prophetic note begins, "And [he] also
hewed out a wine press therein: and he looked that it

should bring forth grapes, and it brought forth wild grapes." Accordingly, no longer will ritual songs such as the Dod songs be sung over the vineyard.[20] Such magical processes will cease for Yahweh will destroy Canaanized Judah. For what Yahweh desires is not magic; he is a being of an utterly different sort from the "darling" of Judah's allegiance. His worship belongs to another category entirely. All that the religion of Canaanized Judah has produced is oppression and the cries of human suffering. What Yahweh looks for and demands is justice and righteousness in human relationships (verse 7).[21] Moreover, while the fertility religion of the Canaanized Judaeans was land-centered, Yahweh's interest was not in land but in men. To Yahweh the real vineyard was not the land of Judah but the society of Judah, the house of Israel, the nation of Judaean human beings. The plants in which he takes delight are not grapevines but the men of Judah. It is justice and righteousness in its outflow toward human beings that Yahweh requires.

5. Micah: The Quintessence of Prophetic Religion

Micah, a contemporary of Isaiah, likewise was a prophet closely akin in spirit to Amos. He was a Judaean from Moresheth, a small town in the maritime plain, five miles north of Gath. He was the spokesman

---

[20] The clause in verse 6b usually rendered "It shall not be pruned" (*lo yezzamer*) is connected with fertility cults and means it shall not be ritually sung. Compare Song of Songs 2. 12.

[21] There is a striking assonance in this sentence wherein words of similar sound are set in sharp opposition to each other. G. W. Wade suggestively renders (*Westminster Commentary*, p. 31):

"He looked for rule but behold misrule;
For redress but behold distress."

of the poor peasantry of Judah and felt keenly the
avarice of the dominant Judaean leadership which was
crushing the heart out of the peasant farmers.   His
prophetic ministry evidently began before the fall of
Samaria, for to him the fountains of iniquity in northern and southern Israel are Samaria and Jerusalem
(1. 5). His speech is solemn and biting. His language
is powerful and penetrates to the conscience. He was
remembered in Judah primarily because of his passionate condemnation of Jerusalem. A whole century
after his time the exact words of Micah against Jerusalem and the Temple were recalled by certain elders,
who used them and the influence they had exercised
upon Hezekiah as a precedent for protecting the life of
Jeremiah in a crisis precipitated by his similar preaching (Jeremiah 26. 17ff.).

It is reasonable to infer from Jeremiah 26. 19, which
describes the responsiveness of Hezekiah to Micah's
preaching, that Micah was an influential factor in the
reform which, late in the eighth century B. C., Hezekiah
put into operation (2 Kings 18. 4). This inference is
in perfect harmony with the total emphasis of his
message. The objective of the reform was the uproot-
ing of stubborn Canaanite elements from the public
worship of Judah—the destruction of the High Places,
the breaking of the *macceboth,* the chopping down of
the *asherah* from each sanctuary, and the destruction of
the brass serpent called Nehushtan, to which incense
was burned, the symbol of a Canaanite deity of healing,
possibly Eshmun.

The key to the correct interpretation of the religious
aspect of Palestinian culture in Micah's day, as W. C.

Graham has penetratingly shown,[22] is the Canaanite fertility cults as they had survived in the Judaean religion. Samaria, the capital of the Northern Kingdom, which was most imbued with this Canaanite influence, is beyond rescue and her certain destruction he announces with evident approval (1. 5-6). Jerusalem, however, he views as "the gate of my people" and even to it, the capital city of Judah, the influences so evident in northern Israel have reached (1. 9). This cuts Micah to the quick. His own "wailing," which he pictures through lamentation features of the fertility cult rites (1.8), is due to this terrible contamination of Judah.

In imagination he then surveys the entire region, addressing the neighboring places of cult where the fertility rites were practiced. The term *"yoshebheth,"* used five times by Micah (1. 11-15) and usually translated "inhabitant," is most probably to be viewed as a sarcastic or contemptuous term which designates the mother-goddess of the local fertility cults.[23]

The centers of cult which have been responsible for introducing these degenerating influences into Judah and Jerusalem are Gath, Ekron, Shaphir, Zaanan, Maroth, and especially Lachish, which is singled out as a most vigorous influence along these lines. Following the translation of the reconstructed text,[24] we note specific features of these fertility rituals. We see the whirling dance (verse 12), the ritual wailing as in the

---

[22] W. C. Graham: "Some Suggestions Toward the Interpretation of Micah 1. 10-16," in AJSL, XLVII (1931), p. 238.

[23] *Ibid.*, p. 239.

[24] *Ibid.*, pp. 250f. He entitles the whole oracle most suggestively "Fertility and Futility."

Adonis rites (verse 10), the sacred prostitution, the processionals of the goddess (verse 11) with the use for that purpose of horse and chariot (verse 13, compare 2 Kings 23. 11), the simulated tearing of the hair (verse 16). All these fertility rites are utterly powerless to bring prosperity and security to Judah. In contrast with the magical, ritual mourning ceremonies, Micah's lamentation is real and from the heart (1. 8), for he is distressed about the moral plight of his people.

It was over against this folk religion which had so largely absorbed the Canaanite fertility cult, that Micah defined with unsurpassed clarity the essence of true worship in words which contain, as G. F. Moore maintains, "the quintessence of the prophetic conception of religion." This forms "one of the most imposing passages of the Old Testament before the spirit of which all other Oriental religions hide their downcast heads."[25] This passage has been denied to Micah, chiefly on the ground of the total impression posterity retained of his teaching (Jeremiah 26. 18-19), which appears to be inconsistent with the positive, constructive tone of these verses. But Micah, whose prophetic activity began shortly before 722 B. C., may well have continued into the beginning of the reign of Manasseh (692 B. C.) which saw a vigorous recrudescence of the fertility cults under the championship of the king.[26] The early reign of Manasseh, at any rate, is the most appropriate cultural background for these mighty words. It was the Canaanized cultic rites of Judah that led Micah to raise

---

[25] E. Sellin: *Introduction to the Old Testament*, p. 178.
[26] So also J. Meinhold: *Einführung in das Alten Testament*, p. 172. Compare J. A. Bewer: *The Literature of the Old Testament*, p. 118.

with hitherto unequaled pertinency and answer with unparalleled simplicity and profundity the question, What does Yahweh require of his worshipers?

With what [that is, bringing what] shall I come to meet
    Yahweh,
Shall I bow myself to the high God? (literally, the God
    of height)?

By rhetorical questions he suggests the answers of the folk religion of Judah, which passionately held that the sacrificial system offered the correct way to approach Yahweh. The Canaanized cult of Judah emphasized the offering of one-year-old calves as whole burnt offerings (Leviticus 9. 3). Oil, an acceptable gift to the deity among the Egyptians and Babylonians, was likewise acceptable to Yahweh in a land of olives and wine (Genesis 28. 18). On great sacrificial occasions (1 Kings 8. 63) where vast throngs participated, the rams for the sacrificial feast might be greatly multiplied and the oil might flow as in rivers (6. 6). The climax of the whole sacrificial system, and that which showed its terrible earnestness and passion, was "the fruit of my body"— human sacrifice. It was practiced, as we have seen, in Canaan, in Phoenicia, in Carthage, and, although vigorously opposed by the prophets, down to a relatively late date, in Israel.

Over against this sacrificial system, viewed here as a totality, stands Micah with his "Everlasting Nay." The whole implication of his words shows that he broke absolutely with it. Sacrifice, be it ever so meticulously and passionately offered, had not been "declared" to Israel, as "good." But what Yahweh deemed "good" had been declared unto Israel, and this alone did he "require" of her and "seek for" in her:

> What is Yahweh seeking for in thee?
> But to do justly, and to love kindness,
> And to show a humble walk with thy God (6. 8).

Micah thus sums up the teaching of his three great predecessors, Amos, Hosea, and Isaiah, respectively,[27] and presents what Professor Borden P. Bowne called "The Magna Charta of spiritual religion."

Nothing in the Old Testament surpasses this statement as a summary of the prophetic view of the requirements Yahweh makes of his worshipers. The true religious genius of Israel throbs in these words. As J. M. P. Smith says, they link ethics with piety, bringing together in a mighty synthesis duty toward God and man. Moreover, Sellin has called attention to the fact that Micah's use of the word man (adham) in "He hath showed thee, O man, what is good," implicitly points toward universalism. We are lifted beyond the thought of Yahweh's requirements of Israel toward his requirements of humanity and are thus carried a step beyond Isaiah. It was the influence of the essentially Canaanite sacrificial cult, with its magical view of religion, as absorbed, practiced, and freshly motivated by Israel that forced into clarity of conception and utterance this prophetic view of Yahweh and the nature of his requirements. Nowhere in the Old Testament is the essence of Yahweh worship expressed with such brevity and adequacy.

---

[27] Amos 5. 24; Hosea 6. 6; Isaiah 7. 9; 30. 15. The root cana (to show a humble walk) suggests the reverse of the arrogant, conceited, self-sufficient spirit.

By these four pioneer minds of eighth-century Israel a dramatic elevation in the nation's long climb toward moral and spiritual heights was attained. As W. O. E. Oesterley has said, "Only the insistent championship of the worship of Yahweh by such men as Amos, Hosea, and Isaiah, ineffectual as it was among the bulk of the people, saved the nation from losing its ancestral religion altogether."[28] Over against the Canaanized features of Israelite religion they hurled their passionate protest. Against that antagonistic background they defined in constructive fashion the nature and the requirements of Yahweh. Hosea alone of the four discovered in Canaanite religion some seeds of positive worth and planted them in the soul of Israel. They were destined to strike root in the nation's religious thinking and bear fruit in the creative epoch of the sixth century.

[28] In S. H. Hooke (editor): *The Labyrinth* ("Further Studies in the Relation between Myth and Ritual in the Ancient World"), 1935, p. 120.

CHAPTER VII

THE FINAL SYNTHESIS

*T*HE issue of the drama of the development of Old Testament religion was a creative synthesis of the greatest elements in Israel and Canaan. Even in the eighth century the prophet Hosea had pointed the way toward this consummation. But it remained for Jeremiah, the greatest Israelite of the seventh century, together with Ezekiel and Deutero-Isaiah, the deep thinkers of the sixth century, to resolve the sharp antagonism of Israel and Canaan into a lofty and all-embracing synthesis.

1. THE HISTORICAL FRAMEWORK

Josiah (638-608 B. C.), one of Judah's noblest kings, son of Amon (638 B. C.), came to the throne in a period of great international turmoil. There was at this time, as Stanley A. Cook maintains, an interconnection of the peoples comparable only to that of the Amarna age. Egypt was self-conscious and ambitious and, under Psammetichus I (663-609 B. C.), was experiencing a revival. The western states during the later years of Ashurbanipal (669-626 B. C.) were freeing themselves from Assyria. The Scythian invasion, which occurred in 635-625 B. C., hastened the decline of Assyria and awakened prophetic activity in Zephaniah and Jeremiah.

In 625 B. C. the viceroy of Babylonia, Merodach Baladan, established the New Babylonian Empire (the

Chaldaean), and in 612 B. C., Nineveh, the capital of
Assyria, fell. Nahum, the prophet, with delirious joy
had preached its certain doom. And the destructive
progress of the New Babylonian Empire stirred the
mind of Habakkuk to grapple with the problem of
suffering in its national aspect (Habakkuk 1. 12ff).

Josiah was another ruler of the stamp of Hezekiah.
In the process of the repair of the Temple, inaugurated
by him, Hilkiah the priest and Shaphan the scribe discovered a document which became the basis of a
national reform. It was the kernel of the book of
Deuteronomy and attempted a reformulation of Israelite law, both civil and religious, in the spirit of the
social ideals of the eighth-century prophets, linking it
to Moses as their germinal source. The roots of the
Deuteronomic reform are thus in the eighth century.
The reformation of Hezekiah (2 Kings 18. 4) had had
as its central objective the purification of the Judaean
Yahweh worship. This was a reform, based, so far as
we can discern, upon no code but upon the living word
of prophecy (Jeremiah 26. 8-19). Deuteronomy, which
means "a repetition of this law" (Deuteronomy 17. 18),
in its original compass (chapters 12-26) is rightly viewed
as the literary deposit of Hezekiah's reform. Most
likely it had the beginnings of its formulation still in
the time of Hezekiah and attained the form it had
achieved when discovered, during the drastic resurgence
of Canaanite and Assyrian paganism under Manasseh
(692-638 B. C.).

Deuteronomy is rightly conceived as a synthesis
of the prophetic religion and the public cult in Israel.
It is one of the most realistic and practical books in

the Old Testament. The Deuteronomic code is a clear expression of the Hegelian dialectic of thesis, antithesis, and synthesis. The thesis is the vigorous and decisive demand for justice, righteousness, piety, and faith, uttered by the prophets without exception from Amos to Micah, over against sacrifice, as the way to Yahweh. The antithesis is the stubbornly entrenched popular cult of Israel, impregnated thoroughly by the Canaanite practices such as the sacrificial system taken over from the Canaanite High Place and Temple. The synthesis is represented by the ideals of the Deuteronomic reform. They embodied the prophetic demands of the eighth century in statutes that were binding upon Israel. But they retained the strongly entrenched sacrificial cult, purging it of its immoralities and connecting it in motivation yet more intimately than the Code of the Covenant had done, with Israelite history (Deuteronomy 16. 1, 3c, d, 6, 12).

Accordingly, the reform which Josiah in 621 B. C. inaugurated had two basic objectives: the abolition of the High Places, where, as we have seen, the cult had become practically Canaanite in nature, and the centralization of all public Judaean worship at the Jerusalem Temple (Deuteronomy 12. 1-7). In no document in the entire Old Testament do we get as clear a picture of the popular public worship of Judah in the seventh century B. C. as in the narrative of this Deuteronomic reform (2 Kings 23), and nowhere else do we see more conclusively that even after the eighth-century prophets had done their work of purging the religion of Yahweh, the public cult of Judah was still scarcely distinguishable from the Canaanite worship.

The reform (2 Kings 23) started in Jerusalem, where the cultic vessels for Baal, and for the *asherah*, and for the host of heaven, were carried from the Temple and buried in the fields of Kidron (verse 4). The *asherah* itself was taken from the Temple and buried at the Kidron (verse 6). Josiah destroyed the houses of the male sacred prostitutes (*qedheshim*, the "Sodomites") which were in the Temple (verse 7). He did away with the idolatrous priests (*kemarim*) who burned incense in the High Places, along with those that burned incense to Baal, to the sun, to the planets, and to the host of heaven (verse 5). He brought all the priests (*kohanim*) out of the Judaean cities and destroyed the High Places where they had burned incense, from Geba in the north to Beer-sheba in the south (verse 8). He attempted to abolish child sacrifice (verse 10). He removed the horses sacred to the sun god at the entrance to the Temple (verse 11). The idolatrous altars, on the roof of Ahaz's upper chamber in the two courts of the Temple, were broken down and pounded to pieces (verse 12). The High Places which Solomon had built for the worship of Ashtart, Chemosh, and Milkom, were destroyed. The *macceboth* were broken in pieces and the *asherim* were cut down (verses 13f.). The altar and High Place at Bethel were destroyed, the High Place was burned and beaten to dust, and the *asherah* was burned (verse 15). Similarly, he destroyed the High Places in the cities of Samaria (verse 19) and slew their priests (verse 20). He put away all necromancers and wizards, all teraphim (images of ancestors), idols, and all elements of Semitic heathendom (verse 24). The whole nation, for the first time in history, was summoned to Jerusalem to observe the Feast of the Passover (2 Kings 23. 21f.; Deuteronomy 16. 1ff.).

Flushed with Deuteronomic triumphs and presumably, like Hezekiah (2 Kings 20. 12-15), favoring Babylon, Josiah attempted at Megiddo to oppose Necho of Egypt, who was advancing against the new Chaldaean empire to assert his supremacy in the Near East, and there Josiah met his death (2 Kings 23. 29).

Necho, now for a brief four years dominant in the west, placed upon the Judaean throne his puppet Jehoiakim (608-597 B. C.), whose luxurious, ostentatious building enterprises and forced labor drew down prophetic criticism (Jeremiah 22. 13f.). Necho was decisively defeated by Nebuchadrezzar II, the Chaldaean, at Carchemish (605 B. C.), who thus became the supreme power in the Near East. Jehoiakim rebelled against Nebuchadrezzar and held his throne only with great difficulty during the last years of his reign against the pressure of invading nomads, Chaldaeans, Syrians, Moabites, and Ammonites who hastened the fall of the Judaean kingdom (2 Kings 24. 2).

Nebuchadrezzar besieged Jerusalem in 597 B. C. (2 Kings 24. 10ff.). Jehoiachin (597 B. C.), who but three months before had succeeded Jehoiakim, surrendered and Nebuchadrezzar carried into captivity the king and the leaders of the nation, placing Mattaniah (Zedekiah) on the throne. At his rebellion against Nebuchadrezzer a few years later (2 Kings 25. 1), the Chaldaeans came, mastered Jerusalem in a three years' siege (586 B. C.), and destroyed it by fire. Zedekiah, who had abdicated, was overtaken at Jericho and carried to Riblah in Hamath. His sons were killed before his eyes. Then he himself was blinded and taken in chains to Babylon. Nebuchadrezzar carried the inhabitants of Judah as captives into Babylonia (2 Kings 25. 11-12), leaving in Judah only a mere remnant of peasants to till the soil.

Jeremiah, with the remnant in Jerusalem, and Ezekiel, among the captives, were the Jews' spiritual guides in the early years of the exile. Jeremiah urged continued loyalty to Yahweh and prayer to him apart from the Temple and its ritual, and, along with Ezekiel, combated the delusion of a speedy return (Jeremiah 29). Ezekiel, after the fall of Jerusalem, in 586 B. C., fought against despair by preaching the possibility of a new future for Judaeans with the restored Temple at the center. He drew up a platform for the restored religious community (Ezekiel 40–48). He attempted to awaken heart and courage in the despondent exiles. Due largely to the work of these two prophets, there was developed and retained in Babylon a loyal nucleus of Yahweh worshipers who watched with growing interest and hope the advance of the Persian Cyrus, prince of Anshan in Elam, as in 559 B. C. he became king of Persia, in 550 defeated Astyages of Media, and in 546 vanquished Croesus of Lydia (in Asia Minor). Deutero-Isaiah (c. 540 B. C.), a great Israelite prophet in Babylon (Isaiah 40-55), interpreted Cyrus as Yahweh's servant (Isaiah 44. 27; 45. 1f.), and hailed him as the inaugurator for the Jews of a new epoch of recovery and advance (48. 20). In 540 B. C. Cyrus opened his campaign against Babylon, and in 538 B. C. entered the city as master, with the acquiescence and welcome of a large part of the people.

2. ZEPHANIAH: THE SUMMONS TO RIGHTEOUSNESS AND MEEKNESS

It was but some six years before the Deuteronomic reform that Zephaniah uttered his criticism of Judah. His prophetic activity was stimulated by the invasion of the Scythians. They were nomads from the steppes north of the Black Sea. For twenty-eight years they lorded it over Asia. As Skinner pictures them, they were "a wild, primeval . . . race, of uncouth speech, cruel and pitiless, moving on horseback, armed with bow and spear, sweeping like a tornado over the land and leaving desolation in their track, prowling like hungry wolves or howling leopards around the fenced cities where the terrified inhabitants have taken refuge."[1] Allied with the Medes and Cimmerians they overran the Near East as far as the Egyptian borders.

Zephaniah viewed them as harbingers of the day of Yahweh, a day of universal judgment (1. 2ff., 7, 14ff.). His primary interest was Judah and Jerusalem. He passionately pronounced the destruction of "the remnant of Baal," the Canaanite Baal worship of the High Places, with its idolatrous priesthood, the *kemarim*, which had stubbornly persisted in spite of the eighth-century prophetic teaching (Zephaniah 1. 4; compare Hosea 10. 5). He inveighed against those who, while bowing down to Yahweh, swore by Milkom (LXX), the old Canaanite king god (1. 5). He also hurled his invective against those who worshiped the host of heaven, that is, the sun, moon, and the planets (1. 5; compare

---

[1] So John Skinner: *Phophecy and Religion*, p. 42. Compare G. A. Smith: *Jeremiah*, p. 73.

2 Kings 23. 4). Place names in Canaan attest the early
worship of the sun and moon, but not until the eighth
century (the reign of Ahaz) do we have reference to the
worship of "the host of heaven," and in the seventh century there is frequent allusion to it.   While the ultimate source of this was Babylonian, the Canaanites were
largely its mediators to Judah.

It was the Judaean religion, as it had been vitally
influenced by the return to Canaanite nature worship,
which had occurred under Manasseh (692-638 B. C.)
and Amon (638 B. C.), that is the object of the prophetic
invective. Zephaniah belongs among the primary line
of prophets who used the imminent threat of universal
destruction occasioned by the Scythian incursions, to
summon Judah to the only thing which could possibly
withhold the expression of Yahweh's righteous wrath,
fundamental repentance, the true seeking of Yahweh
through righteousness and meekness (2. 3; 3. 1ff.).

3. NAHUM: THE DIVINE NEMESIS

Nahum, whose prophetic activity took place when
Nineveh's fall (612 B. C.) was imminent, is the prophet
of the divine Nemesis upon Assyria. His one theme,
upon which he concentrates the high poetic genius of
his passionate soul, is the fall of Nineveh. In interpreting the awesome power of the indignant Yahweh
he referred to three regions where fertility was richest
and which had ancient associations with Canaanite
(Amorite and Phoenician) culture and cult—Bashan,
Carmel, and Lebanon. But they are under the control
of Yahweh. He it is (not the dying Adonis) that is the
cause of their languishing (1. 2-8). He uses for Assyria

the figure which Hosea, largely dependent upon the
fertility cults for his symbolism, had applied to Canaanized Israel, "the harlot":

> Because of the number of fornications of a harlot,
> Good in appearance, a Lady [Baalath] of sorceries,
> Who sells nations by her fornications,

Nineveh is to be humiliated, punished, and destroyed
(3. 4ff.). Imaginatively he represents the maidens of
Nineveh mourning their city's departure from the stage
of history, just as in the lamentations of the women the
departure or death of the fertility god was celebrated
in the Adonis-Tammuz cult:

> Her maidens are lamenting, moaning
> Like the voice of doves,
> Beating upon their breasts (2. 7).

So far as his positive religious teaching is concerned, he
simply expresses the religious attitude of the court party
in Judah which had sponsored the Deuteronomic reform:

> Keep, O Judah, thy feasts;
> Pay thy vows (1. 15).

4. HABAKKUK: RELIGION AS FAITHFULNESS

Habakkuk was but little touched by the Canaanite
influence in Judah. The mighty theme which disturbed
him was the suffering of Judah, particularly at the hand
of the ruthless Chaldaeans. He wrote between 612-600
B. C., after the fall of Assyria and during the early years
of the Chaldaean supremacy. How can the righteous
Yahweh allow the treacherous Chaldaeans to punish
Judah? (Habakkuk 1. 12-13)—this was his perplexing

question and lament. He makes his complaint, then, in imagination, climbs to his watch-tower, "looking forth" to see what answer will come from Yahweh. To the sensitive, waiting spirit of the prophet the insight at length comes. Strong as the Chaldaean may appear, in reality he is hastening toward his ruin. But a just people will have hold upon permanence. "The right-eous (nation) shall live by its faithfulness" (2. 1-4). Habakkuk thus develops Isaiah's central emphasis on trust, reliance upon God, and builds the foundation for the Pauline conception of salvation by faith (Romans 1. 17; Galatians 3. 11).

The influence of Canaanite idolatry may be dis-cerned in his polemic against images of wood (prob-ably *asherim*) and stone (possibly *macceboth*) and of gold and silver veneer. The words uttered to the dumb images, of wood and stone, "Awake!" and "Arise!" re-call the ceremony of the awakening of Melqarth of Tyre, and may be reminiscences of technical terms used in the cult of that Baal. And the lifeless images over-laid with gold and silver form a foil of vivid contrast to the unseen Yahweh in his holy Temple, before whose dynamic, living presence all the earth stills itself to silence (2. 18-20).

5. Jeremiah: Religion as Inner Experience

The prophetic activity of Jeremiah began in 626 b. c. and lasted at least until 585 b. c., after Jerusalem had fallen. His home town was Anathoth, its very name recalling earlier Canaanite days when the cult of the goddess Anath was prominent in Palestine. The early years of his ministry were under the profound influence

of Hosea (Jeremiah 2), who, as we have noted, had
seen more deeply than any other prophet into the heart
of Canaanite religion and had imbibed from it something
of its warmth of personal relationship with deity. This
consciousness of personal relationship to Yahweh,
which was central in Jeremiah's own experience, was
the most distinctive thing in his ministry and his most
abiding contribution to religion. The Canaanite concept
of the worshiper as the habitation of deity, to which
Kittel has directed attention, becomes a reality in Jeremiah's own experience, for he finds Yahweh searching
his heart, examining his dominant affections (12. 3;
17. 10), and he senses Yahweh's word as "a burning fire
shut up in his bones" (20. 9). By his deepest religious
concept, the New Covenant, religion is interpreted with
an inwardness such as no other thinker before him had
understood, and this concept roots in his own rich consciousness of personal relationship with Yahweh. The
time is to come—in Jeremiah's mind it is yet in the
future—when that which he has discovered in his own
inner nature will be a universally experienced reality
in Judaeans' hearts. Yahweh's law, that is, his will and
his teaching, will be followed not as external statutes
to be obeyed, but as an inner impulse of the heart to
be expressed. This intuitive response to Yahweh's will
thus inwardly apprehended, will be experienced by all
and will be accompanied by a joyous sense of emanci-
pation from sin (31. 31-34).

He was deeply imbued with Hosea's central figure of
speech for interpreting the nature of sin, a concept
which had originated in the moralizing of ideas characteristic of the Canaanite fertility cults. Yahweh was

the husband of Israel, and the wilderness was the period
of his betrothal to his sensitive, responsive bride (2.
1-3). But Israel had "played the harlot with many
lovers." Forgetting her earlier exclusive devotion to
Yahweh, her true husband, she had gone after many
lovers, the Canaanite Baalim (3. 1ff.; 9. 14). He here
refers to the Canaanized worship of Yahweh as it still
stubbornly persisted at the High Places where, "upon
every high hill and under every green tree" (2. 20; 3. 2,
6; 17. 2), Israelites participated in the Canaanite fertility
rites, including sacred prostitution with its fertility motivation and its inevitable consequences in illicit passion
(2. 20, 23; 3. 2; 13. 27; 21. 13-14, where forest = grove;
3. 13, for "strangers," compare Lucian, 6). We learn
from him that there were innumerable altars upon
which incense was burned to the Baalim (11. 13).

Jeremiah gives us our most vivid Old Testament picture of the worship of the Queen of Heaven, the Babylonian Ishtar, and, as W. R. Smith maintains, the
Canaanite Astarte, which was performed "in the cities
of Judah and in the streets of Jerusalem," in which the
entire family participated. The children gathered the
wood with which their fathers kindled a fire. The
women kneaded the dough, and shaping it roughly into
female figures "to make images of her" (44. 19, compare "portray," margin), baked it into cakes. They
poured out drink offerings and burned incense unto
her and unto all the host of heaven (7. 17-18; 44. 17-19;
19. 13). While Babylonian in origin, it is primarily
through Canaanite mediation and in Canaanite expression of it that this cult was introduced into Judah. Its
ultimate fertility purpose is clear from the antagonism

which Jeremiah met at the hands of the adherents of
the cult, and their self-defense when he attempted to
root it out of the Jewish colony which had migrated to
Egypt after the fall of Jerusalem (44. 17-19).

Just as Hosea had maintained, in direct opposition to
the Canaanite concept of the Baalim as lords of the
productivity of the soil, that Yahweh was responsible
for Israel's fertility, so Jeremiah asserts that the grain,
the new wine, the oil, the young of the flock and herd,
all are "the goodness of Yahweh" (31. 12).

Jeremiah is at home in the lamentation rites that
were outstanding features in the Adonis cult of Canaan.
The weeping and wailing, especially on the part of the
women (9. 17-21; 6. 26; 9. 10), the shearing of the locks,
and the dirges raised on the bare heights (7. 29), are
all referred to by Jeremiah. Fragments of the Adonis
lamentation ritual seem to be at the basis of the laments

> "Ah! Adonis [*Adhon*]!
> Ah! Hadad!" [2]

which, according to Jeremiah, were to be refused
Jehoiakim (22. 18), and "Ah! Adonis!" which was applied to Zedekiah (34. 5). Kings and members of the
royal family, when they died, were dealt with in Israel
as though they were Adonis, and in Babylon as though
they were Tammuz.[3] It is possible, as von Baudissin
suggests, that in ordinary mourning celebrations the

---

[2] Reading with F. C. Movers, Graetz, and H. Gressmann (*Der
Messias*, 1929, p. 332), instead of *hdh, hdd.*

[3] Jeremiah 34. 5. This becomes the more clear from the lamentation
over the royal son of Jeroboam which the LXX 1 Kings 12. 24m
(Swete) of 1 Kings 14. 13 has preserved: *ouai kyrie*, "Ah! Adonis."
So H. Gressmann: *Der Messias*, p. 333. Compare also F. C. Movers:
Die Phönizier, Vol. I, p. 246.

dead were dealt with as though they were Adonis. The connection of lamentations with the dearth of vegetation is also implied (7. 34), but in Jeremiah's thought it was not the death of the fertility deity that causes it but the will of Yahweh.

It is in contrast to the Canaanite concept of the dying fertility god that we can best understand Jeremiah's unique emphasis upon Yahweh as the living God.[4] In this doctrine Jeremiah is a pioneer in Israel. Yahweh does not live but to die with the decay of vegetation, nor die but to rise again. He is "the fountain of living waters" (2. 13; 17. 13). He is, in contrast to the idols of the Baalim and other gods, "the true God," "the living God," "the everlasting king" (10. 10). He uses a formula of an oath which emphasizes life as Yahweh's outstanding characteristic, "As I live, saith the King, whose name is Yahweh of hosts" (46. 18), "As I live, saith Yahweh" (22. 24). The same oath in the third person, "As Yahweh liveth," is expressed repeatedly (4. 2, etc.) by Jeremiah and once to him by Zedekiah (38. 16). Words of true prophecy are "words of the living God, Yahweh of hosts, our God" (23. 36). To obey the summons of Yahweh is to walk in the "way of Life" (21. 8).

Now, this characterization of Yahweh as the living God is not by any means the exclusive insight of Jeremiah, nor was he necessarily the first to achieve it. In the Davidic narratives, in a source designated by H. P. Smith as having affinities with E and D, the armies of Israel are the armies "of the living God" (1 Samuel

---

[4] Compare for this section W. von Baudissin: *Adonis und Esmun*, pp. 450-510.

17. 26). At the time of the Assyrian invasion of Judah, the Rabshakeh of the Assyrian forces is spoken of by the court chronicler as defying "the living God" (2 Kings 19. 4). In JE's narrative of the conquest of Canaan Yahweh is called "the living God" (Joshua 3. 10). It is most likely that Hosea too held this view of Yahweh (Hosea 4. 15; 6. 2; 1. 10). And it is certainly implicit in Isaiah's unique utterance concerning the spirituality of Yahweh (Isaiah 31. 3). But it was Jeremiah who was most at home in this conception, and it was he who gave it currency in Israel and, as the bridge between the prophets and the psalmists, introduced it into the language of devotion (Psalms 42. 2; 84. 2).

It was largely through Canaanite-Phoenician influence that this concept of the living god was developed in Israel. It could only arise in a religion where the dying of a deity was conceived as a possibility. As we have seen, this was an idea characteristic of the Canaanite nature cults where the death of the deity was associated with the dying vegetation and his coming to life again with its renewal. In Canaanite religion it is through resurrection that the god shows his power to win out over death.

Fragments of early Phoenician cosmogony which embody ideas yet more primary than those of chapter one in Genesis, reveal the conception of a life-creating spirit (*pneuma*) or wind (*kolpia*) as a cosmogonic principle. In the Tell el-Amarna letters we find it applied to the Pharaoh by Ammunira of Beirut (Kn. 141. 2), Zimriddi of Sidon (Kn. 144. 2), Abimilki of Tyre (Kn. 149. 23), and Iapahi of Gezer (Kn. 297. 18) as "breath of my life," a phrase which, like the appellation, "my sun," is a transfer from what men found in deity, to human relationships. The "breath" is here the life principle. The idea of a god who has within himself a principle of life which makes it possible for him to be victorious over death could easily be united with the old Hebrew concept of a lofty, majestic God, and this was done in Israelite prophetic thought. At the same time, however—and this is of supreme importance —the Canaanite concept of a period during which the god was dead was inconsistent with the old Hebrew idea, and hence was definitely rejected along with the cultic practices that were associated with it.

In the Adonis cult, although the resurrection of the god was celebrated, it was never the outstanding feature. The gloomy aspects, the lamentation rites always predominated. The coming to life of the god, as von Baudissin remarks, was not so much the basis of joy as it was comfort in sorrow. This persistent note of solemnity was characteristic of Phoenician religion.

But through Jeremiah's conception of Yahweh as a living God, and indeed through the Israelite conception as a whole, there pulsates the note of masterful creativity. We sense the positive contribution of the Canaanite deification of the life-process. The Canaanite conception of the death-conquering, creative vitality of deity, is taken up into the nature of the majestic, exalted God of Israel. But the Canaanite idea of the periodic death of the fertility deity was definitely rejected and its very rejection enriched by implicit contrast the Israelite view of God. Adonis dies annually, but Yahweh lives. He needs not to be awakened (compare 1 Kings 18. 27). He is the living God. "As

Yahweh lives"—thus comes to express, in contrast to the
Canaanite concept of a dying-rising god, something
unique and central in Yahweh's nature. This emphasis as to the nature of Yahweh was destined to have
great influence upon the development of the Israelite
concepts of resurrection and immortality. Thus Canaanite conceptions were far more creative than Persian
thought in influence upon the Israelite eschatology of
the individual.

In harmony with the entire prophetic tradition since
Amos, and with a definiteness unmatched by any other
thinker in Israel, Jeremiah proclaims that neither burnt
offerings (*oloth*) nor sacrifices (*zebhahim*) were required
of Judah by Yahweh. The whole burnt offering might
be eaten along with the peace offerings, so far as he was
concerned. These formed no part of the initial bond
which he had established with Israel under the leadership of Moses (Jeremiah 7. 21-26). What Yahweh
did then require and still does demand from the nation
is to "hearken unto his voice," and "walk in all the ways
he commands." And these requirements of Yahweh,
moral in their nature, have been made clear to Israel
by a line of prophets reaching from the Exodus down
to Jeremiah's own day (7. 25). But Israel has been
unreceptive and disobedient to the will of Yahweh as
interpreted by the prophets. Instead of showing obedience, the Israelites have violated every moral precept,
have participated in Canaanite and other pagan cultic
practices, and then in magical fashion have presumed
upon the protection of the Temple (7. 4, 8-11).

One of the dark features of Canaanite sacrificial
worship which, as we have seen, had been absorbed into

the religion of Judah and which, even after the Deuteronomic reform, in the latest years of Jeremiah's ministry, was still practiced by the worshipers of Yahweh, was child sacrifice. Jeremiah's indictment of this practice seems limited to the cult as carried on at Jerusalem. Here in the Tyropoeon ravine, in the "valley of the son of Hinnom," they had built "the High Places of Tephath (*Topheth*) (Jeremiah 7. 31), to burn their sons and daughters in the fire. They were offered to the Baal of the place (19. 5), viewed here as Molech = Malk (or Milk) (32. 35), the old Canaanite king deity with whom Yahweh was identified. Jeremiah maintains, with trenchant clarity, that this is contrary to the will of Yahweh, and far removed from his purpose for Israel. It is an abomination to him (7. 31; 32. 35).

To the prophet's mind, such magical dependence upon the Temple (7. 4) and the Canaanized sacrificial cult was futile. From this point of view we are able to evaluate adequately the summons of Jeremiah to an inner reformation which would penetrate beneath the entrenched cultic practices of centuries until the heart of the nation would be reached:

> Till for yourselves the untilled ground,
> And do not sow among thorns.
> Circumcise yourselves to Yahweh,
> And take off the foreskins of your heart (4. 3-4).

The deep, sensitive receptivity and response of Jeremiah's own heart to Yahweh's will and presence is our best commentary on what he means by the paradoxical figure of the "circumcision" of the heart. When this is achieved, when the heart, the seat of the affectional and volitional nature, has been made basic in religion and the right attitude toward Yahweh has become its highest expression, then all the institutional trappings of religion might be destroyed—ark (3. 16), torah (31. 31-34), Temple (7. 14), and even the state itself (29. 4-14), but religion in all its power would remain a reality in the hearts of the individual Judaeans (31. 33).

Likewise outstanding among the prophets was Jeremiah in his emphasis upon Yahweh as healer. In Canaanite-Phoenician religion the healing function in deity was attributed to Eshmun. He was one of the greatest gods of the pantheon, and in addition to his therapeutic functions possessed certain cosmic aspects. The serpent was his symbol. We recall the Mosaic story of the brazen serpent in the wilderness with its healing properties (Numbers 21. 6-9 [E]). This is a cultic legend which attempts to answer the question, "Why is the image of the brazen serpent worshiped in the Temple?" That this image existed in Hezekiah's time (2 Kings 18. 4), when it was called "Nehushtan," is certain. The answer suggested by the myth, in telescopic fashion, carries the origins of this feature of the cult which had not been absorbed until the Canaanite period, back to the wilderness epoch, associating with it the great name of Moses. This concept of the healing deity, already expressed by Hosea (Hosea 6. 1), profoundly influenced Jeremiah. To the latter prophet Yahweh was the great physician (8. 21-22) from whom Israel presumptuously expected healing (8. 15; compare Hosea 6. 1-3). But in the very face of the superficial attempts at healing the hurt of the nation carried on by the contemporary prophets and priests, at its core

the wound remained unhealed (8. 11; 6. 14). Without
fundamental repentance no healing was possible. Yet
Jeremiah's own sore heart had known from experience
the healing touch of Yahweh. And his conviction of
Yahweh's healing passion was sure, its exercise being
solely dependent upon the repentance of Israel (3. 22;
30. 17). His picture of the response of Yahweh to such
repentance on the part of the nation is tender and
beautiful. To the sorely disciplined and torn Israel
he comes bringing "a bandage and a cure" (33. 6, compare margin). It is a striking and arresting fact that
the prophets who were most influenced positively by
Canaanite conceptions were those in whom the emotional nature was deepest and strongest—Hosea, Jeremiah, and, as we shall see, our final prophet, Deutero-
Isaiah.

6. EZEKIEL: THE ANNOUNCEMENT OF RESTORATION AND REANIMATION

Ezekiel, who as a priest was familiar with the Temple
before the exile, at the age of twenty-five (1. 1) had been
carried into Babylonia among the Judaean captives of
597 B. C. In the fifth year of this captivity came his
vision of Yahweh, which was received in a state of
prophetic ecstasy and which mediated to him his prophetic call. He had unquestionably heard the preaching of the prophet Jeremiah, who was perhaps some
twenty-three years his senior,[5] and had been profoundly
influenced by him, although quite different from him
in mental type. As Duhm suggests, while Jeremiah was

---

[5] Jeremiah was about nineteen (Jeremiah 1. 7—so Skinner) in 626 B. C.
Ezekiel was thirty (Ezekiel 1. 1) in 592 B. C.

primarily a man of feeling, Ezekiel was essentially a
man of intellect. He was familiar with remnants of the
Canaanite cult, and his prophetic teaching gives clear
evidence of their obstinate persistence in Judaean life
even into exilic days.

Up until the messenger brings news of the final fall
of Jerusalem (24. 26; 33. 21) he combats popular delusion, preaching the certain destruction of Judah. From
then on, at least until 570 B. C., he is a prophet of hope
and grapples with the prevailing mood of despair.
Canaanite influence determines certain aspects of his
message in both periods. From him we get vivid pictures of the Canaanized cult still persisting at the High
Places, situated on the tops of mountains and on high
hills, in the valleys, and by the ravines, where green
trees and luxuriantly growing terebinths are found (20.
28-32). The positive contribution of the wilderness, of
which Hosea and Jeremiah make so much, he ignores
(23. 3). Already when Yahweh found Israel the nation
was steeped in the idolatrous cults of the Canaanites,
Amorites, and Hittites.

Ezekiel gives the only specific mention in the Old
Testament of the Tammuz cult, which, as we have seen,
was identical with the Adonis rites. While the elders
sat before him in his house, Ezekiel was seized with
ecstasy and reports a visionary experience which came
to him in that state. At the northern gate of the Temple
enclosure at Jerusalem, "there sat the women weeping
for Tammuz" (Ezekiel 8. 14). This is an authentic picture of the most characteristic feature of the Tammuz-
Adonis cult, the lamentation of women for the dead
fertility god. It proves without question that Ezekiel

was familiar with the cult as practiced in Jerusalem, for the visionary experience in its various aspects depended upon features of actual experience, and, accordingly, argues for the presence of this cult in some connection with the public worship of Judaeans at the Temple, in the period just before the exile. It was most likely, as Davidson rightly maintains, that this cult entered Judah not directly from Babylonia, but from Phoenicia, Gebal (Byblos) being its most famous Canaanite center. The weeping of the women mourned the death of the fertility deity, who in this desolate, uncertain period of Judaean life, was evidently in some sense associated with Yahweh. But the lamentation also sought by magical means to restore the deity to life and power. A similar visionary experience reported by Ezekiel, describes the worship by twenty-five Judaean elders, of the Queen of Heaven, the Canaanite Astarte, their backs being toward the Temple, and their faces toward the sun (8. 16). It is possible that the item of the cult specifically mentioned, "They put the branch to their nose" (verse 17), preserves a trace of the Adonis cult.[6] To Ezekiel all this was disgusting and utterly abominable to Yahweh.

In a manner deeply influenced by Hosea and the sacred marriage motif of the Canaanite religion, and in partly parabolic form, he tells how Yahweh found Israel as a babe weltering in idolatry, and when she became a virgin, took her under his protection and married her. He cleansed her, clothed and ornamented

---

[6] So H. A. Redpath: *The Book of the Prophet Ezekiel* (Westminster), p. 40, basing his views upon an illustration from Cyprus of Adonis worshipers holding flowers to their noses. For the illustration see C. H. Toy: *Ezekiel*, p. 112.

her, until she was renowned among the nations. But
she became a harlot, pouring out her amours upon
"strangers" (compare Lucian, 6), upon the Egyptians,
the Assyrians, and the Chaldaeans. Out of what Yahweh
had provided for her, she made High Places, and images
of gold and silver with embroidered garments to cover
them. She set before these idols bread, and oil, and
honey, and burned incense unto them. She even sacrificed children unto them. More passionate than a
common harlot, she bribed her paramours to come
unto her. Now Yahweh will send her paramours
against her in wrath and jealousy. They will stone
her, and spoil her possessions until she will cease from
playing the harlot. Then will Yahweh's anger cease.
As the idolatries of the Hittites and the Amorites are
in her blood, she is more corrupt even than her elder
sister, Samaria, and her younger sister, Sodom (Jerusalem). Yet Yahweh's tie to Israel is not temporary, but
everlasting. Samaria and Sodom will be influential in
bringing Israel to her senses. The covenant bond of
Israel will be renewed, and Samaria and Sodom (Jerusalem) will become to her as daughters (Ezekiel 16).

We note here in parabolic form the parable of the
small and desperate beginnings of Israel in the land of
Canaan, her growth into power in the monarchy, her
political "'flirting" with foreign nations and the consequent syncretism of her religion. We feel especially
the vigorous lure which the Canaanite fertility cults had
for Israel. We see how her political policy augmented
her religious decay. Ezekiel skillfully uses the fall of
the Northern Kingdom (Samaria) and the already
begun fall of Jerusalem (Sodom) as a goad to repent-

ance. His soul thrills at his ultimate hope of a re-united and unified nation, purged of its external alliances, loyal in heart to Yahweh.

Later he returns to the same theme in the harlotry of Oholah (tent-woman), Samaria, and of Oholibah (tent-in-her), Jerusalem. Oholah (Samaria), a harlot from her very youth (in Egypt), before she had been introduced to Yahweh, pursued in harlotry the Assyr-ians, who turned upon her and, after humiliating her, killed her.

Her sister Oholibah (Jerusalem) has failed to learn the lesson which Oholah's fall (722 B. C.) should have taught. She too has pursued the Assyrians and the Chal-daeans. But at length she likewise will be destroyed by the very paramours she has sought. Oholibah (Jeru-salem) will drink of her sister's cup. She will drain it to the dregs. In so harsh a manner, by the political destruction of Judah, harlotry will be rooted from her soul (Ezekiel 23). Ezekiel has a keen realization of the mingling of the political and the religious and sees the intimate connection which existed, as the prophets reg-ularly taught, between Israel's policy of political alliance with foreign powers and the consequent religious cor-ruption.

But the cessation of the political existence of the kingdom of Judah did not represent the horizon of Ezekiel's vision for his people. His concern was Juda-ism, and Judaism is not a political but a religious en-tity. Even before the fall of Jerusalem, Ezekiel had begun to view the individual apart from the state as in direct and immediate relationship to Yahweh, not as a member of the Judaean state but as an individual Jewish soul. As was the case with Jeremiah's teaching of the inwardness of religion, Ezekiel's view arose first in his own solemn inner realization of his prophetic and pastoral responsibility as a watchman over the individual Judaeans in the exilic community (Ezekiel 3. 16-21). From this he advanced to the concept that righteousness is not an affair of the community as a whole, conceived as an entity, but of the individuals who compose it. Every man is but the arbiter of his own fate. However famous he may be, or however great his righteousness, no wicked man can take comfort in his shadow. He will deliver only his own soul from destruction (14. 12-20). From this he goes on to the conception of individual freedom and personal accountability. Every person is a morally independent unit directly related to Yahweh. Neither his father's righteousness nor wickedness can possibly determine his fate. He is himself personally responsible and answerable to God for his own conduct (18. 1-20). Moreover —and this is of great practical significance for Ezekiel's purpose—no man is under the ban of his past. If he will, he can turn from his evil way and live. Thus he laid the foundation for his already announced summons:

> Turn ye, turn ye from your evil ways
> For why will ye die,
> O house of Israel?   (33. 11; compare 18. 30-31).

From now on this is the characteristic tenor of his teaching, which he undergirds and re-enforces by a mighty concept which Canaanite thought has profoundly enriched—that of the resuscitation, the reanimation of Israel. It finds expression in Ezekiel's vision of the valley of dry bones (chapter 37). It no doubt found its origin psychologically, growing out of the brooding of the prophet over the discouraged and dejected utterances of the Jews in the Babylonian exile, when, in 585 B. C., news came (33. 21) that Jerusalem had finally fallen. All hope of a future for Israel was then cut off and the exiles kept saying,

> Our bones are dried up,
> And perished is our hope;
> We are destroyed (37. 11).

How can the dry bones of Israel be reanimated? This was his problem. He seizes upon a conception which is at home in Phoenician cosmogony, and applies it in the realm of human relationships. It is the divine "breath," the "spirit" (*ruah*) which is the animating principle, the life-creating "wind" that is in the control of deity (especially verse 9). This creative life-principle, in Ezekiel's thought an expression of Yahweh's power, moves upon the dry bones, and they come together, "bone to its bone," and sinews with flesh form upon them. Again comes the creative "breath," breathed "into them," and they live and stand upon their feet like a great army.

Strictly speaking, this is not a resurrection from the grave. The bones are not the bones of buried men. They lie upon the ground in the valley. Rather do we have here a resuscitation or a reanimation. It is in intimate harmony with ideas that are most at home in a nature religion where the life-process of the seasons is closely observed and directly connected with the life of the fertility deity. There the deity dies with the death of vegetation and rises with the seasonal reanimation, yet even during the change is viewed as in some sense having hold upon life, inasmuch as he has the power to conquer the experience of death. But as was the case with Jeremiah, Ezekiel definitely rejected any possibility of a period wherein the deity might be viewed as dead, even though the power to win a triumph over death was his. God was to him "the living God," as the frequently expressed oath, "as I live," clearly implies (14. 16, etc.). Yet the Canaanite concepts enriched his idea of the living God, and his application of the animating principle, the "spirit" (*ruah*), the "breath" of God to the dry bones of Israel marked a distinct step of progress toward the concept of individual resurrection which only later developed in Israel (Job. 16. 19; 19. 25f.; Isaiah 26. 19; Daniel 12. 2). Still more clearly than with Jeremiah we see that the impulse toward this development came primarily from Canaanite, not from Persian, thought.

Like Jeremiah, Ezekiel moves in the realm of the healing energies of deity which are at home in the Phoenician Eshmun cult, but he connects them with Yahweh. Wherever the fructifying waters flow which, in Ezekiel's vision, stream forth from under the threshold of the restored Temple, they bring life and healing (47. 1-12, especially verses 9, 11, 12). It is the animating "breath" of Yahweh, and his resuscitating, restoring, healing energies which are the *sine qua non* of Ezekiel's pioneering, imaginative sketch of the restored community (chapters 40-48). This was to have so creative an effect upon the future of Israel, conceived as a religious entity, that H. P. Smith has called him "the father of Judaism."

7. DEUTERO-ISAIAH: THE UNION OF RIGHTEOUSNESS AND REDEMPTION

The prophetic conception of the nature of Yahweh and of his requirements comes to its climax in the utterances of the great prophet of the exile, Deutero-Isaiah, whose prophecy we have in chapters 40-55 of the book of Isaiah. He writes at the end of one age and just before the dawn of another (c. 540 B. C.). Cyrus is on the Near-East horizon. That epoch which Jeremiah had called "a future of hope" (Jeremiah 29. 11), stands just at the doors awaiting the climactic stroke of the Persian advance. This is to inaugurate the first Zionist movement and re-establish Israel as Judaism, a religious, not a political unit, within the vast Persian domain. The prophet writes from Babylon. His work is shot through and through with deep emotion which lifts it into the realm of exalted poetry. Through it throb two major ideas: (1) the restoration of Israel in Palestine (chapters 40-48), (2) the world service of Israel, the Servant of Yahweh (chapters 49-55).

If, as the author believes, Deutero-Isaiah wrote his work in Babylon, it is likely that we must go behind the Canaanite to the Babylonian realm of religious concepts for evidence of the influence of the Near-East fertility cults upon him. During the exile the fructifying and irritating environmental influence of normative Israel was Babylonian rather than Canaanite. Yet we must recall that it was the largely Canaanized Israel which went into exile, and her religious concepts there

remained pretty much what they had been on Judaean
soil, so far as the rank and file of Judaeans were concerned, even as was the case with those who went to
Egypt after the fall of the Judaean state (Jeremiah
44. 15ff.).

Under the direct observation of Babylonian polytheism, Deutero-Isaiah gives the most drastic criticism
of idolatry which the Old Testament has to offer. He
was familiar with the elaborate processionals with Bel
(= Marduk), chief deity of Babylon, where his most
famous temple stood, and with Nebo, herald of the
gods, whose major seat of worship was at Borsippa. The
images of these gods, once borne in solemn pomp and
dignity in festal array by their worshipers, will now be
unceremoniously loaded on the backs of oxen and asses,
powerless to protect their worshipers or to resist their
captors (46. 1-2, 6-7). In ironical, partly humorous vein,
he ridicules idolatry, picturing vividly the whole process of making images of the deities with wood from the
very same fir tree which furnishes the craftsman fuel to
build a fire for cooking (44. 9-17). We are aware in this
prophet of the influence of Hosea's keen ridicule of
idolatry as he had known it upon the soil of Canaan
(Hosea 8. 4-6; 10. 5-6; 13. 2). And over against the futility of idolatry and the utter powerlessness of the gods
which the images represent, he portrays the mighty Yahweh, bearing Israel from his birth and even unto old
age.

> I have borne, and I will carry,
> I will bear, and I will deliver (Isaiah 46. 3-4).

Fertility in the world of nature occupies a great place
in his thought. The probability of his familiarity with

the Babylonian Phoenician Tammuz-Adonis cult lifts
into new force and clarity his ascription of all fertility
to Yahweh, who does not die but whose word, potency,
and presence abide forever. "The grass withers, the
flower fades," not because the fertility god has died but
because the "breath of the Lord blows upon it." He is
the lord of fertility (40. 7).

Moreover, for Israel's sake Yahweh will bring new
fertility to the soil. The poor and needy will not die
of thirst or drought. Yahweh will "open rivers on the
bare heights and fountains in the midst of the valleys."
He will make

> The wilderness a pool of water
> And the dry land springs of water.

He will put

> in the wilderness the cedar,
> the acacia, and the myrtle and the oil tree.

He will set

in the desert the fir tree,
> the elm and the box tree together (41. 18-19; compare
> 43. 20.)

The wilderness regions will become productive, for

> Yahweh hath comforted Zion;
> He hath comforted all her ruins;
> And hath made her wilderness like Eden,
> And her desert like the garden of Yahweh (51. 3).

Just as Yahweh sends the rain and snow that water
the earth, making it productive and fruitful, so he sends
his creative, effective word which will not return unto
him void (55. 10).

These pictures of the fertility of nature are largely

figurative and symbolical of the freshening, spiritual
energies of Yahweh, but he who approaches them
through the Canaanite concepts of the Baalim, lords
of the soil's productivity, sees new beauty and vigor
in the prophet's thought.

Against the background of Canaanite and Babylonian polytheism, the clear, positive monotheism of
this prophet teems with passion and force. We re-
count the triads of the Babylonian deities—Anu, Ellil
(Bel), and Ea; Sin, Shamash, and Adad-Ramman; Sin,
Shamash, and Ishtar. We recall the Canaanite-Phoenician triad of Byblos which was indeed central to all
Canaan, El-Kronos, Baalath (Astarte), and Adonis. We
remember the three deities of Sidon, Astarte, Baal, and
Eshmun, and the Carthaginian triad, Tanith (Astarte),
Baal-Hamman (Melqarth), and Iolaos (Eshmun). To
these Canaanite-Phoenician deities we add the various
trinities of the local Egyptian cults composed of a god,
a goddess, and a god son,[7] and the famed trinity of
the Osiris cult—Osiris, Hathor-Isis, and Horus. To
these we add the endless local Baalim of the Canaanite
fertility cult, which had so profoundly influenced Israel.
Then we are in a position to realize the emancipating
power of Deutero-Isaiah's monotheism.

The eighth-century prophets were practical mono-
theists but Deutero-Isaiah, as John Skinner maintains,
was the first prophet to proclaim monotheism as an
abstract truth and bring it home to his reader's imagination and reason. To him Yahweh is the incompa-
rable being. None can be "likened" unto him (40. 18,

---

[7] For this assembly of triads see W. von Baudissin: *Adonis und Esmun*, p. 16.

25; 46. 5). Before him no god existed and none shall exist after him (43. 10). He is God and there is none else (44. 8; 45. 6, 14f., 18; 43. 11). Therefore he can call unto all peoples, "Turn to me and be ye saved, all ends of the earth" (45. 22). We see how his monotheism has as its inevitable complement universalism. If there is but one God, he exists for the world. With fine imaginative power Deutero-Isaiah represents the nations as "coming over" unto him, "falling down" before him in supplication, and acknowledging him to be the one God (45. 14-15).

In the conception of God held by Deutero-Isaiah we have a remarkable synthesis between the Yahweh of the nomadic period and the Yahweh of the Canaanite era. The Yahweh whom the Israelites brought with them from the wilderness into Canaan was a majestic, awesome deity with certain elements in his being that moved the hearts of his worshipers with terror. There was in his nature what Rudolf Otto has called the *mysterium tremendum,* an almost perfect expression of which is found in an autobiographical section in Isaiah, prophet of the eighth century. Rather than fear the conspiracy of Syria and Israel against Judah, so Yahweh had counseled this eighth-century teacher:

Yahweh of hosts, him shall ye sanctify (call holy);
And let him be your fear,
And let him your awe inspire.
And he shall be [for] a sanctuary;
But [for] a stone causing stumbling and [for] a rock caus-
    ing a fall
To both the houses of Israel,
[For] a gin and [for] a snare to the inhabitants of Jeru-
    salem (Isaiah 8. 13-14).

Never did Yahweh lose this quality from his nature. The Old Testament retained to the end this awe before a God of "dread," sternness, and indignation.

When Israel made the transition from nomadic to agricultural life, however, creative developments were wrought in her religion. The Canaanite environment in which the transition was accomplished, had as its central concept of deity something quite different from that awesome, fearsome Yahweh. In Canaanite religion, as W. von Baudissin has emphasized, the central concept of deity was that of the life-giver and the life-protector. Particularly did the Canaanite-Phoenician god Eshmun embody this healing, helping aspect of deity. His nature, as W. A. Jayne maintains, is more clearly defined than is the case with any other Phoenician god or goddess except Baal Melqarth and Astarte. Now, while Hosea and Jeremiah, themselves deeply touched by Canaanite religious concepts, emphasized this healing, helping aspect of deity which looks toward Yahweh as redeemer, it was Deutero-Isaiah that brought the interpretation of this quality in Yahweh to its climax.

Basic in this thought is the historical aspect of Yahweh's redemption. He summons the exiles to go out from Babylon as by a new Exodus, for "Yahweh hath redeemed his servant, Jacob" (48. 20-21). "He has redeemed Jerusalem." The wasted, destroyed city will break into the joyous song of restoration (52. 9). In the difficult days that are ahead, when Israel must pass through fire and water, she will be protected by Him who has called her by name, her redeemer (43. 1-2).

Yet the purely historical aspect of redemption is but

one expression of something immeasurably deeper. In his very nature he is a Redeemer (*goel*) and a Saviour (*moshia*). Over and over again, in varying contexts, the prophet comes back upon this theme and almost always it is expressed in a connection that brings into a constructive synthesis the exalted Yahweh of primitive Israelite thought and the Yahweh of the Canaanite era, the helper and sustainer of men. Most frequent is the series "Yahweh," Israel's "Redeemer," and "the Holy one of Israel" (41. 14; 43. 14; 48. 17; 49. 7; 54. 5). Similar is the association of appellatives "Our Redeemer, Yahweh of hosts is his name, the Holy One of Israel!" (47. 4). Once we have the combination "the King of Israel, and his Redeemer, Yahweh of hosts" (44. 6). Unique in this prophet is the concept that He who created Israel, that "formed him from the womb," and indeed who "made all things," is Israel's "Redeemer" (44. 24). Another remarkable synthesis, which likewise recalls the Yahweh of even the pre-Mosaic days, defines his nature by three great designations: "I, Yahweh, am thy Saviour (*moshia*) and thy Redeemer (*goel*), the Mighty One of Jacob" (*abhir yaaqobh*) (49. 26). The characterization of Yahweh as Saviour met with in this connection finds frequent expression in Deutero-Isaiah. "I am Yahweh thy God, the Holy One of Israel, thy Saviour" (43. 3). "Besides me there is no Saviour" (43. 11). He is the "God of Israel, the Saviour" (45. 15), "a just God, and a Saviour" (45. 21).

Moreover, we see in this prophet's conception of Yahweh a synthesis of two qualities which we have come to view as being the very essence of prophetic insight—righteousness on the one hand, redemption and salva-

tion on the other (45. 21). In Deutero-Isaiah redemption and salvation are the outflow of righteousness (45.
13; 42. 6; 51. 5, 8). Even the covenant, which goes back
to Mosaic times, was an outgrowth of his righteousness.
Behind every expression of the nature of Yahweh as
helper or sustainer, which concept Canaanite religion
deeply enriched, lies the basic truth and characteristic
Israelite idea of righteousness; as A. B. Davidson describes it, a certain constancy of purpose, a certain
trustworthiness in all his dealings with Israel.[8] Moreover, in this prophet's thought the righteousness of
Yahweh leads to the salvation of man, for it is the
source of God's consciousness of moral obligation, "for
his righteousness' sake" (42. 21). He is the most deeply
obligated being in the universe. To save Israel and
through Israel the world, God is morally obligated to do
his utmost. Even the covenant relationship which
obligated Yahweh to Israel, owed its initial impulse to
his righteousness (42. 6). We see here with unusual
clarity how this prophet held the distinctively Israelite
view of Yahweh as a righteous being, which had been
the characteristic emphasis of Amos, Isaiah, and Micah.
At the same time he brings into this basic and characteristic Israelite concept of righteousness the distinctive emphasis of Hosea and Jeremiah—those prophets
most touched with the positive contributions of Canaanite thought—the saving, helping, redeeming expression of Yahweh. It is Yahweh's righteousness that
sends Israel his servant to carry his light of health and
healing to the world (42. 6-7). Under the sensitive
genius of this spiritual teacher the whole redemptive

---

[8] Compare A. B. Davidson: *Old Testament Theology,* p. 398.

aspect of Yahweh becomes an expression of his righteousness and he passes on to Judaism this unique and
balanced synthesis of the deepest in Israel and in
Canaan.

In Deutero-Isaiah we reach the climax of the dramatic evolution of Old Testament religion. He attained heights in the conception of God and the
interpretation of the mission of the nation, scaled by no
other religious teacher in Israel. The contribution of
a mighty past throbs in his words. To it he was profoundly a debtor. And no small part of that debt he
owed to the irritating yet withal nurturing background
of Canaanite religion. At its best Israelite religion was
the synthesis of two forces, and we see them both best
in him. They are the religion of Sinai and the religion of Canaan.

BIBLIOGRAPHY

Abbreviations Employed

AASOR	Annual of the American School of Oriental Research in Jerusalem, New Haven, Conn.
IAB.	Virolleaud, Ch.: "Un poème phénicien de Ras Shamra, (La lutte de Mot, fils des dieux, et d'Alein fils de Baal)," in Syria 12 (1931), 193-224.
IIAB.	Virolleaud, Ch.: "Un nouveau chant du poème d'Alein-Baal," in Syria 13 (1932), 113-63.
AJSL	American Journal of Semitic Languages and Literatures, Chicago.
AO	Der Alte Orient, Leipzig.
AR	Archiv für Religionswissenschaft, Freiburg, Mohr.
BASOR	Bulletin of the American Schools of Oriental Research, ed. by W. F. Albright, Baltimore, Md.
CAH	Cambridge Ancient History, ed. by J. B. Bury, S. A. Cook, et al., Cambridge, Eng.
CQR	Church Quarterly Review, London.
Enc. Bib.	Encyclopaedia Biblica, ed. by T. K. Cheyne, N. Y., Macmillan, 1899-1903.
Enc. Brit.	Encyclopaedia Britannica[14], N. Y., Enc. Brit. Co., 1929.
ERE	Encyclopaedia of Religion and Ethics, ed. by J. Hastings, N. Y., Scribner's.
ET	Expository Times, London.
HTR	Harvard Theological Review, Cambridge, Mass.
ICC	International Critical Commentary, N. Y., Scribner's.

JAOS	Journal of the American Oriental Society, New Haven, Conn.
JBL	Journal of Biblical Literature, New Haven, Conn.
JMEOS	Journal of the Manchester Egyptian and Oriental Society, Manchester, Eng.
JPOS	Journal of the Palestine Oriental Society, Jerusalem.
JQR	Jewish Quarterly Review, Philadelphia.
JR	Journal of Religion, Chicago.
JTS	Journal of Theological Studies, London.
KAT³	Schrader, E.: Die Keilinschriften und das Alte Testament³, revised by H. Winckler and H. Zimmern, Berlin, Reuther, 1902.
Kn.	Knudtzon, J. A.: Die El-Amarna Tafeln, vol. I, Leipzig.
Migne	Migne, J. P.: Patrologiae cursus completus, Series Graeca Primus (S. G. P.), Series Latina (S. L.), Paris.
OIC	Oriental Institute Communications, Univ. of Chicago.
OLZ	Orientalische Literaturzeitung, Berlin.
PIP	Palestine Institute Publications of the Pacific School of Religion, Berkeley, Cal.
PEFA	Palestine Exploration Fund Annual, London.
PEFQS	Palestine Exploration Fund Quarterly Statement, London.
PJ	Palästinajahrbuch des Deutschen evangelischen Instituts für Altertumswissenschaft des heiligen Landes zu Jerusalem, Berlin.

Ras Shamra 1929 Virolleaud, Ch.: "Les inscriptions cunéiformes de Ras Shamra," in Syria 10 (1929), 304-10.

RB Revue Biblique, Paris.

RGG Die Religion in Geschichte und Gegenwart, Tübingen, Mohr.

RHPR Revue d'histoire et de philosophie religieuses, Strasbourg, Alcan.

RHR Revue de l'histoire des religions, Paris.

RTK Real-Encyklopaedie für protestantische Theologie und Kirche, Hamburg.

RV Reallexikon der Vorgeschichte, ed. by Max Ebert, Berlin, Gruyter, 1924-1932.

SAT Die Schriften des Alten Testaments in Auswahl, ed. by H. Gressmann, H. Gunkel, H. Schmidt, and W. Stärk, Göttingen.

SPCK The Society for Promoting Christian Knowledge, London.

Syria Syria, Revue d'art oriental et d'archéologie, Paris, Geuthner.

ZAW Zeitschrift für die Alttestamentliche Wissenschaft, Giessen, Töpelmann.

ZDMG Zeitschrift der Deutschen Morgenländischen Gesellschaft, Leipzig, Brockhaus.

ZDPV Zeitschrift des Deutschen Palästina-Vereins, Leipzig, Baedeker.

GENERAL WORKS

Barton, Geo. A.: *Archaeology and the Bible*[6], Phil., Am. S. S. Union, 1933.

Breasted, James H.: *Ancient Times,* Boston, Ginn and Co., 1916.

McFadyen, John E.: *An Introduction to the Old Testament,* rev. ed., N. Y., Macmillan, 1933.

Oesterley, W. O. E., and Robinson, T. H.: *History of Israel,* 2 vols., Oxford, Clarendon, 1932.

Oesterley, W. O. E., and Robinson, T. H.: *An Introduction to the Books of the Old Testament,* N. Y., Macmillan, 1934.

Olmstead, A. T.: *History of Palestine and Syria,* N. Y., Scribner's, 1931.

Sellin, E.: *Introduction to the Old Testament,* London, Hodder, 1923.

Smith, J. M. P.: *The Prophets and Their Times,* Chicago, U. of C., 1925.

CHAPTER I—*The Canaanite Background*

1. CANAANITES AND AMORITES, AND CANAANITE RELIGION IN GENERAL

Alt, Albrecht: "Amoriter," in RV I.

Augustine: *Epistolae ad Romanos,* Migne S. L. III, 13, col. 2644.

Bauer, H., and Leander, P.: *Historische Grammatik der hebräischen Sprache des A. T.,* I., Halle, Niemeyer, 1922.

Bauer, Theo: *Die Ostkanaanäer,* Leipzig, Verlag der Asia Major, 1926.

Bertholet, Alfred: *A History of Civilization in Palestine,* London, Harrap, 1926.

Böhl, Franz M. Th.: "Canaan, Canaanites," in Enc. Brit.[14], (Vol. IV).

Gressmann, H.: *Altorientalische Texte* (Vol. I) *und Bilder* (Vol. II) *zum A. T.*[2] Berlin, Gruyter, 1926-7.

Gressmann, H.: "Religion (D) Palästina-Syrien," in RV XI, 99-115.

Guthe, H.: "Kanaaniter," in RTK[3] 9, 732-41; and "Kanaan," in RTK[3] 23, 731-33.

Herodian: *Scripta Tria Emendatiora,* ed. by K. Lehrs, 7, 32.

Karge, P.: *Rephaim,* Die vorgeschichtliche Kultur

Palästinas und Phöniziens, Paderborn, F. Schöningh, 1917.

Kittel, R.: *Geschichte des Volkes Israels*[5, 6], I, Stuttgart-Gotha, Perthes, 1923.

Knudtzon, Jorgen A., Weber, O., and Ebeling, E.: *Die El-Amarna Tafeln,* 2 vols., Leipzig, Hinrichs, 1915.

Meyer, E.: *Geschichte des Altertums,* I[3] (1910-13) and II[2], 1 Abt. (1928); 2 Abt. (1931), Berlin, Cotta.

Meyer, E.: *Sumerier und Semiten in Babylonien,* Abh. der Königl-preuss. Akad., 3, Berlin, 1906.

Paton, Lewis B.: "Canaanites," in ERE 3, and "Phoenicians," in ERE 9.

Ranke, H.: *Early Babylonian Personal Names,* Phil., Univ. of Pa., 1905.

Sethe, K.: *Die Æchtung feindlicher Fürsten,* Abh. der Preuss. Akad. der Wiss., No. 5, 1926.

Albright, Wm. F.: "The Egyptian Empire in Asia in the Twenty-first Cent. B. C.," in JPOS 1928, 223-56.

von Baudissin, W.: "Die Quellen für eine Darstellung der Religion der Phönizier und der Aramäer," in AR 16 (1913), 382-422.

Dussaud, R.: "Observations sur la céramique du IIe millenaire avant notre ère," in Syria IX (1928), 131-50.

Herzfeld, E.: "Archäologische Parerga," in OLZ 22 (1919), 212.

Peiser, F. E.: "Zum ältesten Namen Kanaans," in OLZ 22 (1919), 5-8.

Pfeiffer, R. H.: "The Transmission of the Book of the Covenant," in HTR 23 (1931), 99-109.

Pfeiffer, R. H.: "The Oldest Decalogue," in JBL 48 (1924), 294-310.

Thomsen, P.: "Palästina und seine Kultur in Fünf Jahrtausenden[2]," in AO 30 (1931).

Wood, W. Carleton: "The Religion of Canaan," in JBL 35 (1916), 1-133; 163-279.

2. DEITIES

Albright, Wm. F.: *The Archaeology of Palestine and the Bible*[3], N. Y., Revell, 1935.

Albright, Wm. F.: "Mesopotamian Elements in Canaanite Eschatology," 146ff., in *Oriental Studies in commemoration of Paul Haupt*, Baltimore, Leipzig, 1926.

Alt, Albrecht: "Baal," in RV I.

Asmus, R.: *Das Leben des Philosophen Isidorus von Damaskios aus Damaskos*, Leipzig, Meiner, 1911.

Baethgen, F.: *Beiträge zur semitischen Religionsgeschichte*, Berlin, Reuther, 1888.

Barton, Geo. A.: *A Sketch of Semitic Origins*, N. Y., Macmillan, 1902.

Barton, Geo. A.: *Semitic and Hamitic Origins*, Phil., Univ. of Pa., 1934.

von Baudissin, W.: *Adonis und Esmun*, eine Untersuchung zur Geschichte des Glaubens an Auferstehungsgötter und an Heilgötter, Leipzig, Hinrichs, 1911.

von Baudissin, W.: *Kyrios*, als Gottesname im Judentum und seine Stelle in der Religionsgeschichte, 1-4, ed. by O. Eissfeldt, Giessen, Töpelmann, 1926-29.

von Baudissin, W.: "Sanchuniathon," in A. Hauck's RTK[3] 17, 1906.

Bertholet, A., and Lehmann, E.: *Lehrbuch der Religionsgeschichte*, I, Tübingen, Mohr, 1925.

Budge, E. A. Wallis: *The Gods of the Egyptians*, 2 vols., Chicago, Open Court, 1904.

Cheyne, T. K.: "Baal Zebub," in Enc. Bib. I.

Cicero: *Concerning the Nature of the Gods*, I 25; III 16, 42, ed. by C. D. Yonge, London, Bell, 1911.

Contenau, G.: *La civilisation phénicienne*, Paris, Payot, 1926.

Cook, Stanley A.: *The Religion of Ancient Palestine in the Second Millennium B. C.*, London, Constable, 1908.

Cook, Stanley A.: *The Religion of Ancient Palestine in the Light of Archaeology,* London, Milford, 1930.

Cooke, G. A.: "Phoenicia," in Enc. Brit.[14] 17, 765-72.

Corpus Inscriptionum Semiticarum, Pars Prima (Inscriptiones Phoenicias), Paris, 1881ff.

Cowley, A. E.: *Aramaic Papyri of the Fifth Century B. C.,* Oxford, Clarendon, 1923.

Cumont, Franz: *The Oriental Religions in Roman Paganism,* Chaps. II-V, Chicago, Open Court, 1911.

Damascius: *Quaestiones de primis principiis,* 125., ed. by J. Kopp, Frankfurt, 1826.

Ebeling, E.: *Tod und Leben nach den Vorstellungen der Babylonier,* Berlin, Gruyter, 1931.

Eiselen, F. C.: *Sidon: A Study in Oriental History,* N. Y., Columbia Univ., 1907.

Eusebius: *Praeparatio Evangelica* I, 10 (Philo's Sanchuniathon).

Galling, K.: "Tammuz (Palästina-Syrien)," in RV 13.

Getty, Marie M.: *The Life of North Africans as Revealed in the Sermons of St. Augustine,* Washington, D. C., Cath. Univ. of Am., 1931.

Godbey, Allen H.: *The Lost Tribes a Myth,* Durham, Duke Univ. Press, 1930.

Gressmann, H.: *Die älteste Geschichtsschreibung und Prophetie Israels,* in SAT II, 1, 1921.

Gressmann, H.: "Hadad und Baal," Abhandlungen zur semitischen Religionskunde und Sprachwissenschaft, in von Baudissin's Festschrift, 191-216, Giessen, Töpelmann, 1918.

Harris, Chas. W.: *The Hebrew Heritage,* Chap. XIV, N. Y., Abingdon, 1935.

Herodotus: *History* I, 93, 199; II, 44, 61, 112, ed. by Cary, London, 1854.

Hill, G. F.: *Catalogue of the Greek Coins of Phoenicia* (British Museum), p. 98, Plate XII, 8, 1910.

Jirku, A.: "Zur Götterwelt Palästinas und Syriens," in E. Sellin's Festschrift, Leipzig, Deichert, 1927.

Josephus: *Antiquities* VIII 5, 3; IX 14, 2; *Contra Apionem* I 18; and *Wars of the Jews* IV 1.

Lagrange, Marie-Joseph: *Études sur religions sémitiques*[2], Paris, Lecoffre, 1905.

Langdon, S.: *Semitic Mythology*, Boston, Marshall Jones, 1931.

Lidzbarski, M.: *Ephemeris für semitische Epigraphik*, I-III, Giessen, Töpelmann, 1902-15.

Madden, Mary D.: *The Pagan Divinities and their Worship as depicted in the works of St. Augustine*, Washington, D. C., Cath. Univ. of Am., 1930.

Moore, Mabel: *Carthage of the Phoenicians*, London, Heinemann, 1905.

Pietschmann, Richard: *Geschichte der Phönizier*, Berlin, Grote, 1889.

Philo of Byblos on "Sanchuniathon," in I. P. Cory: *The Ancient Fragments*, ed. by E. R. Hodges, London, Reeves and Turner, 1876.

Polybius: *The Histories*, VII 9, 2, N. Y., Putnam, 1922-27.

Sayce, A. H.: *The Ancient Empires of the East* (Herodotus I-III), London, Macmillan, 1883.

Sayce, A. H.: *"The Higher Criticism" and the Verdict of the Monuments*, London, SPCK, 1894.

Schmökel, H.: *Der Gott Dagan*, Leipzig, Noske, 1928.

Schrader, E.: KAT[3].

Sellin, E.: *Tell Taannek*, Vienna, Gerold, 1904.

Sellin, E.: *Eine Nachlese auf dem Tell Taannek*, Vienna, Hoelder, 1905.

Smith, H. P.: "Theophorous Proper Names in the Old Testament," in *O. T. and Semitic Studies*, I, Chicago, Univ. of C., 1908.

Smith, W. R.: "Baal," in Enc. Bib., Vol. I.

Speiser, E. A.: *Mesopotamian Origins*, London, Milford, 1930.

Tertullian: *Apology*, 9, in Ante-Nicene Christian Library, Edinburgh, Clark.

Albright, Wm. F.: "The Evolution of the West-Semitic Divinity An-Anat-Atta," in AJSL 41, 73 101; 283-5.

Albright, Wm. F.: "The North Canaanite Epic of Al-Eyan Baal and Mot," in JPOS XII (1932), 185 208.

Albright, Wm. F.: "More Light on the Canaanite Epic of Al Eyan Baal and Mot," in BASOR No. 50, (1933), 13-20.

Albright, Wm. F.: "The North Canaanite Poems of Al-Eyan Baal and the Gracious Gods," in JPOS XIV (1934), 101ff.

Barton, Geo. A.: "The Genesis of the God Eshmun," in JAOS 21 (1901), 188-90.

Barton, Geo. A.: "A North Syrian Poem on the Conquest of Death," in JAOS 52 (1932), 221-31.

Bauer, Hans: "Die Gottheiten von Ras Schamra," in ZAW (1933), 81-101.

Cook, Stanley A.: "Notes on the Old Canaanite Religion," in Expositor (1910), 111-27.

Cook, Stanley A.: "Semitic Theism," in JTS 32 (1932), 228-250.

Dussaud, R.: "Nouveaux renseignements sur la Palestine et la Syrie vers 2000 avant notre ère," in Syria 8 (1927), 216-33.

Dussaud, R.: "La mythologie phénicienne d'après les tablettes de Ras Shamra," in RHR 104 (1931), 353-408, Paris, Leroux.

Dussaud, R.: "Les Phéniciens au Négeb et en Arabie, d'après un texte de Ras Shamra," in RHR 108 (1933), 5-49.

Graham, Wm. C.: "Recent Light on the Cultural Origins of the Hebrews," in JR 14 (1934), 306-29.

Hill, G. F.: "Adonis, Baal, and Astarte," in CQR 66 (1908), 118-41.

Meyer, E.: "Untersuchungen der phönikischen Religion," in ZAW 49 (1931), 1-15.

Montgomery, J. A.: "Notes on the Mythological Epic Texts from Ras Shamra," in JAOS 53 (1933), 97-123; 54 (1934), 60-66.

Paton, Lewis B.: "Baal, Beel, Bel," in ERE 2, 283-98.

Pilz, Edwin: "Die weiblichen Gottheiten Kanaans," in ZDPV 47 (1924), 129-68.

Showerman, Grant: "The Great Mother of the Gods," Bulletin Univ. of Wis., No. 43, 1901.

Vincent, L. H.: "Le Baal cananéen de Beisan et sa parèdre," in RB 37 (1928), 512-43.

Virolleaud, Ch.: "The Gods of Phoenicia as Revealed in the Poem of Ras Shamra," in Antiquity 5 (1931), 405-14.

Virolleaud, Ch.: Ras Shamra 1929.

Virolleaud, Ch.: "Le déchiffrement des tablettes alphabétiques de Ras Shamra," in Syria 12 (1931), 15-23.

Virolleaud, Ch.: IAB.

Virolleaud, Ch.: IIAB.

Virolleaud, Ch.: "La naissance des dieux gracieux et beaux, poème phénicien de Ras Shamra," in Syria 14 (1933), 128-51.

3. SACRED PLACES AND PERSONS

Apuleius: *Metamorphoses* (*The Golden Ass*), VIII, 24-29, Adlington trans., N. Y., Macmillan, 1915.

Athanasius: *Contra Gentes* 26, in Migne, S. L. XXV, 52. Translated in Select Library of Nicene and Post-Nicene Fathers, Vol. IV.

Barton, Geo. A.: *Archaeology and the Bible*[6].

Farnell, Lewis R.: *Greece and Babylon*, Edinburgh, Clark, 1911.

Grant, Elihu: *Beth Shemesh*, Haverford, Pa., 1929.

Grant, Elihu: *Ain Shems Excavation*, Parts I, II, and III (*Rumeileh*), Haverford, Pa., 1932-34.

Herodotus: II, 44.

Karge, P.: *Rephaim*.

Lucian of Samosata: *De Dea Syria*, translated in H. A. Strong and J. Garstang: *The Syrian Goddess*, London, Constable, 1913.

Macalister, R. A. S.: *The Excavation of Gezer*, 3 vols., London, J. Murray, 1912.

Petrie, Sir Wm. F.: *Tell el-Hesy,* London, A. Watt, 1891.

Ramsay, Sir Wm. Mitchell: *Cities and Bishoprics of Phrygia,* I, Oxford, Clarendon, 1895-7.

Smith, W. R.: *The Religion of the Semites,* 3d ed., annotated by S. A. Cook, N. Y., Macmillan, 1927.

Socrates Scholasticus: *The Ecclesiastical History,* I 18, London, Bohn, 1853.

Sozomen: The Ecclesiastical History, II 5, V 10, in Nicene and Post-Nicene Fathers, 1855.

Strabo: *Geography,* VI 2, 6; VIII 6, 20; XI 14, 16; XII 2, 3, 6; XII 3, 34, 36; XVI 1, 6; XVI 2, 18, 22, ed. by H. J. Jones, London, Heinemann, 1917-32.

Vincent, L. H.: *Canaan, d'après l'exploration récente*[2], Paris, Gabalda, 1914.

Badè, W. F.: "Excavations at Tell en-Nasbeh (Mizpah) 1926-7," PIP No. 1 (1928).

Badè, W. F.: "Excavation of Tell en-Nasbeh," in BASOR, Nos. 26 (1927), 1-7; and 35 (1929), 24-5.

Badè, W. F.: "Some Tombs of Tell en-Nasbeh," PIP No. 2 (1931).

Badè, W. F.: "The Tell en-Nasbeh Excavations," in PEFQS (1927), 12ff.; (1930), 9-19.

Barton, Geo. A.: "A Liturgy for the Celebration of the Spring Festival at Jerusalem in the Age of Abraham and Melchizedek," in JBL 53 (1934), 61-78.

Dussaud, R.: "Le sanctuaire et les dieux phéniciens de Ras Shamra," in RHR 105 (132), 245-302.

Rowe, Alan: "Excavations at Beisan During the 1927 Season," in PEFQS April, 1928. Compare Museum Journal, June, 1928, 145-69.

Rowe, Alan: Palestine Expedition of the Museum of the Univ. of Pa., Third Report, 1928 Season, in PEFQS April, 1929.

Rowe, Alan, and Vincent, L. H.: "New Light on the Evolution of Canaanite Temples," in PEFQS (1931), 12-21.

Welter, G.: "Stand der Ausgrabungen in Sichem," in Archäologischer Anzeiger, 1932.

4. FESTIVALS

Chwolsohn, D.: *Die Ssabier und der Ssabismus,* II, text I, Chap. V., St. Petersburg, 1856.

Eissfeldt, O.: "Fest und Feiern in Israel," in RGG[2], Tübingen, Mohr, 1928.

Gray, G. B.: *Sacrifice in the Old Testament,* Oxford, Clarendon, 1925.

Hölscher, G.: *Geschichte der israelitischen und jüdischen Religion,* Giessen, Töpelmann, 1922.

Lods, A.: *Israel, from its Beginnings to the Middle of the Eighth Century,* N. Y., Knopf, 1932.

Oesterley, W. O. E.: in S. H. Hooke (editor), *Myth and Ritual,* Essays on the myth and ritual of the Hebrews in relation to the culture pattern of the Ancient East, 111-46, Oxford, Clarendon, 1935.

Dussaud, R.: "La mythologie phénicienne d'après les tablettes de Ras Shamra," in RHR (1931), 353-408.

Gressmann, H.: "The Mysteries of Adonis and the Feast of Tabernacles," in Expositor (1925), 416-32.

Meinhold, J.: "Die Entstehung des Sabbats," in ZAW 29 (1909).

Morgenstern, J.: "The Historical Reconstruction of Hebrew Religion and Archaeology," in JR I, 233-54.

Virolleaud, Ch.: IAB., col. II, 30-5, compare R. Dussaud in RHR (1931), esp. 388ff.

Zimmern, H.: "Sabbath," in ZDMG 58 (1904), 199-202.

5. SACRIFICE, INCLUDING CHILD SACRIFICE

Cooke, G. A.: *North Semitic Inscriptions,* Nos. 42-3, Oxford, Clarendon, 1903.

Diodorus, the Sicilian: *The Historical Library,* XX 14 (child sac.), ed. by Booth, London, McDowall, 1814.

Dussaud, R.: *Les origines cananéennes du sacrifice israélite,* Paris, Leroux, 1921.

Lods, A.: *Israel,* esp. 83-103.

Macalister, R. A. S.: *The Excavation of Gezer,* vol. II.

Plutarch: *De superstitione,* 13 (child sac.), in *Morals,* ed. by W. Goodwin, Boston, Little, Brown, and Co., 1874.

Porphyry: *De Abstinentia* II 56 (child sac.), in T. Taylor: *Select Works of Porphyry,* London, Rodd, 1823.

de Prorok, Byron Khun: *Digging for Lost African Gods* (on child sac.), N. Y., Putnam, 1926.

Schumacher, G., and Steuernagel, C.: Tell el-Muteselim, I (child sac.), Leipzig, Haupt, 1908.

Sellin, E.: *Tell Taannek* (child sac.).

Tertullian: *Apology,* 9, 23 (child sac.).

Watzinger, C.: Tell el-Muteselim, II, 1929 (child sac.).

Dussaud, R.: Brèves remarques sur les tablettes de Ras Shamra," in Syria 12 (1931), 67-77.

Dussaud, R.: "Le sanctuaire et les dieux phéniciens de Ras Shamra," in RHR 105, esp. 285ff.

Moore, G. F.: "The Image of Moloch" (child sac.), in JBL 16 (1897), 161ff.

Virolleaud, Ch.: IIAB., col. IV, 35ff.; col. VI, 22-35; col. IV-V, 4-7.

6. THE ADONIS CULT

Ammianus: *The Roman History,* XIX 1, 11; XXII 9, 15, trans. by C. D. Yonge, London, Bohn, 1887.

Aristides: *Apology,* ed. by J. Rendell Harris, Haverford College Studies 6, 1891.

Athanasius: *Contra Gentes,* 26.

Chwolsohn, D.: *Die Ssabier und der Ssabismus,* II.

Ebeling, E.: *Tod und Leben nach den Vorstellungen der Babylonier.*

Epistle of Jeremiah, ed. by R. H. Charles, in *Apocrypha and Pseudepigrapha of the O. T.,* I, Oxford, Clarendon, 1913.

Eusebius: *Life of Constantine,* III, 55, 58, N. Y., The Christian Lit. Co., 1890.

Farnell, Lewis R.: *Greece and Babylon.*

Firmicus Maternus: *Concerning the Error of the Profane Religions,* ed. by Ziegler, Leipzig, Teubner, 1907.

Frazer, J. G.: *Adonis, Attis, Osiris*[3], Vol. I (1914), Vol. II (1911), London, Macmillan.

Gressmann, H.: *Altorientalische Bilder zum A. T.,* Nos. 665f., and pp. 190f.

Hartland, Edwin S.: *Primitive Paternity,* 2 vols., London, Nutt, 1909-10.

Herodotus, I, 199.

Hieronymus (Jerome): *Explanatio in Ezek.,* ed. by Migne, S. L. XXV, cols. 82f.

Hieronymus: *Epistola LVIII ad Paulinum,* ed. by Migne, S. L. XXII, col. 581.

Hippolytus: *The Refutation of All Heresies,* V 11, secs. 7 and 18, ed. by F. Legg: *Philosophumena,* 120-7.

Kittel, R.: *Die Hellenistische Mysterien Religion und das Alte Testament,* Berlin, Kohlhammer, 1924.

Langdon, S.: *Semitic Mythology.*

Lucian of Samosata: *De Dea Syria (The Syrian Goddess).*

Macrobius: *Saturnalia,* I 23, sec. 11, ed. by Thos. Whitaker.

Mannhardt, W.: *Wald und Feldkulte,* vol. II, Berlin, Bornträger, 1904-5.

Meek, T. J.: "The Song of Songs and the Fertility Cult," in W. H. Schoff: *The Song of Songs, a Symposium,* Phil., Commercial Museum, 1924.

Pseudo-Melito, in *Corpus Apologetarum Christianorum,* IX, 374ff., ed. by de Otto, Jena, Dufft, 1892.

Origen: *Selecta in Ezechielem,* ed. by Migne, S. G. P. XIII, cols. 797-800.

Ovid: *Metamorphoses,* X, trans. by Dryden et al., London, Garth, 1810.

Plato: *Phaedrus,* 276 B, N. Y., Macmillan.

Plutarch: *Of Isis and Osiris,* 15-16 in *Morals,* ed. by W. Goodwin.

Ramsay, Sir Wm. Mitchell: *Cities and Bishoprics of Phrygia,* I.

Sethe, K.: *Dramatische Texte zu altägyptischen Mysterienspielen,* 83ff., Leipzig, Hinrichs, 1928.

Socrates: see under 3.

Sozomen: *The Ecclesiastical History,* see under 3.

Strabo: *Geography,* see under 3.

Theocritus: The Feast of Adonis, in *The Greek Bucolic Poets,* XV, ed. by J. M. Edmonds, N. Y., Macmillan, 1912.

Theodoret: comment on *Ezekiel,* 8. 13f., in Migne, S. G. P. LXXXI, col. 885.

Weston, Jessie L.: *From Ritual to Romance,* Cambridge Univ. Press, 1920.

Barton, Geo. A.: in JBL 53 (1934), see under 3.

Cook, Stanley A.: "Recent Excavations in Palestine," in ET (1926), 487-92.

Gaster, T. H.: "The Ritual Pattern of the Ras Shamra Epic," in Archiv Orientální, 1933.

Gressmann, H.: "Byblos," in ZAW (1925), 225-42.

Gressmann, H.: "Tod und Auferstehung des Osiris nach Festbräuchen und Umzügen," in AO, 23 (1923).

Kittel, R.: "Osirismysterien und Laubhüttenfest," in OLZ 27 (1924), 385-91.

Meek, T. J.: "Canticles and the Tammuz Cult," in AJSL 39 (1922), 1-14.

Virolleaud, Ch.: IAB.

Virolleaud, Ch.: in Syria 14 (1933), see under 2.

Waterman, Leroy: "Critical Notes" (*Dodhi* in the Song of Songs), in AJSL 35 (1919), 107.

CHAPTER II—*The Religion of the Hebrew Fathers*

Alt, Albrecht: *Der Gott der Väter,* Stuttgart, Kohlhammer, 1929.

Barton, Geo. A.: *Archaeology and the Bible*[5], 316ff.

von Baudissin, W.: *Kyrios*, III.

Bertholet, A., and Lehmann, E.: *Lehrbuch der Religionsgeschichte*, I.

Breasted, James H.: *Ancient Records of Egypt*, vols. I-III, Chicago, 1906-7.

Breasted, James H.: *The History of Egypt*[3], N. Y., Scribner's, 1919.

Brightman, Edgar S.: *The Sources of the Hexateuch*, N. Y., Abingdon, 1918.

Burney, C. F.: *The Book of Judges*[2], lxxiv-lxxix, London, Rivingtons, 1920.

Chiera, E., and Speiser, E. A.: "A New Factor in the History of the Ancient Near East," in AASOR VI (1926), 75-92.

Cooke, G. A.: *North Semitic Inscriptions* (Nabataean and Palmyrenian), 214-340.

Garstang, John: *The Hittite Empire*, N. Y., R. R. Smith, 1930.

Guthe, H.: *Geschichte des Volkes Israels*, Freiburg, Mohr, 1899.

Kittel, R.: *Geschichte des Volkes Israels*[4], I.

Knudtzon, J. A., and Weber, O.: *Die El-Amarna Tafeln*.

Kraeling, E. G. H.: *Aram and Israel*, N. Y., Columbia Univ. Press, 1918.

Meyer, E.: *Die Israeliten und ihre Nachbarstämme*, Halle, Niemeyer, 1906.

Noth, Martin: *Die israelitischen Personennamen im Rahmen der gemeinsemitischen Namengebung*, Stuttgart, Kohlhammer, 1928.

Noyes, Carleton: *The Genius of Israel*, Boston, Houghton Mifflin, 1924.

Olmstead, A. T.: *The History of Palestine and Syria*, Chaps. XI-XVI.

Pedersen, J.: *Israel, Its Life and Culture*, London, Milford, 1926.

Smith, H. P.: *Old Testament History*, N. Y., Scribner's, 1903.

Speiser, E. A.: "Ethnic Movements in the Near East in the Second Millennium B. C.," in AASOR XIII (1933).

Böhl, Franz M. Th.: "Das Zeitalter Abrahams," in AO 29 (1930).

Dhorme, P.: "Abraham dans le cadre de l'histoire," in RB (1928), 367-85; 481-511; (1931), 364-74, 503-18.

Jirku, A.: "Die Wanderungen der Hebräer im dritten und zweiten vorchristlichen Jahrtausend," in AO (1924).

Langdon, S.: "The Habiru and the Hebrews," in ET 31 (1920), 324-9.

CHAPTER III—*The Religion of Moses*

Barton, Geo. A.: "Yahweh Before Moses," in *Studies in the History of Religion,* presented to C. H. Toy, N. Y., Macmillan, 1912.

Breasted, James H.: *The History of Egypt*[3].

Budde, K.: *The Religion of Israel to the Exile,* N. Y., Putnam, 1899.

Cornill, Carl H.: *The Prophets of Israel* (on Moses' relation to them), Chicago, Open Court, 1897.

Driver, S. R.: *Exodus,* Cambridge Bible, 1911.

Eissfeldt, O.: "Fest und Feiern II, in Israel," in RGG[2], II.

Glueck, Nelson: "Explorations in Eastern Palestine," I, in AASOR XIV (1934), 1-113.

Gressmann, H.: *Mose und seine Zeit,* Göttingen, Vandenhoeck und Ruprecht, 1913.

Holzinger, H.: *Exodus,* in Marti's Kurzer Hand-Commentar zum A. T., Tübingen, Mohr, 1900.

Jack, J. W.: *The Date of the Exodus,* Edinburgh, Clark, 1925.

Kennett, Austin: *Bedouin Justice,* N. Y., Macmillan, 1925.

Knudson, Albert C.: *The Religious Teaching of the Old Testament,* N. Y., Abingdon, 1918.

Lods, A.: *Israel.*

Meyer, E.: *Die Israeliten und ihre Nachbarstämme.*

Nielsen, Ditlef: *Handbuch der altarabischen Altertumskunde,* I, Kopenhagen, A. Busck, 1927.

Noyes, Carleton: *The Genius of Israel.*

Oesterley, W. O. E., and Robinson, T. H.: *Hebrew Religion,* N. Y., Macmillan, 1930.

Smith, W. R.: *The Religion of the Semites*[3].

Volz, Paul: *Das Dämonische in Jahwe,* Tübingen, Mohr, 1924.

Woolley, C. L., and Lawrence, T. E.: "The Wilderness of Zin," in PEFA (1914-15).

Albright, Wm. F.: "The American Excavations at Tell Beit Mirsim," in ZAW (1929), 1-16.

Flight, John W.: "The Nomadic Idea and Ideal in the Old Testament," in JBL 43 (1923), 158-226.

Hartmann, Richard: "Zelt und Lade," in ZAW (1917-18), 209-39.

Peters, J. P.: "The Religion of Moses," in JBL 20 (1901), 101-28.

Phythian-Adams, W. J.: "The Volcanic Phenomena of the Exodus," in JPOS (1932), 86ff.

Phythian-Adams, W. J.: "The Mount of God," in PEFQS (1930), 135-49; 192-209.

Vincent, L. H.: "The Chronology of Jericho," in PEFQS (1931), 104-5.

Ward, Wm. Hayes: "The Origin of the Worship of Yahweh," in AJSL 25 1909), 175-87.

CHAPTER IV—*Clash and Transition*

1. WHEN ISRAELITE MEETS CANAANITE

Bertholet, Alfred: *Die Religion des Alten Testaments* (Religionsgeschichtliches Lesebuch), Tübingen, Mohr, 1932.

Böhl, Franz M. Th.: *Kanaanäer und Hebräer,* Leipzig, Hinrichs, 1911.

Burney, C. F.: *The Book of Judges*[2].

Burney, C. F.: *Israel's Settlement in Canaan*, London, Milford, 1918.

Curtis, Edward L.: "The Tribes of Israel," in (Yale) *Biblical and Semitic Studies*, N. Y., Scribner's, 1902.

Driver, S. R.: *Deuteronomy*, ICC, N. Y., Scribner's, 1895.

Garstang, John: *The Foundations of Bible History*, Joshua and Judges, N. Y., R. R. Smith, 1931.

Gressmann, H.: *Der Ursprung der israelitisch-jüdischen Eschatologie*, Göttingen, Vandenhoeck und Ruprecht, 1905.

Moore, G. F.: *Judges*, ICC, N. Y., Scribner's, 1910.

Mueller, W. Max: *Asien und Europa*, Leipzig, Engelmann, 1893.

Noyes, Carleton: *The Genius of Israel*.

Sellin, E., and Watzinger, C.: *Jericho*, Leipzig, Hinrichs, 1913.

Skinner, John: *Genesis*, ICC, N. Y., Scribner's, 1910.

Smith, Geo. Adam: *The Early Poetry of Israel*, London, Frowde, 1912.

Steuernagel, C.: *Die Einwanderung der israelitischen Stämme in Kanaan*, Berlin, Schwetschke, 1901.

Goff, Beatrice L.: "The Lost Jahwistic Account of the Conquest of Canaan," in JBL 53 (1934), 241-9.

2. ANTAGONISM

Burney, C. F.: *The Book of Judges*[2].

Lods, A.: *Israel*, 190-210; 327-66.

Sale, Geo.: *The Koran*, Boston, 1862.

Wallis, Louis: *The Sociological Study of the Bible*, Chicago, Univ. of C., 1912.

Hempel, J.: "Westliche Kultureinflüsse auf das älteste Palästina," in PJ (1927), 83ff.

3. TRANSITION AND MERGING

Bertholet, Alfred: *Die Religion des Alten Testaments.*

Cooke, G. A.: *The Book of Judges,* Cambridge Bible, 1918.

Gressmann, H.: *Die Anfänge Israels*[2], in SAT I, 2, Göttingen, Ruprecht, 1922.

Moore, G. F.: *The Book of Judges,* ICC.

Wallis, Louis: *Sociological Study of the Bible.*

Morgenstern, J.: "Two Ancient Israelite Agricultural Festivals," in JQR 8 (1917-18), 31-54.

4. THE PHILISTINE STIMULUS

Breasted, James H.: *The History of Egypt*[3].

Breasted, James H.: *Ancient Records of Egypt,* Vols. III and IV.

Cook, Stanley A.: "The Rise of Israel," in CAH, II.

Davidson, A. B.: *The Called of God,* Edinburgh, Clark, 1917.

Garstang, John: *The Foundations of Bible History,* 359-60.

Macalister, R. A. S.: *The Philistines,* London, Milford, 1914.

Petrie, Sir Wm. F.: *Beth Pelet,* I (Tell Fara), London, Brit. Sch. of Arch., 1930.

Albright, Wm. F.: "The Excavations at Ascalon," in BASOR, No. 6 (1922), 11-18.

Cook, Stanley A.: "Recent Excavations in Palestine," in ET 37 (1926), 487-92.

Garstang, John: "The Fund's Excavation of Askalon," in PEFQS (1921), 12-16; pls. I-III.

Garstang, John: "The Excavation of Askalon," in PEFQS (1921), 73-5; pls. I-II.

Garstang, John: "Askalon Reports. The Philistine Problem," in PEFQS (1921), 162f.

Garstang, John: "Excavations at Askalon," in PEFQS (1922), 112-19; pls. I-III.

Garstang, John: "Askalon," in PEFQS (1924), 22-35; pls. I-III, Figs. 1-5.

Garstang, John: "The Excavations at Askalon," Annual Report of the Smithsonian Institute, 509-16, Washington, D. C., 1924.

Hempel, J.: "Westliche Kultureinflüsse auf das älteste Palästina."

Nelson, H. H., and Hölscher, Uvo: "Medinet Habu," in OIC No. 5 (1924-28), Chicago, Univ. of C.

Phythian-Adams, W. J.: "History of Askalon," in PEFQS (1921), 76-90.

Phythian-Adams, W. J.: "Pre-Philistine Inhabitants of Palestine," in PEFQS (1921), 170-2.

Phythian-Adams, W. J.: "Stratigraphical Sections," in PEFQS (1921), 163-9.

Phythian-Adams, W. J.: "Report on the Stratification of Askalon," in PEFQS (1922), 60-84; pls. I-IV; Figs. 1-4.

Wainwright, G. A.: "Caphtor, Keftiu, and Cappadocia," in PEFQS (1931), 203-16.

5. SAMUEL AND ECSTATIC GROUP PROPHECY

Allen, Grant: The Attis of Caius Valerius Catullus, London, Nutt, 1892.

Apuleius: Metamorphoses (The Golden Ass), VIII, 24-9.

Driver, S. R.: The Hebrew Text of the Books of Samuel², Oxford, Clarendon, 1913.

Heliodorus: An Aethiopian History, IV 16, Underdowne's translation, London, Chapman and Dodd, 1924.

Hepding, Hugo: Attis, Seine Mythen und Sein Kult, Giessen, Ricker, 1903.

Hölscher, Gustav: Die Profeten, Leipzig, Hinrichs, 1914.

Hurgronje, C. Snouck: Mekka, II, Haag, M. Nijhoff, 1889.

Kern, Otto: Reformen der griechischen Religion, Halle, Niemeyer, 1918.

Kittel, R.: *The Religion of the People of Israel,* London, Allen and Unwin, 1925.

König, E.: "Prophecy (Hebrew)," in ERE 10 (1919).

Lucian of Samosata: *De Dea Syria (The Syrian Goddess).*

Oesterley, W. O. E.: *The Sacred Dance,* Cambridge, Univ. Press, 1923.

Origen: *Contra Celsum,* VII 8, 9.

Pliny: *Natural History,* Bk. 8, 71, ed. by J. Bostick and H. T. Riley, London, Bohn, 1855-57.

Smith, H. P.: *The Books of Samuel,* ICC, N. Y., Scribner's, 1899.

Tiele, C. P.: *Histoire comparée des anciennes religions de l'Égypte et des peuples sémitiques de la Syria,* Paris, Fischbacher, 1882.

Gunkel, H.: "Secret Experiences of the Prophets," in Expositor (London), May, June, July (1924).

Nöldeke, Th.: "Die Selbstentmannung bei den Syrern," in AR X (1907), 150-2.

6. COALESCENCE

Arnold, W. R.: *Ephod and Ark,* Cambridge, Harvard Univ. Press, 1917.

Dibelius, M.: *Die Lade Jahves,* VIII in Forschungen zur Religion und Literatur, Göttingen, 1906.

Gray, G. B.: *The Book of Numbers,* ICC, Edinburgh, Clark, 1903.

Gressmann, H.: *Die Lade Jahves und das Allerheiligste der salomonischen Tempels,* Berlin, Kohlhammer, 1920.

Gunkel, H.: *Genesis*[4], p. 486, in Nowack's Handkommentar, Göttingen, Vandenhoeck, 1917.

Hoffmann, G.: "Versuche zu Amos" (on *Abbir*), in ZAW 3 (1883), p. 124.

Meyer, E.: *Die Israeliten und ihre Nachbarstämme.*

Moore, G. F.: "Idolatry and Primitive Religion," in Enc. Bib. II, 2152-8.

Pedersen, J.: *Israel, its Life and Culture.*

Reichel, Wolfgang: *Ueber vorhellenische Götterculte,* Vienna, Hoelder, 1897.

Stade, B.: *Biblische Theologie des A. T.,* I, esp. p. 121, Tübingen, Mohr, 1905.

Wallis, Louis: *God and the Social Process,* Chicago, Univ. of C., 1935.

Budde, K.: "War die Lade Jahves ein leerer Thron?" in Theologische Studien und Kritiken (1906), 489-507.

Hartmann, R.: "Zelt und Lade," in ZAW (1917-18).

Mowinckel, S.: "A quel moment le culte de Yahvé à Jérusalem est-il officiellement devenu un culte sans images?" in RHPR (1929).

CHAPTER V—*Yahweh or Baal*

1. THE INFLUENCE OF SOLOMON

Barnes, W. E.: *The Books of Kings,* Cambridge Bible, 1908.

Cook, Arthur B.: *Zeus: A Study in Ancient Religion,* 2 vols., Cambridge, Univ. Press, 1914-25.

Cook, Stanley A.: *The Religion of Ancient Palestine in the Light of Archaeology.*

Gressmann, H.: *Altorientalische Bilder zum Alten Testament*[2] (for plan and description of the temple).

Gressmann, H.: *Die Lade Jahves und das Allerheiligste der salomonischen Tempels.*

Gunkel, H.: *Die Psalmen,* in Nowack's Handkommentar, Göttingen, Vandenhoeck, 1926.

Knudtzon, J. A., Weber, O., and Ebeling E.: *Die El-Amarna Tafeln.*

Jirku, A.: *Altorientalische Kommentar zum A. T.,* 220ff. Leipzig, Scholl, 1923.

Mowinckel, S.: *Psalmstudien II-IV,* Kristiania, Dybwad, 1922-24.

Pedersen, J.: *Israel, its Life and Culture.*
Winckler, H.: *Geschichte Israels,* I, 123, Leipzig, Pfeiffer, 1895.

Böhl, Franz M. Th.: "Hymnisches und Rhythmisches in den Amarnabriefen aus Kanaan," in Theologisches Literaturblatt, No. 15, Leipzig (1914).
Guy, P. L. O.: "New Light from Armageddon," in OIC No. 9, Univ. of Chicago (1931).
Jirku, A.: "Kanaanäische Psalmenfragmenta in der vor-israelitischen Zeit Palästinas und Syriens," in JBL 52 (1933), 108-20.

2. THE PROPHETIC PROTEST
Binns, L. E.: *From Moses to Elijah,* The Clarendon Bible, Vol. II, Oxford, Clarendon, 1929.
Harris, Chas. W.: *The Hebrew Heritage,* Chaps. XVII-XX.

Mowinckel, S.: "A quel moment" etc., see under IV, 6.

3. THE DYNASTY OF OMRI
Cheyne, T. K.: "Baal-Zebub," see under I, 2.
Jack, J. W.: *Samaria in Ahab's Time,* Edinburgh, Clark, 1929.
Josephus: *Antiquities* VIII 3, 1, 2, and *Contra Apionem* I, 18.
Kittel, R.: *Geschichte des Volkes Israels*[3], II.
Reisner, G. A., Fisher, C. S., and Lyon, D. G.: *Harvard Excavations in Samaria,* 2 vols., Cambridge, Harvard Univ. Press, 1924.

Crowfoot, J. W.: "Recent Discoveries of the Joint Expedition to Samaria," in PEFQS (1932), pp. 132-133, Plates I-III.
Crowfoot, J. W., and Crowfoot, G. M.: "The Ivories from Samaria," in PEFQS (1933), 7-26, Plates I-III.
May, H. G.: "A Supplementary Note on the Ivories from Samaria," in PEFQS (April, 1933).

4. THE PROPHETIC REVOLUTION

Benzinger, I.: *Die Bücher der Könige*, ın K. Marti's Kurzer Hand-Commentar zum A. T., Freiburg, Mohr, 1899.

Burney, C. F.: *Notes on the Hebrew Text of the Books of Kings*, Oxford, Clarendon, 1903.

Gunkel, H.: *Genesis*[4].

Heliodorus: *An Aethiopian History*, IV 16.

Jack, J. W.: *Samaria in Ahab's Time*.

Lagrange, Marie-Joseph: *Études sur religions sémitiques*[2].

Oesterley, W. O. E.: *The Sacred Dance*.

Sellin, E.: *Der israelitische Prophetismus*, Leipzig, Deichert, 1912.

Thenius, O.: *Die Bücher der Könige*, Leipzig, Hirzel, 1873.

Wellhausen, J.: *Israelitische und jüdische Geschichte*[7], Berlin, Reimer, 1914.

5. THE CANAANIZING OF THE ISRAELITE CULT

Gray, G. B.: *Sacrifice in the Old Testament*.

Harford, Geo.: *Exodus*, in Peake's Commentary, 187, col. 2.

Hölscher, Gustav: *Die Profeten*.

Holzinger, H.: *Exodus*.

Lagrange, Marie-Joseph: *Études sur religions sémitiques*[2].

Mowinckel, S.: *Psalmstudien II-IV*.

Oesterley, W. O. E., and Robinson, T. H.: *Hebrew Religion*.

Oesterley, W. O. E.: in S. H. Hooke: *Myth and Ritual*, 111-46.

Taanit IV. 8, in Mishnah, ed. by Rodkinson, *The Babylonian Talmud*, VIII, N. Y., 1899.

Thackeray, St. J.: *The Septuagint and Jewish Worship*, London, Milford, 1921.

Tiele, C. P.: *Histoire comparée des anciennes religions de l'Égypte et des peuples sémitiques de la Syria*,

Waddington, Wm. H.: *Inscriptions grecques et latines de la Syrie,* Nos. 1855-6, Paris, Didot, 1870.

Dussaud, R.: "La mythologie phénicienne d'après les tablettes de Ras Shamra," in RHR (1931), 354-408.

Gaster, T. H.: "The Ritual Pattern of the Ras Shamra Epic."

Hooke, S. H.: "The Mixture of Cults in Canaan in Relation to the History of Hebrew Religion," in JMEOS 16, pp. 17ff.

Meek, T. J.: "The Interpenetration of Cultures as Illustrated by the Character of the Old Testament Religion," in JR (May, 1927).

Morgenstern, J.: "Two Ancient Israelite Agricultural Festivals."

Wood, I. F.: "Borrowing Between Religions," in JBL 46 (1927), 98-105.

Chapter VI—*The Prophetic Clarification*

1. THE HISTORICAL BACKGROUND

Barton, Geo. A.: *Archaeology and the Bible*[6].

Meyer, E.: "The Development of Individuality in Ancient History," in *Kleine Schriften zur Geschichtstheorie und zur wirtschaftlichen und politischen Geschichte des Altertums,* Halle, Niemeyer, 1910.

2. AMOS: RELIGION AS RIGHTEOUSNESS

Cook, Stanley A.: in CAH II, 398.

Cripps, R. S.: *A Critical and Exegetical Commentary on the Book of Amos,* London, Macmillan, 1930.

Driver, S. R.: *The Book of Amos,* Cambridge Bible, 1915.

Dussaud, R.: *Les origines cananéenne du sacrifice israélite.*

Eiselen, F. C.: *The Prophetic Books of the O. T.,* 2 vols., N. Y., Abingdon, 1923.

Gressmann, H.: *Die älteste Geschichtsschreibung und Prophetie Israels,* in SAT II, 1 (1921).

Graham, Wm. C.: *The Prophets and Israel's Culture,* Chicago, Univ. of C. Press, 1934.

Knudson, Albert C.: *Beacon Lights of Prophecy,* N. Y., Abingdon, 1914.

Knudson, Albert C.: *The Prophetic Movement in Israel,* N. Y., Abingdon, 1921.

Lidzbarski, M.: *Ephemeris für semitische Epigraphik,* III, 261-4.

Nowack, W.: *Die Kleinen Propheten,* in Nowack's Handkommentar, Göttingen, Vandenhoeck, 1897.

Philo of Byblos: in Fragment 24 of Eusebius' *Praeparatio Evangelica,* I, 10.

Smith, Geo. Adam: *The Historical Geography of the Holy Land*[25], London, Hodder, 1931.

Smith, W. R.: *The Religion of the Semites*[3].

Zimmern, H.: *Die Beschwörungstafeln Surpu,* p. 11, lines 179ff., in Beiträge zur Kenntnis der Babylonischen Religion, Leipzig, Hinrichs, 1901.

Cook, Stanley A.: "Chronicle: O. T. Religion and Related Works," in JTS IX (1908), 632 note.

Cook, Stanley A.: "Semitic Theism," see under I, 2.

Graham, W. C.: "The Religion of the Hebrews," in JR 11 (1931).

3. HOSEA: RELIGION AS ETHICAL UNION WITH GOD

Brown, Sydney L.: *The Book of Hosea,* Westminster Commentary, London, Methuen, 1932.

Cumont, Franz: *The Oriental Religions in Roman Paganism,* Chap. II.

Glueck, Nelson: *Das Wort Hesed,* Giessen, Töpelmann, 1927.

Kittel, R.: *The Religion of the People of Israel.*

Knudson, Albert C.: *Beacon Lights of Prophecy.*

Mannhardt, W.: *Wald und Feldkulte,* II.

Scott, Melville: *The Message of Hosea,* London, SPCK, 1921.

Smith, W. R.: *The Prophets of Israel*[2], London, Black, 1895.

May, H. G.: "The Fertility Cult in Hosea," in AJSL 48 (1932).

Peters, J. P.: "The Worship of Tammuz," in JBL 36 (1912).

Schmidt, Hans: "Die Ehe des Hosea," in ZAW (1924), 245-72.

4. ISAIAH: RELIGION AS TRUST IN THE SOVEREIGN GOD

Hill, G. F.: *Catalogue of the Greek Coins of Phoenicia* (British Museum), p. 98; pl. XII, 8.

Hölscher, Gustav: *Geschichte der israelitischen und jüdischen Religion*, 106-10.

de Lagarde, Paul: *Symmicta* I, p. 105, Göttingen, 1877.

Philo of Byblos: in Eusebius' *Praep. Evan.* I, 10, Frag. 26.

Procksch, O.: *Jesaia I*, in Sellin's Kommentar zum A. T., Leipzig, Deichert, 1930.

Skinner, John: *Isaiah I-XXXIX*, Cambridge Bible, 1910.

Wade, G. W.: *Isaiah*, Westminster Commentary, N. Y., Gorham, 1912.

Graham, W. C.: "Notes on the Interpretation of Isaiah 5. 1-14," in AJSL 45 (1929), 167-78.

5. MICAH: THE QUINTESSENCE OF PROPHETIC RELIGION

Bowne, Borden P.: *The Essence of Religion*, Chap. IV, Boston, Houghton Mifflin, 1910.

Hooke, S. H. (editor): *The Labyrinth: Further Studies in the Relation Between Myth and Ritual in the Ancient World*, London, SPCK, 1935.

Meinhold, J.: *Einführung in das Alte Testament*[2], Giessen, Töpelmann, 1926.

Moore, G. F.: *The Literature of the Old Testament*, N. Y., Holt, 1913.

Sellin, E.: *Introduction to the Old Testament.*
Smith, J. M. P.: *Micah,* ICC, N. Y., Macmillan, 1914.

Graham, W. C.: "Some Suggestions Toward the Interpretation of Micah 1. 10-16," in AJSL 47 (1931), 237-58.

CHAPTER VII—*The Final Synthesis*

1. THE HISTORICAL BACKGROUND

Barton, Geo. A.: "The End of the Babylonian Exile," Chap. XX, in *Archaeology and the Bible*[6].
Driver, S. R.: *Deuteronomy.*
Herodotus: I, 103-6.

2. ZEPHANIAH: THE SUMMONS TO RIGHTEOUSNESS AND MEEKNESS

Davidson, A. B.: *The Books of Nahum, Habakkuk, and Zephaniah,* Cambridge Bible, 1920.
Skinner, John: *Prophecy and Religion* (for Scythians), Cambridge, Univ. Press, 1922.
Smith, Geo. Adam: *Jeremiah,* Baird Lecture (for Scythians), London, Hodder, 1923.
Stonehouse, Geo. G.: *The Books of the Prophets Zephaniah and Nahum,* Westminster Commentary, London, Methuen, 1929.

3. NAHUM: THE DIVINE NEMESIS

Stonehouse, Geo. G.: *The Books of the Prophets Zephaniah and Nahum.*

4. HABAKKUK: RELIGION AS FAITHFULNESS

Sellin, E.: *Introduction to the Old Testament.*
Wade, G. W.: *The Book of the Prophet Habakkuk,* Westminster Commentary, London, Methuen, 1929.

5. JEREMIAH: RELIGION AS INNER EXPERIENCE

von Baudissin, W.: *Adonis und Esmun,* esp. 490-509.

Calkins, Raymond: *Jeremiah the Prophet*, A Study in Personal Religion, N. Y., Macmillan, 1930.

Damascius: *Quaestiones de primis principiis*, 125.

Duhm, B.: *Das Buch Jeremia,* in Marti's Kurzer Hand-Commentar, Tübingen, Mohr, 1901.

Gressmann, H.: *Der Messias* (Forschungen), Göttingen, Vandenhoeck und Ruprecht, 1929.

Jayne, Walter A.: *The Healing Gods of Ancient Civilizations,* New Haven, Yale Univ. Press, 1925.

Kittel, R.: *The Religion of the People of Israel,* 120.

Movers, F. C.: *Die Phönizier,* 2 vols., Bonn, Weber, 1841-56.

Skinner, John: *Prophecy and Religion.*

Smith, Geo. Adam: *Jeremiah,* Baird Lecture.

Smith, W. R.: *The Religion of the Semites*[3].

6. EZEKIEL: THE ANNOUNCEMENT OF RESTORATION AND REANIMATION

Damascius: *Quaestiones de primis principiis*, 125.

Davidson, A. B.: *The Book of the Prophet Ezekiel,* Cambridge Bible, 1916.

Duhm, B.: *Theologie der Propheten,* Bonn, Marcus, 1875.

Redpath, H. A.: *The Book of the Prophet Ezekiel,* Westminster Commentary, London, Methuen, 1907.

Smith, H. P.: *Religion of Israel,* N. Y., Scribner's, 1914.

Toy, C. H.: *Ezekiel,* N. Y., Dodd, Mead, 1899.

7. DEUTERO-ISAIAH: THE UNION OF RIGHTEOUSNESS AND REDEMPTION

von Baudissin, W.: *Adonis und Esmun,* esp. 16f., note 1; 514-20.

Davidson, A. B.: *Theology of the Old Testament,* N. Y., Scribner's, 1912.

Knudson, Albert C.: *Religious Teaching of the Old Testament.*

Otto, R.: *The Idea of the Holy*, London, Milford, 1923.

Skinner, John: *Isaiah XL-LXVI*, Cambridge Bible, 1914.

Smith, Geo. Adam: *The Book of Isaiah*, Vol. II, rev. ed., N. Y., Doran, 1927.

Torrey, Chas. C.: *The Second Isaiah*, N. Y., Scribner's, 1928.

INDEX TO BIBLICAL REFERENCES

INDEX OF SUBJECT MATTER AND AUTHORITIES

[(d) designates a deity]

277